D0982618

THE DILEMMA OF
MEXICO'S DEVELOPMENT

THIS BOOK HAS BEEN PREPARED

UNDER THE AUSPICES OF

THE CENTER FOR INTERNATIONAL AFFAIRS

HARVARD UNIVERSITY

Created in 1958, the Center fosters advanced study of basic world problems by scholars from various disciplines and senior officers from many countries. The research at the Center, focusing on the processes of change, includes studies of military-political issues, the modernizing processes in developing countries, and the evolving position of Europe. The research programs are supervised by Professors Robert R. Bowie (Director of the Center), Alex Inkeles, Henry A. Kissinger, Edward S. Mason, Thomas C. Schelling, and Raymond Vernon. A list of Center publications will be found at the end of this volume.

THE DILEMMA OF
MEXICO'S DEVELOPMENT

The Roles of the Private and Public Sectors

Raymond Vernon

HARVARD UNIVERSITY PRESS

Cambridge, Massachusetts

1963

To Josh, who wasn't much help;

and to Karin, who was in no position to be

Foreword

BY EDWARD S. MASON FOR THE CENTER
FOR INTERNATIONAL AFFAIRS

This is the first of a series of studies of the relative roles of private enterprise and government in a number of developing countries. These studies, under my direction, are a part of the research program of the Center for International Affairs at Harvard. The countries have been chosen to give some notion of the rather wide spectrum of relationships between the public and private sectors at different stages of development and in different areas of the world. Latin America is represented by studies of Mexico and Brazil; Asia by Iran and Pakistan; and Africa by Nigeria. There is, however, no claim that these countries are representative in the sense of being typical of government-business relations in those continents. The fact is that until a larger number of careful studies of the process of development have been made, it will be difficult to say whether any set of public-private relationships is typical of a particular stage of development in the non-Communist world as a whole or any large sector thereof.

In addition to these "country studies," a number of inquiries into various aspects of the more general question have been undertaken by the Center. Two of these have already been published. *United States Manufacturing Investment in Brazil: The Impact of Brazilian Government Policies, 1946–1960,* by Lincoln Gordon and Engelbert L. Grommers, was issued in 1962 by the Harvard Graduate School of Business Administration. *Entrepreneurs of Lebanon: The Role of the Business Leader in a Developing Economy,* by Yusif A. Sayigh, was issued by Harvard University

Press, also in 1962. The Sayigh volume was a joint undertaking of the Center for International Affairs and the Center for Middle Eastern Studies. Two other studies have been completed but not yet published. Montague Yudelman's volume entitled *Africans on the Land* is an inquiry into the conditions affecting African agricultural productivity in South, Central, and East Africa, with special reference to Southern Rhodesia. The late Max Thornburg had finished before his death a manuscript entitled *From People to Policy: Lessons from the Changing Middle East,* which is concerned with the peoples of traditional societies and how they adapt to modernization.

All of these studies have been financed in part by a generous grant from the Ford Foundation to the Center for International Affairs for research on the relation of government to private enterprise in economic development.

Author's Preface

This is a book constructed out of thousands of little fragments. Its historical interpretations were drawn painfully out of tomes of published materials in Mexico and the United States, and out of endless discussions with Mexican intellectuals. Its analysis of Mexico's current situation was built up from stubbornly resistant and perversely inconsistent data, from contemporary newspapers, magazines, and other publications, and from the conflicting interpretations of my many Mexican friends.

So much of what has been written and said about Mexico, by foreigners as much as by Mexicans, is laced with fantasy and passion. So much is painted in pitch black or glistening white. Much of what has happened in Mexico, however, seems to me to have been quite mixed in tone. The national villains of Mexico, however evil their motives, have usually managed to make some constructive contribution to the country in spite of themselves. The national heroes of the country, however virtuous their aims, have rarely failed to exhibit some of the strains of unreality and otherworldliness of Cervantes' Don Quixote.

Developments in Mexico have been mixed in still another sense, a sense particularly important to the theme of this book. Labels often suffer from over-easy use by Mexicans and from over-simple translation by foreigners. Thus, "the Revolution," "the left," and "the public sector" stand for more complex institutions and conceptions in Mexico than one might at first be led to suppose; and much the same can be said of terms like "reaction," "the right," and "the private sector" as they are applied in that country.

Anyone who attempts to preserve some of the complexity of

Mexican life, to depart from the love-or-hate, white-or-black tradition of describing or prescribing for Mexico, may have to pay a price. He must accept the risk of losing a considerable part of his audience — especially that part of his Mexican audience which has been reared in the tradition of passionate and unqualified versions of the country's history. One does not love with footnotes and qualifications. And he who does not love Mexico is suspected of hating it.

Reluctantly, I have decided to accept the risk, hoping at the same time that my analysis may be able to contribute a little to a deeper understanding of the Mexican process.

I have hesitated a long time over the decision whether to list the names of the Mexicans who did so much to help me with this study. The names of some of them will be evident enough when a companion volume to this book is published — probably early in 1964. That volume will contain a series of monographs written by a number of my associates in this enterprise, analyzing the relations between the private and public sectors in certain selected areas of the Mexican economy. But there were scores of others who helped too — businessmen, bankers, politicians, teachers, government officials, and ordinary people. In the end, I have decided that I would be doing a doubtful service to those whom I might have listed. Those who helped me most have no doubt of my deep gratitude. Some, however, might suffer embarrassment by being associated with conclusions they did not share. None would acquire any added kudos by being listed here.

There are some acknowledgments, however, that I cannot fail to make. In addition to the financial support of the Center for International Affairs — from funds of the Ford Foundation as mentioned by Professor Mason in his Foreword — this study was also supported in part by the Harvard Business School's Division of Research, from grants of the Ford Foundation and the Associates of the Harvard Business School. Then, too, there was the stalwart help of Marian Berdecio, whose voracious scanning of the Mexican press put meat on the bones of many an hypothesis in this study;

and of my wife, long-time decipherer and typist extraordinary, who stepped out of that role to win her spurs as a researcher in the preparation of this book.

Raymond Vernon

Cambridge, Massachusetts
February 5, 1963

Contents

CHARTS

TABLES

THE DILEMMA OF
MEXICO'S DEVELOPMENT

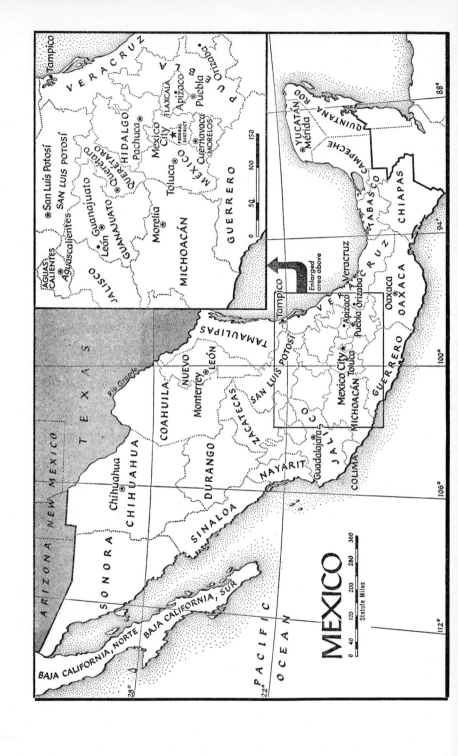

Chapter I

Mexico Today

For those who are concerned with the economic development of the less-developed areas of the world, the elusive philosopher's stone is the secret of achieving growth without the suppression and destruction of the individual. Many countries seem to have achieved this goal. Others seem to have floundered. Still others appear well on the way to achievement, caught up in a process which appears self-sustaining and irreversible.

As we look at the list of the successes, the failures, and the aspirants, generalizations about the causes of failure or success are not easy and obvious. To be sure, the developed nations in general have many characteristics which distinguish them from the aspirants, including a higher level of education and more fully developed "overhead" facilities such as transportation, communication, and power. But the possession of these characteristics is no guarantee of sustained growth; witness the slowdown of Argentina since the 1930's. Besides, one cannot always be certain whether the observed characteristics are cause or effect — whether they generate growth or growth generates them.

Of the many riddles concerning the development process, some of the most contentious have to do with the relative roles of the public and the private sectors.

In the first place there are questions as to what the historical facts are. Competing theories about the origins of British growth, of United States growth, even of Russian development, have usually been distinguished by their differing interpretations of the significance of public and private initiatives. Observers of change in the less-developed countries, such as the nations of West Africa and of South Asia, have commonly been at odds over the relative importance of government and private activities in the past growth of these areas. Some have tended to downgrade the importance of government activity; others have judged it to be both a necessary and sufficient condition for satisfactory economic growth.

The really prickly differences, however — the differences which have supplied the grist for the bitterest international disputes — have turned more on issues of ideology and on systems of values than on questions of historical fact. In this sphere, the questions have been framed in terms of whether the public sector or the private sector "ought to" be the instrument responsible for one activity or another associated with economic growth. Here, the disputants have commonly entered the lists placing different values, implicitly or explicitly stated, on the relative importance of national growth versus individual equity, of deferred returns versus immediate consumer satisfactions, of national discipline versus personal choice, of national self-sufficiency versus national interdependence.

The debates have been all the more confused and complex because of the imprecision of such concepts as "government," "public sector," "private sector," and "private enterprise." In developed capitalistic countries such as France, the Netherlands, Belgium, and Austria, investment policy, wage policy, and pricing policy are commonly determined through complex processes of consultation which so thoroughly integrate governmental and private interests that it would be a distortion to try to identify the unique contribution of each. Even where the entities in advanced countries can readily be labeled "public" or "private" in accordance with the identity of their owners or directors, the label need not provide a reliable clue to their motivations and behavior. In Italy, the country's major oil company, though publicly owned, sometimes ignores its own government on critical questions of policy, whereas in Britain we encounter privately-owned oil companies whose acceptance of governmental guidance is legendary.

In the less-developed nations, too, it is commonplace to find public agencies taking on a life and tradition of their own which defy the control of the government apparatus, and private entities that passively do as they are directed by the government authorities. Enterprises owned jointly by government and private interests behave in some cases as if they were altogether public, and in other cases as if they were altogether private. Functions which are commonly thought of as endowed with a public interest are sometimes discharged by private groups while activities of a trivial and parochial character are under the wing of public bodies.

Despite these variations and anomalies, an inquiry into the relative roles of the public and private sectors in less-developed countries is far from meaningless. Such an inquiry requires subtlety and caution — a constant awareness of the potentially misleading character of the words "public" and "private," and of the existence of hybrid and ambiguous institutions and relationships. Still, such a study can address itself to major distinctions and to vital issues. For at the margin of their institution-building and policy-making processes, the developing countries are forever being confronted with choices, running the gamut from government ownership and operation to private ownership and laissez-faire. Complex as the subject may be, it is reasonable to expect that a study of the experiences of various countries may demonstrate that patterns have in fact existed in the past, and that cause-and-effect relationships can in practice be traced. Once these patterns are identified, they may well provide some added guidance to nations looking for a course that will contribute to their goals of economic development.

THE CASE OF MEXICO

A study of any one country offers something less than an adequate basis for generalization. But in any list of countries whose experiences may suggest fruitful hypotheses, the case of Mexico surely ranks high. Ever since economists began to produce the relevant data by which economic growth is measured, they have been aware that Mexico was growing, sometimes at a modest pace, sometimes very rapidly. In the twenty years from 1939 to 1960, the country's physical output of goods and services — calculated about as carefully as such magnitudes are usually calculated in countries with sparse and uncertain statistics — seems to have tripled.* Table 1 gives us some perspective for gauging this per-

TABLE 1

Annual Growth Rates of Physical Output of Goods and Services, Total and Per Capita, Selected Countries[a]

(in per cent)

Country	1938–1954[b]		1950–1959	
	Total	Per capita	Total	Per capita
Mexico	5.7	2.9	5.2	2.3
U.S.A.	4.6	3.2	3.3	1.1
Argentina	3.2	1.1	1.7	c
Brazil	4.8	2.4	4.8	1.9
Canada	5.1	3.3	4.0	0.9
Chile	4.0	2.3	2.4	c
Germany	3.0	1.4	7.4	5.4
Israel	—	—	9.9	2.9
Japan	13.5	11.1	7.9	5.6
Peru	5.1	3.1	4.3	1.4
South Africa	4.5	2.2	5.1	2.6

[a] For some countries, the figures are based on measures of gross national product, for others, gross domestic product, and for still others, national income.
[b] For Mexico, 1939–1954; Japan and South Africa, 1946–1952; Brazil, 1939–1953; Chile, 1940–1952; Peru, 1949–1952.
c Less than 0.1 per cent.
Sources: For Mexico, our own estimates based upon various official sources. For other countries, 1938–1954: *U.N. Statistical Papers*, series H, nos. 8 and 9, table 2. For other countries, 1950–1959: output data, *U.N. World Economic Survey, 1959*, tables 1-1, 2-9, 3-1; population data, *U.N. Demographic Yearbook, passim*.

formance by comparing Mexican growth rates with those of a variety of other countries, both developed and otherwise. Mexico's growth rates, as the table shows, have been fairly impressive, both in total output and on a per capita basis. The country has grown

* Trends in gross domestic product and its principal components, 1939–1960, are shown in Chart 2 (Chapter 4), and the underlying data are in Appendix Table A-1.

faster than any of the Big Three of South America, though not so fast as truly spectacular performers like postwar Japan and Germany.[1]

By 1960, Mexico's per capita annual income had risen to slightly over 300 U.S. dollars, a figure far above the levels characteristically encountered in Africa, Asia, and many parts of Latin America itself.[2] By that year, too, Mexico's output had acquired a composition characteristic of a reasonably advanced economy. Output of the manufacturing industries made up about one fifth of the gross national product; if the petroleum and electric power industries are added to manufacturing, this enlarged "industrial" sector accounted for about one quarter of the total. Agricultural output, it is true, still came close to matching that of manufacturing in value; but more than three quarters of it by this time was commercial rather than subsistence agriculture.

The appropriateness of studying Mexico as an instructive case of economic development, however, stems from more subtle indicators of successful progress. Mexico today is a nation, not a collection of loosely-joined localities or an appendage of a foreign power. It has a well-developed public sector, consisting of its government agencies and its government-controlled enterprises, which by now have acquired a sense of continuity and of effective performance. It has a firmly established indigenous private sector producing not only in the traditional agricultural activities but also in the modern areas of industry, banking, and commerce. Indeed, the human and material resources which spark Mexico's growth today are largely indigenous. The men who design the dams, roads, and factories of the country, direct its businesses and financial institutions, plan its educational system, provide its advanced training, and guide its agricultural research are principally Mexican nationals. The funds that finance its capital formation in every major sector of its economic life come predominantly from Mexican sources. Foreign contributions, both in human and material terms, are still important — just how important is the subject of continuous acrimonious debate. Despite the debate, however, no one any longer doubts that Mexico has the internal human and physical resources, the social organization, and even the level of income which most other countries of the underdeveloped world would be content to achieve thirty or forty years hence.

For the scholar who is probing to understand the actual and potential roles of the public and the private sectors in the development process, the Mexican case is attractive on other grounds as well. Both sectors have had vigorous parts to play in the development of the country. In some countries and for some periods, it is easy to describe the performance of one of the two sectors as "dominant" — as both the necessary and the sufficient condition for growth. Egypt since the middle 1950's, for instance, has been dominated by the activities of the public sector. Peru, on the other hand, owes its recent growth principally to activities in the private sphere. But no such obvious statement can be made about Mexico.

The importance of the public sector in Mexico is not apparent on first impact. Table 2 indicates that the public sector — when measured in terms of its direct contribution to the nation's gross national product — seems to occupy a minor role in the economy. To be sure, the government owns the petroleum industry, the bulk of the electric power industry, and the railroads; some major steel plants, fertilizer plants, and railroad equipment plants; a number of commercial and industrial banks; organizations engaged in the distribution of foodstuffs and newsprint; and a variety of other institutions. Still, the activities of these enterprises plus those of the governmental institutions proper — which together comprise the public sector as a whole — account for less than one tenth of the gross national product.

The position of the public sector looms somewhat larger when it is measured by its relative importance in the capital formation of Mexico. The rather infirm figures on this subject suggest that in recent years public investment has been running at about 5 per cent of gross national product, while domestic private investment has been about 9 per cent.[3] The largest part of public investment goes into such overhead items as transportation and communica-

TABLE 2

*Contribution to Mexico's Gross National Product
by Public and Private Sectors, 1959*

	Public sector[a]		Private sector	
Activities	Millions of pesos	Percentage of activity in sector	Millions of pesos	Percentage of activity in sector
Petroleum	4,243	100.0	0	0
Electric power[b]	626	74.8	231	25.2
Transportation	1,222	44.4	1,529	55.6
Mining	134	5.4	2,362	94.6
Manufacture	873	3.6	23,458	96.4
Construction	4	0.2	2,511	99.8
Agriculture	0	0	22,298	100.0
Other[c]	4,469	7.1	58,040	92.9
Total	11,571	9.6	110,429	90.4

[a] Includes most enterprises in the public sector plus federal, state, and local governments.

[b] After 1959, the Mexican government purchased most of the remaining private interests in the electric power industry, raising the public sector's position to nearly 100 per cent.

[c] Principally trade and services, including services of government agencies.

Sources: Secretaría del Patrimonio Nacional and Banco de México.

tions, electric energy, and petroleum; but a significant part also goes into agriculture and manufacturing. One gains the impression, therefore, of a vigorous — but hardly a dominant — public sector.

The importance of the public sector, of course, cannot be gauged solely by the size of its output or by its contribution to investment. Since the public sector consists not only of enterprises but also of government agencies, there is also the question of the role of public regulation as it affects the country's growth. On this subject impressions are necessarily qualitative and subjective; but there are a number of points on which wide agreement would exist.

In some countries the existence of a national "plan" offers a clue to some of the goals which the public sector has set for itself. In Mexico, little light comes from this quarter. Until very recently, Mexico had no development plan, at least no development plan with articulated quantitative objectives and an articulated strategy of achievement. From time to time, statements of general priorities, labeled as "national plans," were issued by one administration or another. In addition, some of the operating agencies of the government maintained internal projections for use in connection with their own programs. But there were no integrated targets for gross national product, for capital formation, for steel production, and the like. Today, quantitative targets of this sort have begun to be produced inside the Mexican government and to receive the president's stamp of approval. At this writing it is too early to say whether the targets are part of an operating plan, which will include a strategy of achievement and which will command the allegiance of all the branches of government concerned with its execution, or whether they are a sterile quantitative exercise of the sort which the requirements of the Alliance for Progress have made popular in many Latin American capitals.

In any case, one is bound to say that the Mexican government is unequivocally committed to the objective of economic growth. And it does consistently accept the responsibility for at least three major courses of action which bear on national development.

One is the improvement of the education, health, and general well-being of the ordinary citizen. It is true that official performance in the immediate discharge of this responsibility has sometimes been fairly feeble as governments have wrestled with conflicting objectives, such as the desire to hold down taxes and avoid inflationary financing. But no government since the Revolution of 1910 has failed to assert its fealty to these objectives nor to contribute a little toward their achievement.

A second acknowledged responsibility of all governments since the Revolution has been to provide the basic industrial "overhead" facilities, including transport, communication, power, and water. Though motives and emphases have differed from one administration to the next, no administration has failed to make substantial contributions to the building of the nation's infrastructure.

The third cause to which all recent governments of Mexico have adhered has been to encourage import replacement as a matter of high priority. It has been taken as an article of faith that as soon as the domestic demand for a product was large enough to offer some hope of domestic production on a scale appropriate to the technology of the industry, every effort should be made to stimulate the necessary domestic investment and to eliminate imports.

While operating on these lines, Mexico's governments of the last two decades have not shown any particular ideological hostility to the concept of private enterprise. On the contrary, a private investor intent on producing a hitherto imported product could be reasonably well assured that the competition of imports would be suppressed or eliminated; that he would be given some relief from income taxes and from import duties on his materials and machinery; and that he would have access to relatively cheap governmental credits. He could even assume that if some bottleneck existed in the form of inadequate public facilities — inadequate power, for instance, or inadequate transportation — there would be a sympathetic governmental response to his difficulties and a genuine effort to meet his needs.

If the private investor is Mexican, his assurances on all these points are fairly clear and unequivocal; but if he is a foreigner he may run into various difficulties. His risks will not seem obvious from a reading of Mexican law; in fact, on first blush, the law will seem reassuringly nondiscriminatory in most respects. Except for some significant restrictions on landowning rights, some limitations on foreign ownership in a few strangely assorted industries, and some flatly discriminatory tax legislation in the field of mining and metal processing, the foreigner's opportunities will appear on a par with those of Mexican nationals. In practice, however, the consummation of any major foreign investment is likely to turn on the granting of a variety of licenses, beginning with the issuance of articles of incorporation and continuing with licenses to import the necessary machinery or raw materials and licenses to permit foreign managerial personnel to work in the country. Therefore, the foreigner who is considering any large direct investment in Mexico is obliged to determine if the contemplated investment is acceptable to the Mexican government. And at this stage, notwithstanding the blandly neutral character of the legal structure, the foreigner is likely to discover that in a considerable number of industries the existence of a large Mexican equity interest in the investment is indispensable to the granting of the necessary licenses.

Though there is no obvious hostility to domestic private investment in official Mexican government policy, neither is there any ideological barrier which restrains the Mexican government from investing in any branch of economic activity when it believes the investment to be in the public interest. For instance, if private investment is not forthcoming speedily or in quantity in some important import-replacing field of production at a stage when such an investment appears feasible, the government may well take a direct hand in that sector. This is what accounts for some of the government enterprises in the steel, fertilizer, and paper industries. Nor is the government strongly inhibited from making *ad hoc* investments in industry, whether or not they contribute to import substitution, when some bottleneck problem arises or some political interest would be served. So we find the government investing heavily in the production of rail cars, in the promotion of a local motion picture industry, and in a dozen other miscellaneous pursuits, most of them representing the uninhibited responses of a government unhampered by any well-articulated limitations on public investment.

The readiness of the government to provide easy credit to favored segments of the private sector explains the existence of numerous public banks and investment institutions, set up to provide loans for activities as diverse as manufacturing, cooperative agriculture, and foreign trade. The existence of this public credit system affords one more crude means of comparing the importance of the public and the private sectors. In recent years, the outstanding credits of private lending institutions have been a little greater in the aggregate than those of the public credit agencies. The private sector has led heavily in the making of short-term loans, and the public institutions have led slightly in long-term ones. Once more, therefore, we come away with the impression of two very active sectors, neither obviously dominated by the other. Thus the case of Mexico offers attractions to those who are interested in discovering the implications which the relationships between a public sector and a private sector have for the development process. The comparatively advanced state of Mexico's development, the experimental and eclectic character of Mexico's use of the two sectors, the vigor with which both sectors have operated — all these commend the Mexican case for study.

THE POLITICAL SETTING

The political machinery of any nation represents the brain and nerves of its public sector, the conduit through which the goals and strategies of the public sector are defined. Here, therefore, is where our inquiry begins.

The first impression which one gains of the Mexican political structure is one of tremendous discrepancies between legal form and solid substance, leading to an enormous concentration of power in the office of the president. Nominally, Mexico has a federal government composed of twenty-nine states, two territories, and a federal district. In reality, however, the federal government dominates the states, both in administrative and in fiscal terms. The measure of its fiscal dominance is suggested by the fact that the revenues of the federal government are typically four or five times as great as those of all the states and municipalities combined. The degree of administrative dependence of the states is indicated by the fact that no state governor could attain office if he were *persona non grata* to the president of the Republic.

According to the constitution, the federal government consists of three independent branches — an executive arm, a two-house legislature, and a judiciary. But in practice, the legislature is a passive creature which hardly ever fails to carry out the wishes of the president; independent action on its part is almost unknown. The decisions of the judiciary are almost as predictable, particularly in fields in which the executive has taken an unmistakable position.

The structure of the executive branch is fascinating in its complexity. Endless ministries, commissions, institutes, semi-independent committees and corporations seem to depend from the presidency. One authoritative compilation lists twenty-one executive ministries and departments; fifteen interministerial committees; sixty independent administrative commissions charged with tasks ranging from the control of imports to the administration of colonization projects; seventy-eight decentralized institutions operating directly in such fields as petroleum, railroads, or banking; and scores of individual firms producing in the many branches of industry to which we referred earlier.

However, though the complexity of the executive branch is real enough, the points of major power — at least as far as economic matters are concerned — are comparatively few.

One of those points is the finance ministry. Among the ministries and departments, the finance minister stands out as *primus inter pares*. He exerts an extraordinary measure of direct control over the current budgetary expenditures of the government agencies; and by means of that control he affects staffing patterns, operational policies, and even capital budget expenditures throughout the executive branch. At the same time, by means of his control over the policies of the nation's central bank and of its principal development bank, the finance minister is able to exert a ubiquitous influence upon the development process.

A second source of economic power is located in the larger decentralized institutions, particularly in those charged with running the nation's petroleum, railroad, and electric power industries. Since the decentralized agencies in these three industries typically account for about 40 per cent of the public sector's total capital investment in any year, and since the area of their operations is so critical to the growth of the rest of the economy, they are a force with which the rest of the economy must reckon.

For all that, it is universally recognized that the ultimate arbiter in disputes within the executive branch — the ultimate arbiter *de facto* as well as *de jure* — is still the president. In other countries, an aggrieved ministry inside the executive branch might openly or clandestinely enlist the support of allied business groups, friendly newspapers, or legislative committees, not only in order to put pressure upon other ministers but even to force a favorable decision from the president. It might be risky to say that this tactic has never been used in Mexico, but if it is used, the tracks of the miscreant official must be very well covered. For the ultimate authority of the president in Mexico must never be overtly questioned, and his freedom of action never overtly compromised by any member of the executive branch.

The impression of a monolithic governmental structure centering in the office of the presidency gains strength as one examines the party structure of the country and the process of succession. One party, the Partido Revolucionario Institucional, or PRI, controls all the branches of the federal government and all the state governments. Other parties exist, to be sure. A few, such as the Partido Popular Socialista, lay claim to being the uncorrupted heirs of Mexico's revolutionary tradition. One party, the Partido de Acción Nacional, or PAN, represents pro-enterprise, antisocialist opposition to PRI. None of these opposition parties suffers from obvious oppression by the government, except in the usual sense that any "out" group may be handicapped in its opposition to a party fully in control of the political machinery. But none of these parties has more than a few hundred thousand members and none garners more than 5 or 10 per cent of the national popular vote. Here and there, a local official is elected with their support. In addition, a few seats in the legislature are usually captured by or assigned to these opposition groups. But their opposition has more symbolic than tangible significance; it is merely evidence of the fact that Mexico's monolithic political structure today is not the product of brute suppression and force.

Not until one observes the operation of Mexico's economy at close quarters does he begin to sense the great diffusion of political power and political viewpoints that exists despite the monolithic façade of the presidency. Though the president's right to call the tune on any critical economic issue is not seriously challenged from any quarter, the president is constantly aware that he must use his staggering power with discretion, on pain of destroying the system which has given him the power. This is a key point in any understanding of Mexican political behavior. The elements behind the precarious position of the presidency are complex, but a few points can be made here in the nature of a preview.

In the first place, though the president is backed by the overwhelming power of his party at the polls, one can look in vain for a tight ideological bond cementing its many splinters. The universal allegiance of the leaders of PRI to the Revolution has only slightly more substance than the asserted allegiance of the United States politician to the Founding Fathers. Allegiance to the Revolution implies adherence to such general goals as the equitable distribution of land and decent conditions for labor, but it leaves the adherent uncommitted in choosing his methods and timing for the achievement of these goals. The PRI adherents, in short, encompass only a little less than the 180 degrees of opinion in the fan of the typical European parliamentary structure. And all of these splinters must have some measure of access and some significant degree of persuasion upon the policies of the presidency if the pitch of dissension inside the PRI is to be held within tolerable limits.

More important still, the PRI is far from being the only effective channel of communication to the ear of the executive. In fact, some would say that it is far from being an effective channel at all. The president always has to be wary not only of dangerous pressures inside the PRI but also of threatening forces which are not a part of the PRI machinery. Accordingly, the day-to-day operation of government in Mexico entails an incessant process of consultation, conciliation, and compromise between the seeming governors and the governed. Though the governed sometimes make themselves heard through the mechanism of the PRI, far more often their channels of communication are through organizations quite out-side the formal political structure. Some of these channels, such as the national chambers of commerce and industry, are recognized by law and entail compulsory membership for business enterprises of stated kinds. Other channels, however, depend upon the com-manding position of individuals or small groups whose economic power and potential political strength have won them a special right to the ear of key ministers or of the president himself.

THE PRIVATE SECTOR

Measured in output terms, Mexico is an economy of private enterprise; over nine tenths of its production comes from the private sector.* A few words about the composition of this sector, therefore, are needed to set the stage.

Any description of the structure of Mexico's private sector, as it bears on the problem of economic development, gets us into a good deal of conjecture; but some points are clear. One is that agriculture, when measured in terms of sheer manpower, is the dominant activity of the private sector. Though the output of agriculture is roughly equal to that of private manufacturing activ-ities (as Table 2 showed), agriculture nonetheless engages four or five times as much manpower as manufacturing; indeed agri-culture accounts for more than half of Mexico's total labor force.

Mexican agriculture, however, is far from a homogeneous activ-ity. For one thing, about half of the land under cultivation in the country is held under individual title and the other half is held under collective title. There is a gulf between the two kinds of holdings, both in legal and in operational terms. True, the collec-tively held land, organized through the collective village or the *ejido,* is almost always worked by individual farmers rather than by the collective group. But the position of the ejidal farmer differs from that of the private landowner principally in two respects: in

* When Mexicans use the phrase "el sector privado," they usually mean to exclude agriculture and labor. Here, however, the phrase is applied to all the economic activity outside the public sector.

the inability of the farmer on ejidal land to mortgage the land, and in the somewhat equivocal character of his rights of continued possession and of inheritance.

Partly as a result of these differences but partly also for other reasons such as location and quality, the agricultural lands owned by individuals channel a larger proportion of their output into commercial outlets than do the ejidal lands; as a rule, the individual lands operate with larger credit resources, more irrigation water, more fertilizer, and more machinery per unit of land or labor than the ejidal lands; and, on the whole, the individual lands yield more per acre, measured in value terms, than do the ejidal lands. Of course, there are numerous exceptions to all these generalizations. The individual proprietors of tiny parcels of land, for instance, are more closely akin to the ejidal farmers in their operating patterns than to the individual proprietors of larger land parcels.[4] But the distinctions are useful nonetheless, and they are reflected in a rather different relationship between the government and the landowning farmers than prevails between the government and the members of the ejidos.

The attitude of the government toward the ejidos is constantly solicitous and paternalistic, at least as far as the outside observer can tell. It would be surprising if it were otherwise. The ejidos in large part are the creatures of the government, constituted or regenerated by one administration or another since the Revolution as a vehicle through which land reform and redistribution are achieved. A special government bank, noted for its disposition not to press too hard on loans in arrears, is the principal source of credit for the ejidal farmer. Special dispensations are made to the ejido in the public provision of water, fertilizer, and machinery. In return, the ejidos form an overtly acquiescent and dutiful part of the PRI, a part which can generally be counted on to support official policy without apparent demurrer.[5]

The seeming preference of the government for the ejido does not mean that the individual landowner, particularly the large landowner, suffers from excessive discrimination at the government's hands. On the contrary, his final performance — as recorded by his inputs of water, fertilizer, and machinery and his outputs of agricultural products — points to the opposite conclusion. But the individual landowner differs from the collective farmer in the means by which he achieves results. To begin with, he feels that he owes nothing to the government for the possession of his lands. On the contrary, any large landowner is always confronted with the threat that some of his property may be expropriated under the discretionary powers of the land reform laws. For many large landholders, there is also the nagging worry that some of the extra-legal means by which they hold the oversized parcels may be exposed and that control over some of the land may be lost.

Worried or not, the individual landowner has no hesitation in demanding government credits to match the credits which are granted to the ejidal farmers. In fact, such credits have been funneled through credit unions to the individual farmer in aggregate amounts exceeding those extended to the ejido. Unlike the ejidal farmer, however, the individual landowner also draws heavily upon private domestic banks; and in the north of Mexico, where production is strongly oriented to the export markets, the individual landowner even draws a considerable part of his financing from foreign sources.

In the individual landowner's demand for the things that only the government can provide — notably, in his efforts to obtain roads and irrigation works — he seems to work on a much more aggressive and individualistic basis than do the farmers of the ejido. Many landowners, for instance, elect not to join that sector of the PRI which is reserved to agriculture but instead to exert their influence in the party through the so-called "popular sector," which is much the most aggressive and individualistic of the various party sectors. Others will have nothing to do with the PRI and prefer to exert their influence through direct intervention in the government ministries. Some of these farmers, especially in northern states, react on this pattern out of a long-time hostility to the government party. Some, including those who are farmers only in the sense that they provide the financing for fairly large-scale commercial agriculture, avoid the party simply because it can be more efficient for a businessman of substance to take his problems directly to the officials and technicians concerned.

Outside agriculture, a number of major groups in the private sector serve as the principal organizational structures for the purpose of dealing with the government. The bankers, for instance, use as their main organizational channel an Asociación de Banqueros; the manufacturers, a Confederación de Cámaras Industriales (CONCAMIN); the merchants, a Confederación de Cámaras Nacionales de Comercio (CONCANACO). But this does not mean that each group is a homogeneous package.

Consider the case of Mexico's private banking community. A certain element of homogeneity exists, to be sure. Except for one or two mavericks, for instance, practically every member of the banking community is devoted to two general propositions: that the credit restrictions imposed by the Banco de México are too severe and too particularistic, leaving little room for the exercise either of creativeness or discretion on the part of the private banking fraternity; and that the competition of government banks has been both unfair and destructive of the development of an effective credit mechanism. These are standard affirmations of faith essential to continued good standing in the banking community. But each of the country's major banks, apart from its support of these general positions, appears to have a distinct personality in its relations with the government, developed over many years of operations. The Banco Nacional de México, the country's leading commercial bank, enjoys the reputation of being a responsible and sympathetic collaborator with recent government administrations. The Banco de Londres y México is generally considered more remote and unbending in its relations with the government. A number of other banks, typically newer and smaller, are commonly thought of as institutions "on the make," concentrating on the use of inside government connections to build their affiliated industrial enterprises. And so it goes. Each of a dozen or so banks is sufficiently large and sufficiently well connected that it need not rely upon the collective strength of the Asociación de Banqueros to press its points effectively before the government. A certain measure of heterogeneity also exists inside the organizations which represent the nation's industry and commerce. Once again, there are common elements of interest to which a clear majority subscribes; for example, taxes on corporate profits should be kept low; government enterprises should not engage in unfair competition with existing Mexican industry; foreign investment should be restrained in some degree; and machinery and materials used by any particular industry for its operations should be admitted into Mexico without restriction, whereas the end-products of the industry should be protected from foreign competition. But there are also striking differences. First, there is the traditional aloofness of the Monterrey industrial group — a group whose origins go back beyond the 1910 Revolution and whose traditions are those of open hostility to the "socialistic and godless" central governments of the Revolution. Then there is the difference in emphasis between the industries which in general feel their interests best served by a minimum of government activity in the economic sphere and those which still feel the need for government help.

This split over government activity finds its principal expression through the public utterances on the one hand of the manufacturers' CONCAMIN and the merchants' CONCANACO, and on the other hand of the Cámara Nacional de la Industria de Transformación (CNIT), a constituent group of CONCAMIN consisting principally of small manufacturing enterprises. CONCAMIN and CONCANACO tend to be under the control of entities which are capable of generating their own internal sources of credit or of borrowing from private domestic or foreign sources, and which therefore show a predilection for keeping the government's role in economic activity under considerable restraint. CNIT, on the other hand, consists largely of smaller, newer, and on the whole more "indigenous" units, lacking adequate credit and fearful of the competition of foreign capital; hence their preference for extensive government intervention in these areas.

Broad national organizations such as CONCAMIN, CONCA-NACO, and CNIT are not the only structures through which Mexican business tries to pool its strength. Of considerably more importance in the day-to-day contacts between business and government are the dozen or so major groups which have been created in Mexico through the linking of the country's principal enterprises. A large proportion of the major industrial and banking enterprises of Mexico belong to one or another of these groups.[6] Nonetheless, though the existence of the groups is an important and indisputable fact of Mexican business life, it is not easy to define them precisely. Each group characteristically incorporates a banking institution or two and an assortment of industrial enterprises. Sometimes a dominant personality or principal stockholder is the chief link among them, as in the case of the Antonio Sacristán and Carlos Trouyet groups; sometimes it is a common major source of credit, as in the case of the Banco Nacional de México group; sometimes it is a community of interest blended of credit sources, family connections, or geography, as illustrated by the complex composed of Monterrey and Banco de Londres y México interests or by some of the smaller groups of the provincial cities. Even the public sector can be said to have its group, composed mainly of Nacional Financiera — the government's principal development bank — and the thirteen companies in which it has a controlling interest.

To add to the complexity, many of the groups work with others in an intricate system of alliances. Some groups work more easily with the government-controlled enterprises than do others. Some frequently operate in tandem, as in the case of the Carlos Trouyet and Raúl Bailleres groups. Others have so many interconnections that one may think of them either as separate groups or as parts of a single group, as in the case of the Banco Nacional de México and the Carlos Prieto interests.

Whatever the patterns may be, however, the motivations which have generated the patterns are clear. One such motivation is the need of businessmen for an assured source of credit. The pooling of enterprises means, in effect, that the profits of the slow growers in the group can be made available to those expanding more rapidly. It also means that the collective borrowing power of the whole group is available to any of its members; thus a group can go to foreign sources or to government credit agencies such as Nacional Financiera, and negotiate for credits on a scale which gives it a decided advantage over unconnected firms. Negotiations are carried on not only for credits but for other purposes; indeed, another major motivation for the creation of the groups has been the general enhancement of bargaining power vis-à-vis the government. The fact that a central core of entrepreneurs could call on the resources of a number of enterprises has meant that proposals to the government could be put together, modified, or expanded to achieve the most favorable possible reception. For example, the ability of the group to command large resources means, as it does in most countries, that the government's contracting agents look more benignly on a bid for public business from some enterprise in the group. If the group is trying to obtain import permits for an oversized drill press or for supplies of stainless steel, its offer to have an affiliate produce some intermediate product for a government-owned plant may create an important friend in court. If an enterprise in the group is faced with the need to use scarce Mexican materials in a manufacturing process in order to qualify for a tax exemption under the law, its ability to command those materials from a related company gives it an important advantage. And so on.

In short, in a manner which suggests the operation of the Galbraithian doctrine of countervailing power, the industries of Mexico have tended to group themselves in a way which permits them to deal more effectively with the Goliath represented by the Mexican government.

One final aspect of the private sector of Mexico's economy needs to be introduced at this point, namely, the influence of foreigners in the economy's operation and control. Most Mexicans are extraordinarily sensitive on the subject, for reasons which will become perfectly clear to the reader as he works his way through the chapters that follow. The existence of that sensitivity makes the facts more than usually difficult to come by. Nevertheless, the situation is clear on a number of points, which we shall summarize here and elaborate in later chapters.

The pervasive influence of United States consumer tastes and United States technology is evident throughout the Mexican economy. United States brand names and United States designs are paraded before the Mexican public through publications, moving pictures, tourism, and a dozen other channels. United States technology flows into the country through the *ad hoc* visits of outside technicians, through formal technical assistance or licensing contracts, and through the channels established between subsidiaries and their parent companies.

Actual foreign control of Mexican private enterprise, however, is far more limited than foreign influence of the sort just discussed. In agriculture, one would not be risking much if he were to surmise that a certain amount of United States capital has been quietly invested in the lands devoted to Mexican export crops — such as cotton, tomatoes, and cattle — in the northern states close to the United States border. But outside these areas, foreign ownership in agriculture is probably of very little importance. In mining, electric power, and transportation, the facts are easier to verify; foreign ownership, which once dominated all these sectors, is being squeezed back to a minority position in mining and has been practically extinguished in the others. Only in manufacturing is foreign ownership and control of much significance. Here, as one scans the list of major Mexican manufacturing companies, there is no question that a significant proportion is controlled by foreign interests, principally United States interests. In terms of output, the United States-controlled manufacturing companies probably account for something on the order of one fifth or one sixth of total Mexican production in the manufacturing sector; but since the foreign-controlled activity tends to be concentrated in well-known nationally distributed products, the general impression is one of even greater foreign dominance. This dominance — its continuation, its expansion, its reduction, or its suppression — is never far from the center of the stage in the interplay between the public and the private sectors.

THE CONFRONTATION

In a country whose private sector accounts for more than nine tenths of its output, the question of the interplay with the public sector may not seem of transcendental importance. The importance of the subject is fully appreciated only when we recognize that Mexico's government takes a major hand in rationing the supply of three factors which are perennially scarce at this stage of Mexico's growth, to wit, credits, imports, and public facilities.

The scramble for long-term and short-term credits is one of the critical activities of any entrepreneur in Mexico, a life-and-death matter in any growing enterprise. But the Mexican government's control of such credits is pervasive, selective, and particularistic. The government's interest in credits begins with its desire to reserve a certain part of the available supply for the financing of public investment. Then, it tries to channel what is left into activities of the private economy which it considers of high priority, while choking off the flow to "nonproductive" pursuits. In the "high priority" category, for instance, one would usually find industry and agriculture, and in the "nonproductive" category, the construction of high-cost housing and the financing of commodity inventories. Beyond these objectives — reserving credits to the public sector and channeling the rest to "productive pursuits" — the government has still another objective in sitting astride the flow of credits, namely, that of holding down foreign claims and foreign investment in the Mexican economy. To thread one's way through the resulting system of government roadblocks, regulations, and incentives in the field of credit, therefore, becomes an absorbing problem of management.

In the regulation of imports, the stakes are often just as critical to the existence of the private sector. Though imports account for no more than one fifth of the total goods consumed in the country, there is scarcely a major branch of Mexican industry or agriculture which is not affected directly and significantly by the government's import policy. The government uses its powers in the field of foreign trade with vigor and flexibility. It "closes the border" to any product whenever it believes that the public interest would be served by such action. And it raises or lowers official import duties with unusual frequency; indeed, whenever the government sees fit, it exempts selected importers from duties while continuing to apply the duties to other importers.

The motivations behind these measures are neither simple nor invariant. They include the desire to stimulate the domestic production of consumer goods; to force existing Mexican producers toward greater use of Mexican materials and machinery; to conserve scarce foreign exchange; to increase government revenue from customs duties; to raise prices on some products and lower them on others, in order to force an internal redistribution of income; to discourage foreign investors and encourage domestic ones inside the country; and so on. The objectives continually change and clash as the situation of the country and the strategy of the government evolve. Scarce wonder that the representatives of the private sector are always preoccupied with the puzzling question of the government's import policy and looking for a path through the maze.

The parceling out of scarce public facilities is the third critical area in the relations between the public and private sectors. At times, the initiative for securing government action comes from existing enterprises; at other times, the initiative comes from the government in the expectation that the facilities will generate new lines of economic activity. Spectacular illustrations are easy to find. The development of the cotton crop of Mexico has depended almost entirely upon the decisions of the Mexican government on whether to build irrigation works and where to place them. The scale and location of Mexico's industry have been influenced critically by the government's decisions on the structure of Mexico's power rates and on the location of Mexico's power and transportation facilities. Once again, the ability to penetrate the structure of the government's decision-making machinery has been decisive in the fortunes of much of Mexico's private sector.

Of course, much of what has been said so far about the importance of the interrelations between the public and private sectors in Mexico could be said with some measure of validity for any modern nation in the world. If there are differences between Mexico and other nations, they stem largely from two related features of the Mexican government's regulatory activities: first, the relative pervasiveness and vigor of the government's regulatory measures; second, the extraordinary degree of particularity and discrimination in the application of those regulatory powers. Enough has already been said to offer a glimpse of the ubiquitousness of the Mexican government's directive efforts. But a word or two may still be in order on the subject of particularity and discrimination.

No writer can free himself altogether from the taint of ethnocentricity. And a writer from the United States cannot avoid being impressed — perhaps overly impressed — with what appear to be fundamental differences in the approach to government regulation as between the two countries. Most federal law and regulation in the United States operate from the premise that there are objective standards to be applied, indeed guaranteed, on a nondiscriminatory basis to all comers. Of course, the actual performance is sometimes at variance with the ideal, as graft, favoritism, and error creep into the administrative machinery; but the ideal persists as a living, operating norm.

Mexican administration, on the other hand, places less emphasis upon the rights and guarantees of the individual, and more emphasis upon the discretionary rights of the state, acting as the agent of the public interest. Therefore fewer cases are decided automatically by general rule and more are determined by specific *ad hoc* decisions. This, in turn, means that the degree of predictability and uniformity of the government's treatment of its citizens tends to be lower than in, say, the United States. Importer A may find his import duties waived on a particular product, but Importer B may not. Foreigner X may be required to sell a half interest in his firm to Mexican investors, but Foreigner Y may continue to hold the full equity in his operation. The cotton crop of the State of Nuevo León may be assessed an export duty of 22 per cent, but that of the State of Sonora may be taxed only 10 per cent. Price control may be imposed and enforced on one critical drug, but price control of another critical drug may be nonexistent. The differences in treatment may be justifiable under the criteria being used by the government — or they may not. The important point is that the private sector operates in a milieu in which the public sector is in a position to make or break any private firm.

At the same time, the style of Mexican politics and Mexican government operations is such that there is continual personal contact between government officials and businessmen. There is no wide ideological barrier, no explosively sensitive public opinion which demands that contact be only at arm's length. The atmosphere varies, of course, from one government agency to another, and from one presidential regime to the next. But it would be wrong to think of Mexico as a battleground on which the public sector and private enterprise are belligerently arrayed. It is altogether possible for Nacional Financiera to arrange a major financing operation jointly with some powerful private financial group, and for the Compañía Nacional de Subsistencias Populares — the government food-marketing agency — to enter into extensive arrangements with the private food-distribution industry. Frictions, suspicions, and uncertainties exist, to be sure, but they are not so great as to paralyze participation by either sector.

It would be conceivable at this point to frame the obvious syllogism and to close the book: Mexico has developed its own special system of relationships between the public and private sectors; Mexico has grown substantially over the past several decades;

therefore the Mexican system of public-private relationships, at the very least, is not inconsistent with satisfactory growth.

But even this timid and tentative conclusion could well be wrong. For the Mexican institutions of today are different in many ways from those that existed twenty years ago and strikingly different from those of the pre-Revolutionary era. As a result, all kinds of alternative propositions suggest themselves. Could it be that the growth of Mexico in the modern era is based upon the impetus generated by its public and private institutional structures of earlier decades, rather than by the present structure? Can the country's modern growth be taking place despite drawbacks in the existing structure, rather than because of that structure? Is the recent slowdown in growth perhaps a reflection of inadequacies in the structure, and a forerunner of greater difficulties in the future? To get the glimmerings of answers to questions such as these, one needs to go at least a century back into Mexican history.

Chapter 2

Juárez and Díaz

O**UT** of the clash and synthesis of current ideas and historic experience, most countries have managed to generate their own unique sets of interacting expectations between the governors and the governed. In any given country the governed will expect, on the part of the state, aggressive or passive behavior, variable or uniform treatment, efficient or inefficient performance, solicitousness or indifference, insolence or civility. The state, in turn, will have developed its own expectations about the behavior of the governed — participation or remoteness, adherence or avoidance, passivity or aggressiveness. In every century, these two-way expectations deeply affect the nature of the political process, color the form of laws and regulations, and influence the character of their enforcement.

In modern-day Mexico, we find a fairly well-defined set of expectations on the part of the private sector concerning the behavior of the government, and an equally clear set running in the other direction. Some of these expectations are a product of fairly recent history; no Mexican of the nineteenth century, for instance, would have expected the government to maintain free clinics in the principal cities or to promulgate minimum-wage laws. But other — and, on the whole, more basic — elements in the modern-day relations between the citizen and his government go deep into Mexican history, lending a touch of credence to such shopworn clichés as "ancient Mexico" and "the timeless land."

JUÁREZ AND THE REFORM

When Benito Juárez became president of Mexico in 1858, he inherited a country whose ruling institutions, traditions, and habits of mind had been solidly established in three centuries of rule by the Spanish Crown. These institutions and attitudes, however, implied roles for the state and its citizens that were utterly repugnant to the Juárez philosophy. Juárez represented a tiny group of rebel intellectuals in Mexico whose ideology flowed out of the political doctrines of Quesnay, Rousseau, and Jefferson, and whose economic views derived from Adam Smith and John Stuart Mill.[1] Though many differences of view were expressed within the group, the society which most of them conceived of as ideal was one in which the state performed an essentially passive and impersonal role, a role as guarantor of the basic economic and personal rights of the individual. In economic terms, it was a society in which the individual, not the state or the corporate body, was the instrument of economic growth.

The Mexico of 1858, however, still accepted the old values. For three centuries, ending in 1821, the prevailing theory of property had been that all use of property was a concession by the Crown to its subjects. All rights lay ultimately with the Crown; hence, to the extent that the Crown demanded it, such rights had to be bought and paid for.

The system of the Spanish Crown, therefore, was one of pervasive law and regulation. Economic life was organized by highly detailed and particularistic provisions, aimed at granting and maintaining a complex web of privileges and monopolies. Trade with any country other than Spain was illegal. Import and export licenses for trade with Spain could only be obtained through a board, sitting in Seville, controlled by Spanish merchants. Trade inside Mexico was controlled almost as rigorously as foreign trade; local monopolies, trading privileges, and tax exemptions proliferated in every area of the colony. And production was controlled even more than trade. In principle, nothing fabricated in Spain could be produced in Mexico; and what was produced in Mexico was subject to the minutest regulation.[2]

This conception of the relation of business to the state still prevailed in the mid-nineteenth century, thirty years after the end of Spanish rule. And a related state of mind prevailed with it. As long as the law was so pervasive in its scope and so particularistic in its application, it was inevitable that corruption would exist. First of all, the pervasiveness of regulation meant that any operating business was at the mercy of the law. There was always some provision or other that constituted a threat, actual or potential, to the continued existence of a going business; so any business that hoped to stay afloat had to find some way of securing immunity from a hostile application of the regulations. Second, the particularistic character of the regulations was an invitation to every businessman to buy a monopoly or a favor — or to buy relief from the monopolies and favors of others.

So bribery in one form or another was an unavoidable part of the system; indeed, one wonders if the word "bribery," with all its pejorative implications, appropriately describes the process. It might be more accurate to say that businessmen, engaged at the time primarily in mining, agriculture, and trade, bought their favors from the government or its lieutenants in accordance with the system.

The fact that protection and exemption could be bought had another implication which is important in understanding the political and economic milieu of Mexico. The man who could not buy protection could not count on getting it as a matter of right. Though the Indian on the hacienda had certain paper rights, they were meaningless as a buffer between himself and his omnipotent employer. The half-Indian artisan in Mexico City or Puebla was hardly in any better position, with no real redress if the authorities dispossessed him of his trade.

In an environment lacking an impersonal and impartial system of protection under law, a measure of security was found, nonetheless, by a different route. Throughout the social structure of Mexico, men looked for some patron, leader, or protector who could give them the security they needed. A social structure was built on the relationship between protector and protected. The hacienda owner allied himself to the local military chief, the general swore allegiance to the governor, and so on. As a matter of survival, loyalty ran to the protector rather than to some abstract concept such as the state.

One of the institutions which provided a measure of protection to the humble rural Mexican was the Catholic Church. If any force existed to protect the ordinary Mexican from slavery in the mines or excessive abuse in the haciendas of the Spaniards, it was the rural priest and the hierarchy on which he could call. Of course, there were many well-documented instances in which the Church administrators themselves were venal, abusive, and exploitative. But a large part of the enormous landholdings of the Church was typically administered in a style which does not suffer by comparison with the private enterprises of the time. Trained administrators maintained the large establishments of the Church on a basis of local self-sufficiency, often in a spirit of benign paternalism. This pattern, which had developed before the era of Independence, survived 1821 and was another major factor in the social structure of the Juárez era.

In any such setting a certain amount of regional separatism would have been inevitable. In the case of Mexico the tendency to regionalism was aggravated by the country's disconcerting geography — by its remote and impenetrable mountains and jungles, set off by great stretches of thinly populated arid wasteland. The geography of the country not only handicapped the overland movement of goods but also encouraged the retention of major linguistic and cultural differences. The physical scene was such as to challenge the authority of any central government. Local rebellion was easy; and wherever local rebels gained autonomy, they usually imposed the only kind of law they knew — systems of monopoly and personal privilege.

Juárez faced a nation, therefore, which was not yet a nation in an economic sense. The local powers-that-be throughout Mexico, in order to enforce their local privileges and at the same time to generate government revenues, were levying taxes on any goods that tried to penetrate their little markets from outside. Manufactured goods from foreign countries were usually favored with a lower tax rate than goods from other parts of Mexico, because they tended to be less competitive with the local product (being of higher quality) and because they were destined for the homes and tables of the well-to-do. At times, too, the local authorities levied taxes on goods that tried to leave their areas, especially items wanted for local processing or for consumption. What difficult transportation problems and great distances had already achieved in part, was more fully achieved with the help of local law; Mexico was divided into an infinite number of tiny markets.

Prospective investors were unlikely to risk much in the economic development of such a country. Juárez was confronted with the fact that investment, when it did take place, was either investment by the Church in real property or investment by individuals in enterprises which they had a chance of protecting with a force of local retainers — that is, ranches, haciendas, and plantations.

There were occasional exceptions, of course. From time to time Mexican governments in the period before Juárez had made sporadic efforts to stimulate the industrialization of Mexico. In these efforts, import prohibitions, government credit, and tax exemptions had been used.[3] Here and there, some stubborn entrepreneur, borrowing from the swiftly developing technology of the United States and the United Kingdom, had managed to overcome fantastic obstacles and to import the machinery and methods of large-scale plants into Mexico.[4]

But the only significant investments in the pre-Juárez period portending a change in the economy of Mexico had come from misled foreign investors, mostly British, who were victims of the persistent legend of the boundless riches of Mexico. "The inhabitants of the British Isles," says J. Fred Rippy in a discussion of investments in Latin America, "indulged in a wild speculation spree in the 1820's, investing large sums in the bonds of foreign governments and in the securities of hundreds of joint stock companies organized for operation at home and abroad. Clever salesmen, scheming attorneys, and gamblers of every description swarmed through the business streets, subsidized journalists, induced members of Parliament to grant company charters and peddled engraved paper . . ." But the profits went to the salesmen, not to the investors. For instance, an issue of Mexican government bonds, bought from the Mexican government at 58 per cent of par in 1824, was down to 22 per cent in 1828. On the whole, English investment in Mexico in that era proved less profitable than in any other major Latin American country, bringing losses or only nominal returns.[5]

Confronted by a body of legal traditions, a political history, and a physical geography which bore not the remotest relationship to Western Europe or the United States, the Juárez liberals nonetheless drew upon the United States constitution as a model for the Mexican government. They sought to make a single nation of Mexico by reserving for the national government such powers as the maintenance of armies, the issuance of currency, and the regulation of foreign trade. They prohibited monopolies and special privileges to industry, they forbade the states to interfere with the internal trade of the country, and they abolished slavery and forced labor. At the same time, however, they looked to the private sector, not to the national government, as the principal engine for economic growth. In this spirit, they adopted a federal and not a central form of government for the nation; the states were conceived as the instruments of the federal government in the execution of its programs and as the repository of all rights not expressly reserved to the federal government.[6] As a result of superimposing this grand design on the fragmented Mexico of that day, two fundamental concepts of the 1857 constitution were in conflict from birth: the concept of a free, open, internal market, and the concept of a weak, decentralized government.[7]

The 1857 constitution called unequivocally for the abolition of the internal trade barriers that had been frustrating the concept of a free internal market; but these obstacles to trade were indispensable to the maintenance of local privilege and protection. A rule so long entrenched and so stoutly defended by powerful local interests could not be wiped out simply by a declaration from a remote capital city. Besides, there was no source of local revenue that could easily replace the revenue generated from these local barriers. The State of Aguascalientes derived about two thirds of its income from taxes on goods moving into the state, that of Hidalgo nearly one half, Oaxaca more than one third, and so on. Even the federal government itself imposed such duties on the movement of goods into the Federal District, in which Mexico City is located. So most states paid no attention to the constitutional provision despite considerable public agitation for its enforcement.

Nevertheless, energetic and determined men like Juárez' finance minister, Matías Romero, struggled to break the system down. And in some small ways their struggle produced a limited success. But the experience of the period suggested that one or the other basic concept of the 1857 constitution would have to go. Either the central government would have to exercise considerable power or the concept of a single national market would never be achieved.

The push toward a strong central government was generated not only by the necessity to overcome internal man-made trade restrictions but also by the strong desire of Mexico's national leaders to overcome natural transport barriers. Railroad building had begun in Mexico in 1837, barely twelve years after the inauguration of the world's first rail line in Great Britain. But when Juárez resumed office in 1868, after the bizarre interregnum of the Emperor Maximilian, the rail line which had been started thirty-one years earlier to link Mexico City with Veracruz was still unfinished. To get the railroad finished, Juárez took extraordinary measures — measures which seemed to flout basic principles rooted in the 1857 constitution. First, he granted substantial subsidies to a British concessionaire to complete and operate the line, a clear departure from the laissez-faire economic theory of the constitution's draftsmen. Second, he undertook not to subsidize any competing line for a period of seventy-five years, an obvious detour from the strictures against preferences and privileges. Third, he had the government buy stock in the company and assume the right to appoint a stated minority of the directors.

From Juárez' point of view, government participation seemed the only course despite the concepts on which his government was based. The social gains to be achieved for Mexico through an adequate railroad system seemed enormous; yet Mexican private investors would not even consider the possibility. For one thing, it is doubtful that there was much liquid wealth available in Mexico at the time, except perhaps in the treasures of the Church. For another, the insecurity of a railroad investment, when compared with rural land or urban structures, was so great as to rule it out at once. Few non-Mexicans would touch the proposal either; in the eyes of most of the world Mexico was then a land of bandits and revolutions. Only the perennially gullible British investors, inured to the risks and lured by the gains of overseas investments, would take the gamble — and then only if the risks could be held to seemingly manageable proportions by government subsidy and participation.

The Jeffersonian principles of the Juárez regime demanded freedom not only for internal trade but for international trade as well; a high level of international trade was seen as a spur to national growth. But this doctrine too was destined to clash with harsh realities. Though the regime made some preliminary gestures in the direction of lower tariffs, in the end it maintained a generally high wall of protection against imports. The forces pushing the government in this direction were exceedingly powerful. About half the income of the federal government came from customs revenues. Besides, the organized pressure of protectionist groups was strong enough to prevail against any general theory in favor of freer trade. Struggles over the duties on such basic products as wheat, flour, and cotton indicated where the balance of power lay.

There were other deviations between the asserted objectives and the actual performance of the Juárez regime. Perhaps the most tragic of these was the misfiring of the Juárez land policy.[8]

True to their general principles, the drafters of the 1857 constitution had pictured Mexico as a community of landed yeomen, of free private landholders selling their produce and buying their wants in an open market. Two kinds of landholdings stood in the way of that concept, those of the age-old cooperative Indian communities, and those of the Church. Therefore a series of enactments in the 1850's — some before and some after the date of adoption of the constitution — forced the Indian villages and the Church to give up their holdings.

The trouble with the theory was that the communal Indian had neither the attitudes, the training, nor the resources to assume the role of a sturdy yeoman. He had no recourse to a system of strong institutions that could protect him from local economic pressure or physical force. He lacked experience with land management and he lacked the cash or credit to buy the land. To make matters more difficult, any peasant who exercised his legal right to buy Church land was certain to be subjected to the frightful perils of excommunication. In these circumstances, the ordinary rural Mexican was powerless. At the same time, any individual with liquid funds or solid credit was offered a rare windfall from the sale of Church lands, provided he was willing to brave the excommunication threat. Some found the courage. All over Mexico, great estates were acquired at rock-bottom prices, frustrating the intent of Juárez and his followers.

The weakening of the communal system of agriculture and the appearance of great estates under the control of lay owners were changes of consummate importance to Mexico's later development. They contributed to the achievement of one objective in which Juárez was interested: the appearance of a market economy in Mexico. They dealt a blow to the self-sufficient agriculture which was characteristic of the Church and the Indian communities, and they opened the way for the more extensive harvesting of commercial crops. But the Juárez policy misfired because the ordinary rural Mexican did not benefit.

The history of the Juárez era, therefore, can be characterized as one in which a group of men with high ideals and personal dedication sought to apply a set of principles out of joint with the place and the times. Not that failure was altogether inevitable. Given the best possible good luck and a long period of political stability, the gamble might have worked. Despite the internal contradictions, outright errors, and pervasive uncertainties of the Juárez regime and of the Lerdo regime which followed, and despite the continual conflicts with the values of the Spanish heritage, there seems no overwhelming reason for assuming that a workable adaptation might not have taken place in time. In general, the Juárez and Lerdo administrations managed to recruit men of devotion, competence, and imagination. They dealt with Congresses which on the whole behaved neither much worse nor much better than Congresses are wont to behave in a democratic nation. Such fragmentary data as can be found indicated that Mexico's economy expanded a little under Juárez and Lerdo. In addition to completing Mexico's pioneer railroad, these regimes extended the all-weather highway grid, initiated drainage and canal projects, and financed port improvements, all on a modest scale. Unflaggingly optimistic of Mexico's future, they were always planning for Mexico's continued growth.

It requires no violent wrench of the imagination, therefore, to picture an evolutionary course for Mexico's economy, in which the principles of 1857 would eventually have found some compromise with Mexico's regionalism and with the counterproductive habits and preconceptions of Mexico's entrepreneurs and investors — a compromise which almost certainly would have given the national government a more aggressive political and economic role than first had been contemplated. It is altogether possible that the process might gradually have elevated Mexican agriculture and brought the submerged three quarters of Mexico's economy out of its vegetable existence into the modern world. But the era of Porfirio Díaz intervened, pushing the changes initiated by Juárez in quite another direction.

THE PORFIRIAN ERA

When Porfirio Díaz seized control of Mexico in 1876, the economy with which he had to deal was still overwhelmingly agricultural in character. A few signs of industrialization existed, of course; some textile plants, glass works, and sugar mills, and numerous artisans' shops, were scattered about the country. Besides, a few groups of active and able intellectuals — lawyers, doctors, teachers, and writers — could be found in Mexico City and the major provincial cities. But most of the Mexican leaders who might constitute a threat to the Díaz tenure had close ties to the land. As landed gentry devoted to a pattern of easy living and absentee ownership, they probably had little interest in promoting the economic development of Mexico.

Despite that fact, the Porfirian government seemed bent on achieving development. Why Díaz and his closest aides were interested in such an objective is not at all clear. Perhaps they saw development as the only way to pull together the scattered regions of Mexico into a working political unit which they could control. Or perhaps they felt the need to emulate the countries which they considered the "successful" powers of the world — France, Britain, Germany, and the United States.

Whatever the motives, the Porfirian era produced the first Mexican government with a strategy directed toward economic development. The substance of the strategy was to take any measures necessary to encourage large amounts of foreign investment to come to Mexico, on the theory that the capital, skills, and markets which foreigners had at their command were critical for Mexico's growth. The Porfirian concept of the Mexican economy, therefore, was a trichotomy. There was (1) the government, charged with maintaining the conditions which would attract outside capital; (2) the foreign private sector, charged with promoting the country's growth through investment; and (3) the domestic private sector, some chosen parts of which were bound to benefit from the creative activities of the foreigners.

Development and production

The stamp of Porfirian policy was so deep on Mexico's economy that the traces can still be glimpsed in the 1960's. The Porfirian policy regarding foreign capital, for instance, still provides part of the emotional backdrop against which foreign investors are judged today in Mexico's economy. Moving much less hesitantly than Juárez, Díaz invited foreign capital to finance the building of Mexico's railroad system. And following the tentative lead of Juárez, Díaz offered all kinds of monetary inducements to investors to reduce the risk of investment. Before Díaz was finished, he had added 15,000 miles of right-of-way to the 400 miles which Juárez and Lerdo had built. At the same time, the archaic trappings of ancient Spanish landholding laws and tax laws, aimed at protecting local privilege and monopoly, were swept away to give the foreigner easy access to the Mexican economy.

There was no preconceived plan in the pattern of growth. Mexico's railroad system, like every railroad system that is compelled to operate at a profit (and like many that are not), was laid out to meet the most immediate and obvious transportation needs of the nation. The government granted concessions for routes which investors were willing to finance; and investors were willing to finance the routes which gave most promise of returning a profit. These were first of all the routes which passed through the heavily populated plains of central Mexico. After that, they were the routes which might haul the bulky products of mines and plantations to the United States border or to coastal ports for shipment overseas. Accordingly, many of the more remote corners of Mexico were not reached by railroad and were left behind in the not-so-splendid isolation of the pre-railroad age.

How long this policy of railroad building through foreign capital would have gone on in Mexico is anybody's guess. But in the last years of the Porfirian regime, there were the faint rumblings of change. In 1906, José Ives Limantour — the best known and most powerful of Díaz' ministers — had bitter things to say about the "inadequacy" of the existing railroad grid and the threat of domination by foreign interests, using the very arguments which Díaz' critics would later use in condemnation of the Díaz regime.[9] And in 1908, Limantour was largely responsible for having the government buy a controlling interest in Mexico's main railroad lines. The era of laissez-faire railroad building could well have been coming to an end anyhow; but what would have replaced it is something we shall never know.[10]

The growth of Mexico's railroads was indispensable to the achievement of a major Mexican objective — an objective which had dominated the policies of Juárez and Lerdo and which now influenced the policies of the Porfirian era. This was the conversion of Mexico from a country of isolated little markets, chopped up by a difficult geography and by man-made trade restrictions, to one in which goods could move easily and freely. Railroad-building, of course, was not enough; there was also the problem of controlling the state and local trade barriers which flourished all through Mexico in spite of the 1857 constitution and in spite of the tentative efforts of Juárez and Lerdo to trim them back. In 1884 and 1886, Díaz amended Juárez' constitution so that the illegality of these internal restrictions was made clear beyond question. And in 1896, Díaz put his constitutional amendments into practical effect.

Mexico's private economy responded strongly to the breakdown of its internal barriers, sometimes in spectacular and unanticipated ways. A foretaste of the extent and unpredictability of the impact had been provided during the Lerdo era by the railroad line from Veracruz to Mexico City. The principal product of the line — 30 per cent of all its domestic cargo — proved to be pulque, the poor man's "beer" of Mexico. Behind that statistic lay a dramatic alteration in the character of the pulque trade up and down the length of the line. Producers of pulque in the vicinity of the maguey-growing area of Apizaco suddenly found the rich market of Mexico City open to them. Pulque producers in Mexico City, more remote from adequate sources of supply, were no match for the Apizaco producers; Mexico City lost its high-cost producers while Apizaco grew. Cheap Apizaco pulque also made its way for the first time to the port of Veracruz, adding to the consumer choices — and the law-enforcement difficulties — of the city. In short, Apizaco became a major center for the region's pulque production with all the attendant advantages of an inexpensive source of supply and large-scale production.[11] In the Porfirian period, there were scores of illustrations of this sort — illustrations of the principle that cheap and rapid transportation could drive down costs by widening the market for the private producers who were most strategically located and giving them new opportunities for large-scale production.

One of the most dramatic illustrations was that of cotton. For a long time, Mexico's cotton growers had been protected from foreign competition by a high protective tariff. Nonetheless, at the beginning of the Porfirian period, Mexico's internal transport was so primitive and so unreliable that the textile manufacturers located their plants near the coasts and relied principally on the imported raw material rather than on the domestic product. The result was that large clusters of mills were found in and near Veracruz and Orizaba, where access to the imported product was easy. At that stage, therefore, Mexico's domestic cotton production tended to locate near the mills, close by the Gulf of Mexico.

As the railroads reached northward, however, they opened up new cotton land, much superior to that of the Gulf areas. At first, the mere opening of the new lands had little effect on cotton production; on the contrary, production declined for some years after the railroads appeared, perhaps because of some new uncertainties in land tenure which the Porfirian era introduced. But in the latter years of the era, production expanded spectacularly in the northern states of Sonora and Nuevo León. By 1910, Mexico's cotton production had risen to over 40,000 tons, doubling the production of the late 1870's. By that time, Mexico was very close to a self-sufficient basis in cotton despite a significant expansion in its use.

The Porfirian policy, besides seeking to create an easier flow of goods inside Mexico, had another strand that was reminiscent of Juárez and Lerdo — its approach to the regulation of international trade. Like the leading spokesmen of the Juárez period, the Porfirian group thought they saw a hope for Mexico's economic development through a great expansion in its exports; this view was all of a piece with the concept that foreign capital would be the salvation of Mexico. Díaz lowered export taxes and gave every impetus to increased exports. On the import side, the savants of the Porfirian era, like the economic philosophers of 1857, were disposed in general to favor the classical free-trade doctrine, though the writings of the later group — for example, of Joaquin D. Casasús, Francisco Bulnes, and Limantour himself — show perhaps slightly less enthusiasm for the lowering of import barriers than the writings of the 1850's. In its actual performance the Porfirian regime ran up against pressures somewhat similar to those of the Juárez era and behaved in approximately the same pattern. Except in drought years, the traditionally high protection on agricultural products was retained. When manufacturers tried to break down this barrier in order to get access to cheaper raw materials, they usually lost the debate. To the extent that manufacturing itself received protection against imports, it was usually with the justification that the duties were needed for revenue, rather than with the purpose of protection.[12]

But if there were similarities in economic performance between Porfirio Díaz and his predecessors, there were also enormous differences. In sweeping away the web of restraints which had inhibited foreign capital in the past and in enforcing peace and security for such capital, Díaz assigned a role to foreigners in Mexico's internal economy which has very few parallels in the history of modern states. Attracted by opportunities in Mexico, United States investments rose from 200 million United States dollars in 1897 to about 1100 million by 1911. The British increased their investments from $164 million in 1880 to over $300 million in 1911, and the French increased their investments from under $100 million in 1902 to something in the neighborhood of $400 million in 1911.[13] Though the figures seem just barely short of incredible, the available estimates suggest that, of Mexico's total investment outside agriculture and the handicraft industries, foreign interests accounted for two thirds.

In order to appreciate some of the implications of this foreign investment for Mexico's development, it is important to draw some sharp distinctions among the different elements that made up the total. To begin with, there were the investments financed by the perennial victims of the investment bankers of the period, mostly channeled into the railways and Mexican government bonds; these investments alone accounted for considerably more than one half of the foreign total in 1911. Though the productiveness of much of these investments was evident, notably in the form of the growing railroad grid, investments in this category were destined in the end to be defaulted and to be settled at large discounts.

Second in importance were the export-oriented investments, those concerned with generating products for sale in foreign markets. These investments were unquestionably far more profitable, and they led to a rapid expansion of Mexico's output during the two decades which straddled the beginning of the twentieth century. Production and exports of precious metals, copper, lead, zinc, graphite, antimony, and other mining products rose swiftly. So did the output of cattle and cattleskins, cotton, chickpeas, rubber, vanilla, sugar, guayule, henequen, chicle, and ixtle, and all these joined the list of major exports.

The third category of foreign investments, though least important in quantity, was in some ways the most significant. These were the investments made by immigrants, mostly Frenchmen and Spaniards, supplemented by a few British, Germans, and North Americans. Their interests lay largely in the development of industries serving the internal markets of Mexico. Part of their funds came with them from the mother country, and part was provided by their overseas contacts. The immigrants tended to invest in banking, trade, and the spindling manufacturing industries which Mexico's internal markets by this time were beginning to support.

The role of the immigrants in starting up industrial plants during the Porfirian era was extraordinarily important.[14] Most of the major cotton textile plants that came into being during this period claimed a Frenchman as a major partner, usually a dominant one. The new large breweries of the period, such as those of Toluca, Monterrey, Guadalajara, and Orizaba, usually reported a German group among their founders. And in paper, cement, explosives, and steel, French, British, United States, or Spanish entrepreneurs were prominent. The *1914 Mexican Yearbook,* reporting on twenty-seven large manufacturing firms in Mexico, provides data which suggest that eighteen were completely "foreign" and that at least twenty-five had some measure of "foreign ownership." [15]

Nonetheless, we begin to see also the solid beginnings of a Mexican indigenous industrial class. In the first place, the immigrants themselves were Mexicanized in the course of time, sometimes rapidly. True, many of the families concerned were still being referred to as foreigners — "Frenchmen," "North Americans," "Germans," and "Jews" — several generations after they had acquired Mexican citizenship. But the group survived the Revolutionary era which followed their arrival and made a solid contribution to the creation of the modern Mexican industrial class. In addition, Mexicans of longer standing were also active in the industrial beginnings of the Porfirian era. To be sure, most Mexican capital was still reluctant to leave the haciendas and retail trade and go into risky manufacturing ventures. Still, there were exceptions. Some Mexicans joined the foreigners as partners in their newly established enterprises. Others started their own firms, probably small firms on the whole, in the more familiar lines such as textile plants and sugar mills. In the aggregate, according to one estimate, new domestic investment in manufacturing during the period from 1886 to 1910 exceeded new foreign investment in manufacturing by more than two to one.[16]

As one looks at Mexico's performance in the Porfirian era, this aspect of the era — the beginnings of the emergence of a modern indigenous industrial base — seems a development of the highest importance. The process by which this feeble beginning was made, therefore, is worth a little further exploration. The process appears to have started with the expansion of Mexico's exports. As Table 3

TABLE 3

Indexes of Exports and Imports of Mexico, 1888–1910
(1900–01 = 100)

Period[a]	Annual quantity of exports[b]	Annual quantity of imports	Ratio of export price index to import price index[c]
1888–1894	57.0	54.6	0.76
1895–1899	90.8	80.4	0.93
1900–1904	113.0	111.6	1.02
1905–1910	143.1	143.1	1.05

[a] The data are actually for fiscal years beginning in the indicated calendar year. Data for fiscal years beginning 1890, 1891, and 1908 are missing and are not included in the averages. The quantities are estimated by deflating value figures with price indexes and using base weights of 1900–01.
[b] The export index, so-called, is actually based on the quantity of exports of merchandise plus the quantity of production of precious metals.
[c] The price of silver is not included in the export price index, hence is not reflected in the ratio.
Source: El Colegio de México, *Comercio exterior de México, 1877–1911* (Mexico, D.F.: Talleres Gráficos de Impresiones Modernas, 1960), pp. 157, 163.

shows, the prices at which Mexico was able to sell its goods to the world grew increasingly favorable to Mexico, favorable in the sense that Mexico's export prices increased faster than the prices of the goods Mexico was buying from abroad. The one major departure from this generally helpful trend was in the price of silver, which persisted in falling during most of the Porfirian regime as the United States demonetized the metal. This, of course, was a departure of some significance in view of the importance to Mexico of silver exports; but even this handicap did not prevent the swift growth of Mexico's overseas earnings and of her capacity to import goods from abroad.

Not all of Mexico's imports were financed by her exports; some were financed by the fresh capital which kept pouring into Mexico during the Porfirian period. And not all of Mexico's exports were available to finance her imports; some of the proceeds were used to pay the interest, dividends, and other home remittances generated by the foreign investment in Mexico. On balance, as shown in Table 3, Mexico's imports grew swiftly, and at about the same rate as her exports of goods plus her production of precious metals — this latter sometimes being defined as her "capacity to import." (It is difficult to know just how these figures should be adjusted to reflect smuggling; presumably imports would be adjusted upward somewhat.)

Though the expanded exports were valuable to the Mexican economy for the imports they financed, the most important legacy which Mexico's expanded exports left to the country was the 15,000 miles of railroad grid. As we have already suggested, the advent of the railroad had irreversible consequences on the markets for manufactured products. Before the railroad appeared, the only producers of manufactured goods operating on a large-scale basis with wide-flung markets were the larger textile mills. Textiles, with their comparatively simple technology, low capital investment, and easily transported final product, could be produced on a large scale long before most products. On the other hand, the dairy products, leather, jewelry, glass, shoes, porcelain, ironwork, beer, and wine produced by local workshops before the railroad era usually were consumed close to the areas in which they were produced.

As Mexico's internal markets widened under the impulse of the railroad, modern manufacturing grew at a swift pace. Table 4 reflects the trend in a few major products, indicating the rapid rates of growth recorded in the era. Nor was manufacturing confined to the products shown in the table. With the advance of the

TABLE 4

*Index of Physical Output of Selected Manufactured
Products in Mexico, Selected Years*
(1900–01 = 100)

Fiscal year	Cotton textiles	Sugar	Rum	Tobacco products
1877–78	26.2	43.4	75.2	—
1893–94	42.9	64.3	127.1	—
1900–01	100.0	100.0	100.0	100.0
1910–11	130.4	195.1	149.2	135.2

Source: Fernando Rosenzweig Díaz, *El Porfiriato: La vida económica,* unpublished manuscript to appear in the series *Historia moderna de México,* ed. Daniel Cosío Villegas (Mexico, D.F.: Hermes).

Porfirian era, modern beer factories appeared in various major cities, notably in Monterrey, Orizaba, Mexico City, and Mérida. Glass factories developed to supply the growing beer industry; shoe plants emerged to displace the output of artisan shops; commercial soap factories developed to exploit the growing supply of cotton-seed oil; and so on.

Even the more basic lines of manufacturing, lines which were substituting for imports rather than displacing artisans, began to show signs of considerable growth. Mexico's first modern steel mill appeared in Monterrey in 1903 and showed an impressive growth rate until the end of the Porfirian era; in 1911 it produced over 60,000 tons of iron and steel. Equally impressive records were made by new electric power plants and by factories turning out paper, cement, plate glass, and explosives. All told, Mexico's gross national product is estimated to have grown 37 per cent in the first decade of the new century, a rate equivalent to 23 per cent in per capita terms.[17] By 1910, one could begin to see the possibilities that Mexico might eventually emerge as a modern industrial state.

Welfare and change

If one were to stop here in his review of the Díaz regime, however, the net impression would be a gross distortion of what transpired in those thirty-five extraordinary years. We can be reasonably sure that when Porfirio Díaz took office in 1876, the economic and political philosophies of the 1857 constitution were far from his mind. On the contrary, his prime preoccupation seems to have been to build a political machine which would give his regime stability and power. To do this, he used the time-tested recipe of the skillful politician — a recipe which, with suitable adaptations and changed objectives, was followed for many years after the Porfirian era. He made it worthwhile for his major potential adversaries to join him. He made it easy for the landowners to expand their already extensive holdings. He commissioned the leaders of the major bandit armies into the Mexican forces, paid them and their troops well, and gave them slack rein in the enforcement of local law and order. He eased the anticlerical curbs just enough to eliminate the Church's incentive to foment rebellion. He gave lip service to the 1857 constitution and offered the intellectuals government jobs and diplomatic commissions. And — at least at first — he winked at the local monopolies of business, the labor impressment systems of the mines and haciendas, and the illegal levies of states and municipalities.[18]

There was one major group in the structure of Mexican society, however, whose adherence Díaz felt no need to buy — the peasant on the land. Mexico's history is dotted with revolts by the rural Mexican responding in desperation to the poverty and suppression under which he lived. But whenever the peon had been a real threat to any Mexican regime, it was principally because some other power had mobilized and used him — the intellectuals, the generals, or the Church. He had served as manpower in the generals' armies, drawn in by force or by the promise of loot. He had served as soldiers for the Church, whipped to a killing fervor by exhortation and superstition. But he had rarely evidenced much ability to organize on his own account in order to redress his basic grievances.

From Díaz' point of view, therefore, there were very few risks and many advantages in continuing the process which Juárez had unintentionally begun — the process of separating the peasant from his land. The Díaz political machine would be strengthened by helping the landowners extend their holdings, and by satisfying the needs of the haciendas which were short of labor. At the same time, foreign investors would be given better conditions for investment, because labor would be made available for the mines in the North and the plantations of the Gulf Coast.

The techniques of the Porfirian land-grab do not matter here; they are unlikely to serve as a model for economic development programs elsewhere. In general, however, the new land laws of the regime established a method by which any land whose title was in any way beclouded would revert to the state for redistribution. Through all the turmoil and change of Mexico's history, few landholders in Mexico had clear, unblemished title to their properties. Besides, there were extensive lands in Mexico, many of them inhabited by squatters, for which no private title at all was in existence. Wherever the right of possession was beclouded, those on the land were ejected and title was passed to a small coterie of new owners. As an indication of the consequences of these transfers, one family in Chihuahua came to control about 33,000,000 acres, and four individuals in Baja California controlled about 28,000,000.

By 1910, over 80 per cent of Mexico's rural families were landless,[19] and the prevailing agricultural system of Mexico was that of the giant hacienda. Small-holder agriculture was no longer of any importance except in a few pockets such as those in Nuevo León and Oaxaca. Though the number of haciendas in Mexico totaled only a few thousand, about 50 per cent of Mexico's rural population lived on them.[20] True, many of these huge landholdings were not worth very much according to the prevailing prices of land, but their sheer spread meant that the people on them had no choice but to work for the owner on his terms and to accept his brand of local justice. Familiar systems of bondage, built around the company store and perpetual debt, gave a quasi-legal cast to the peonage system. More than anything else, the landholding aspect of the Porfirian program turned the peasants into revolutionaries when later they saw their chance.

There was another aspect of the Porfirian land policy which helps to explain the events that followed. Some of the beneficiaries of the redistribution were foreigners. Well-financed United States land companies moved down into northern Mexico, acquiring the land under the Porfirian rules of the game. Spanish and British companies entered other areas. By 1910 foreigners owned about 72,000,000 acres of Mexican land, roughly one seventh of the land surface of the country. Here lay one more source of the anti-foreign sentiment which later would dominate Mexican political thinking.

In general, therefore, Díaz managed to establish political stability by reverting to a system of preferences and privileges for men of power — for Mexican hacienda owners, generals, and politicians, and for foreign investors as well. But this system of privilege and power was distinctly different from that of the old Spanish rule and of the Mexican governments before Juárez, and it had very different implications for Mexico's growth.

The system of privilege of the governments before Díaz had taken for granted the physical fragmentation and local isolation of Mexico's many areas. Monopoly grants, therefore, were usually local in character. Díaz and his intellectuals, however, were living in a different world. In this world of the late nineteenth century they began to realize, as many others were realizing in Europe and North America, that an individual with a little capital, a little government help, and the freedom to use both as he wished had enormous opportunities open to him. The widening of internal markets and the development of large-scale methods of manufacture had changed the outlook for men of energy and influence. The intellectual bases for a new theory to justify the uninhibited use of these opportunities had already been half developed. Adam Smith, John Stuart Mill, and Alfred Marshall had demonstrated that on certain carefully defined assumptions the interference of government by regulation could hamper the optimum performance of a nation's economy. Charles Darwin and Herbert Spencer had suggested in biology and human society, respectively, that there were the weak and the strong in every system and that the fittest tended to survive. It was only a step from these doctrines to a theory which in one fell swoop would justify Díaz' suppression of the Indian, the grant of concessions to a favored group of Mexicans and foreigners, and the use of government as an aid and support to an otherwise unhampered business community.

According to the *científicos* of Díaz' period, the superior culture of the late nineteenth century was that of Europe and North America, and its superiority was based on the innate qualities of its people. The Indian culture was innately inferior and eventually would have to succumb. While Mexico was growing, the Indian would have to be harnessed to the only jobs of which he was capable, those of field hands and untrained mine and factory labor. For the superior elements of society, however, there should be maximum freedom of opportunity and maximum opportunities for growth. In the end, the efforts of the superior group would elevate Mexican society as a whole, including the Indian along with all the others.[21]

This bizarre application of laissez-faire and positivist doctrine was vigorously espoused in Mexico from the early 1890's to 1910. It produced considerable growth but it also had unintended consequences. Though the haciendas had benefited at first from the land grab which the Díaz regime had authorized, in the end their position was weakened in various parts of the country by other policies of the regime.

The hacienda's existence depended partly on its ability to absorb and immobilize the labor around it, so that labor would be available for its peak needs at sowing and harvest time. Its position in this regard was strongest if there were no rival economic opportunities for the hacienda's labor force. The Díaz regime's developmental policies produced those rival opportunities. The hacienda system gave a nominal daily credit to its labor — usually one quarter or one half a peso a day — and kept the labor in perpetual debt through sales at the company store. The foreign mining companies, desperate to lure away some of the labor tied up by the haciendas, paid far higher rates for their dangerous work. The wage most commonly offered by the mining companies in the latter stages of the Porfirian period seems to have been about one and a half pesos a day, though for some jobs the rate was as high as three pesos. The occasional reports of tension between the hacienda owners and the foreign mining companies, therefore, were hardly surprising.

It was not only mining that weakened the labor market of the haciendas but the "modern" agriculture of the Porfirian period as well. When large-scale irrigated cotton farms appeared in the north of Mexico, the wage rates they offered to agricultural labor were significantly higher than the prevailing agricultural wage. From the viewpoint of the haciendas of the area, this was piling injury on injury, since the cotton growers also were competing for scarce water in some areas. The new sugar plantations had a similar effect on wage rates wherever they appeared. So did the pull of jobs in cities. Collectively these forces generated rapid, unsettling changes in the population distribution of the country, speeding the growth of the largest cities, transforming villages into towns, and generating streams of migrants out of states such as Jalisco and Guanajuato into other areas such as Veracruz and Yucatán.[22]

The strain on the hacienda which these developments implied may well have been matched by strains in other parts of the body politic. Though it is hard to be sure after a lapse of over fifty years, it seems likely that other institutions of local privilege were also on the defensive. The elimination of local import duties and monopolies on the transit of goods in the 1890's undercut many local business interests. The same measures dried up lucrative sources of revenue to local governments. The reform of the banking system in the same decade curbed the power of the local monopolies to issue money and — at least in theory — substituted a more impersonal and more extensively regulated banking system. Finally, Limantour's foray against American railroad investors and his assumption of control of major portions of the Mexican railroad system in 1908 generated a wave of uneasiness among Díaz' foreign supporters.

Another source of strain for Porfirio Díaz stemmed from the fact that many consumers failed to gain anything from the economic growth of the period. Before 1890, in fact, it is altogether possible that Mexico's standard of living declined quite generally. The cataclysmic upheaval in landholdings, according to the fragmentary data, cut the total production of the basic consumption crops — of corn, wheat, and beans — even though export crops grew.[23] After 1890, however, food production seems to have increased.

Part of the growth came about through the recovery in the production of corn, the staple food crop of Mexico. This was not the sort of spectacular growth that was occurring in the export crops. Indeed, from 1890 to 1910, the increase in production of corn, wheat, and beans together barely exceeded the growth in population. But the Porfirian regime alleviated the situation somewhat by importing considerable quantities of corn in the serious drought years; meanwhile, throughout the period, private traders rapidly increased their imports of wheat, sugar, flour, milk, lard, salted meat, and fish.

Many of the reasons for buying these products abroad, rather than at home, were perfectly sensible, given the conditions of Mexico at the time. For one thing, some of the more spectacular shifts in agricultural land use during the Porfirian period took place near Mexico's borders — in the northern states, adjoining the United States boundary, where United States interests financed extensive cattle-raising operations, and in Veracruz and Yucatán, facing the sea, where foreign money financed the production of tropical export crops. From a transport-cost point of view, some of these areas were — some still are — closer to foreign sources of supply than to Mexico's food-surplus areas. On top of this, Mexico's hacienda-dominated agriculture was not organized ideally for the increased production of foodstuffs. Many haciendas produced for the market, to be sure, but these establishments were principally engaged in raising cotton, cattle, and tropical crops. It is doubtful that production under the hacienda system was particularly sensitive to changes in the market demand for basic foodstuffs such as corn and wheat.

Much of the growth in Mexico's food consumption, therefore, was achieved by imports from abroad. Exactly what these quantities meant in final consumer satisfactions for the people of the Porfirian era — exactly how much fish is needed to match a given quantity of corn — is hard to say. As best we can tell, however, the physical quantities of food consumed by Mexico went up about 40 to 45 per cent between the early 1890's and the years just before 1910, while total population was rising about 20 per cent.[24]

But averages are a deceptive measure. The probabilities are that the gains were concentrated among people living in cities. In short, though the social structure all about them was stirring and straining, the rural Mexican saw very little benefit from the change.

One ought not to infer, however, that the new economic opportunities in the cities necessarily contributed to the stability of the Díaz regime. It is true that a literate urban middle class was beginning to appear in Mexico, as reflected by such indexes as a quadrupling of newspaper circulation between 1893 and 1907, a marked increase in white-collar occupations, and a sharp rise in the literacy rate. But it was a middle class, according to various accounts, which was locked into a restraining social and economic structure. It was a middle class which could not easily aspire to the top positions in the social structure or in business fields which were dominated respectively by the landed gentry and by foreigners. It was, in short, a middle class with a gnawing grievance.

Add one more dimension to Díaz' position. Mexico's greatly increased exports, helpful though they may have been to Mexico's economic development, also exposed Mexico to the vagaries of international price movements. The first decade of the twentieth century was a period of considerable instability in world-traded products. In 1907, especially, a depression in world henequen prices bankrupted many of the newly expanded henequen plantations of the Veracruz region, and at the same time the cotton growers and the producers of industrial minerals felt a sudden shrinking of foreign markets. Twenty or thirty years earlier, the banking system had been of only marginal importance to Mexico's economic life. But as time went on, the importance of the system increased. By 1907, the banks were increasing their credit to Mexico's illiquid agriculture, renewing old loans as a matter of course until they seemed perpetual obligations. With the shortage of funds in 1907, the margin of safety of the banks was suddenly imperiled. Banks were forced to curtail credit sharply; and despite efforts by the government to bail out the banks, the swollen debt of the haciendas was squeezed back. Even the landowners, therefore, must have had mixed feelings about the Porfirian regime when Francisco Madero hauled up the revolutionary banner in 1910.

With the loyalties of the landowners shaken, with the attitudes of the foreigners uncertain, with the growing middle class chafing for freedom, and the peons burning with the outrages of thirty-five years of oppression, scarcely anyone appeared to defend Díaz. It could well be that, by this time, there were few who were entirely sure that he was worth defending.

JUÁREZ, DÍAZ, AND DEVELOPMENT

Juárez and Díaz represent the two great regimes of Mexican history which were premised on the concept that the state's role in economic development should be largely passive in character — that the state should be the guarantor of security and stability, but that the private sector should be the principal engine of the nation's development. Neither regime adhered to this role with total consistency; each assumed from time to time a more aggressive role for the public sector. But both, on the whole, were wedded to the doctrine that the main sources of initiative and growth must come from outside the public sector.

Juárez, for his part, had pitifully little to work with. During his regime, the domestic private sector of Mexico was in no condition for bold initiatives, having been shaken by half a century of war and revolution. At the same time, foreign investors saw little about the Mexican economy to attract them, as long as internal security in Mexico continued to be so uncertain. The only possible source from which security might have been guaranteed and the initiatives for growth might have come was the federal government. But Juárez, restrained by his conviction about the relative roles of the individual and the state, could not find it in him to use the full power of his position to create an integrated nation and to generate an increase in living standards. Little by little, it is true, he and his successor, Lerdo, began to experiment with the more extensive use of central power. It was this willingness to bend to the realities of the Mexican environment, this willingness to recognize the overwhelming need for some direction from the center, which advanced Mexico even a little toward the goals of an integrated state and a rising living standard. In time, Juárez and Lerdo might well have used their powers more extensively and more effectively. But before that stage could have been reached, Porfirio Díaz had taken over.

Díaz, with no concern at all for the well-being of the great majority of Mexicans, capitalized upon the growth in the world's demand for Mexico's materials and created some of the indispensable elements for its later growth. During his regime, the isolated localities of Mexico were linked in some degree; the elements of a national infrastructure were put in place; a productive middle class began to develop; and the first signs of an indigenous modern industry began to appear. Some of these results were the conscious objectives of Porfirian policies. Some occurred as the unintended and unexpected consequences of those policies. Whether intended or not, they provided part of the platform on which subsequent Mexican growth would be built.

From the economist's point of view, the route which Díaz chose to stimulate Mexico's growth was almost classic in its form. To reduce the process to a simple caricature, foreign investment and exports were the dominant features in the development; they, in turn, increased domestic incomes and established the basis for a system of internal transport; and the increased incomes and internal transport, by broadening the size of the market available to domestic producers, set the stage for the beginnings of modern large-scale industry.

At the same time, however, Díaz took brutal measures which despoiled and suppressed the people on the land, and offensive measures which denigrated Mexican culture and elevated the foreigner to an exalted status in the country. Were these essential elements in the pattern of growth? From the stereotyped Mexican viewpoint, the answer would be provided without the slightest hesitation. All that Díaz did, according to this view, was of a piece. Large foreign investments and heavy exports of raw materials could only take place if local labor were exploited, and if the nation were directed by persons subservient to those foreign interests.

From almost any other viewpoint, however, the analysis is not so simple. A peaceful and secure Mexico in the late nineteenth century unquestionably required a tough and clever leader at its center, given its history of localism and its unhappy geography; but there is no need to assume that the situation required the near-psychotic ruthlessness of Porfirio Díaz. A prosperous Mexico in the late nineteenth century probably required heavy foreign investment, given the underdeveloped character of its domestic investors and the limited human and financial resources of the state; but there is no reason to assume that such investment demanded the debasement of Mexican values and the elevation of foreign interests to the degree that Porfirio espoused.

Unfortunately, however, economists cannot often conduct their experiments in a test tube. They are usually reduced to placing their best interpretation upon events as they occur. We shall never know for sure, therefore, whether a somewhat altered version of the Porfirian era, while laying the basis for a modern Mexico, might also have avoided sowing the seeds of the holocaust that was to follow.

Chapter 3

The Revolution and After, 1910–1940

THE advent of the Revolutionary era in Mexico laid the basis for a deep-seated change in the relationships between the public and the private sectors. Gradually, the state enunciated more positive versions of its obligations and its goals. Gradually, it assumed a more aggressive role in the production of goods and services and in the distribution of income.

The word "gradually," however, needs to be stressed. For during most of the first decade of the Revolutionary era, a national state hardly existed in Mexico. The institutions which made up the central government were a feeble version of a modern state. There was neither a genuine national currency nor a central bank, neither a true national army nor a civil service. Besides, during much of that early period, the very jurisdiction of the national government was in question; there were only a few areas of Mexico in which the basic authority of the state was not being seriously challenged.

The period from 1910 to 1940, therefore, was an era in which Mexico was developing the essential preconditions for the new role of the state. During those thirty years, the state regained physical control over the nation; it began to shape and define a new philosophy for its existence and a new role in the performance of its goals; it manufactured a new set of powers and generated a new crop of institutions; and it began to flex its muscles by attempting new programs and new approaches to the old problems of credit, transportation, water resources, and land tenure in the country.

During these thirty years, however, the private sector also was going through a swift and heady evolution. Even at the beginning of the period, an extensive railroad grid, a limited system of all-weather roads, and a nucleus of electric-power plants had provided Mexico's small crop of indigenous entrepreneurs with some of the critical facilities essential for national markets and specialized production. With the return of some measure of security on the roads and in the countryside, the chances of profitable activity grew greater still. The increasing disposition and ability of the public sector to tackle bottlenecks in transportation, communication, and power kept adding to the scope of the private sector's opportunities. By 1940, the creative potentials of the private sector had grown to such a point that there was little chance of the sector's being overwhelmed by the growing effectiveness of the state.

The process itself, however, was far from being an uninterrupted upward march. Indeed, even today, many Mexicans would insist that it was not an upward march at all. In both the public and the private sectors, the three decades were punctuated with setbacks and detours. Inevitably, as the spotty and uncertain process of economic change began to evolve, some areas of the country and some segments of the nation's population lost ground. Still, the direction of political and economic change, viewed from the perspective of a quarter century later, seems unmistakably to have been one of consolidation and growth.

THE POLITICAL CHANGE

On the political front, the thirty-year period began with an interval of seeming destruction and retrogression. When Porfirio Díaz was swept out of office in 1910, his political apparatus went with him. Francisco Madero, the first national leader of Mexico's revolution, did not inherit the web of relationships and understandings which had given the Díaz regime its earlier stability: the system of neatly balanced bargains with political chieftains and generals in the provinces; the allegiance of hopeful heirs-apparent in the capital; the support of foreign governments whose investors had been made secure. Nor did Madero inherit a constitutional system to which anyone paid automatic allegiance. The political machinery provided in the 1857 constitution, which had never had a chance to become deeply fixed in Mexican habits, was by now rusty from disuse and neglect.

Madero's program was not enough to fill the political vacuum. His early rallying cry, "Effective suffrage, no re-election," responded to the wants of only a handful of Mexican intellectuals. For those who had done well under the Díaz system, Madero's program seemed filled with vague threats of a return to impersonal government, based on nondiscriminatory law rather than on negotiated bargains — the old vision of Juárez and Lerdo. For those who had done badly under Díaz, there was no promise of early succor. Although there were allusions to the need to bring the foreign companies to heel, there was no real substance in these allusions. Although there were mild promises to return some land to the landless field workers, there was no prospect of a swift redress of their grievances.

For the first time, perhaps, in Mexico's history, these grievances could not safely be put aside. A few rural leaders, who had acquired enough exposure to the outside world to be aware that poverty was not in the inevitable nature of things, mobilized the latent discontent of rural Mexico. Many other Mexicans, feeling the relaxation of iron-bound discipline which Díaz had imposed, reacted quickly to the intoxicating sense of freedom — all the more quickly, no doubt, because the railroad had made travel and exposure to the outside world so much more common. The motivations of the peasants to acquire some land and to strike back against the harsh restraints imposed by the system inherited from the Díaz era were almost irrepressible. A reactionary *coup* which destroyed Madero in 1913 was the signal for a new Revolutionary surge. The social structure of rural Mexico was pulled down as lands were seized, haciendas were burned, and rural tradesmen were robbed and murdered.

In the decade of turmoil that followed Madero's death, Mexico

lapsed quickly back into the sectionalism that its sparse popula-
tions and difficult geography had always encouraged. Whereas the
Russian Revolution produced a Lenin to follow its Kerensky, the
Mexican Revolution followed a different pattern. No disciplined
cadre existed to play the role of the Bolsheviks; no common
philosophy prevailed in revolutionary circles; no military group
was altogether dominant. It seemed evident that anyone aspiring
to leadership in Mexico could achieve his position only by coali-
tion. After various abortive efforts, Venustiano Carranza managed
to create the necessary merger of interests. Without having much
stomach for the demands of the rural "radicals" or for the principles
of numerous socialist-oriented urban groups which had sprung up
in the turmoil, Carranza nevertheless agreed to a constitutional
convention at which these groups might have the opportunity to
incorporate their goals into Mexico's basic law.

Mexico's constitutional convention of 1917, however, was far
from being an engineered affair. The delegates to the convention
included people of incredibly diverse political views and aims. Almost every major brand of political thinking in the world had some
representation; in fact, the only major political position without
vocal support in the convention seems to have been the philosophy
of Karl Marx. Among the delegates were a few of the erstwhile
adherents of Porfirio Díaz, one or two in important roles. The
classical economists and the agricultural utopians were there,
though less important than in 1857. There were a few representatives of the incipient labor movement of Mexico, usually holding
the anarcho-syndicalist ideas of the Spanish nineteenth-century
radicals. Also on hand were a few well-placed Mexican intellectuals, familiar with the reformist ideas of Woodrow Wilson and
Lloyd George and anxious to assign a more aggressive regulatory
role to government in order to prevent the abuse of private power.
In fact, the views represented at the convention were so diverse
that there were only two propositions on which there was near-
universal agreement. One was that the groups which heretofore
had dominated the Mexican political structure — the Church, the

foreigner, and the landowners — would have to surrender their power. The other was that the state would have to assume in more affirmative fashion the responsibility for the well-being of the Mexican people.[1]

Despite the clear shift in direction which the new constitution was to embody, the delegates paid due obeisance to the shade of Benito Juárez by accepting the 1857 constitution as the starting point of the 1917 document. Step by step, however, they whittled away at the laissez-faire doctrine of the Juárez document and its structure of decentralized governmental powers. Though the basic system of an independent executive, judiciary, and legislature still seemed right to the drafters, they felt the need for a stronger presidency — a presidency which would not be hamstrung, as Juárez and Lerdo had sometimes been, by the opposition of the other branches. Accordingly, they enlarged the president's power by granting him the right of veto, the right to initiate legislation, freedom from easy impeachment, and the right to issue personal decrees in special circumstances.[2] Then, having strengthened the power of the president to the point at which he might be a threat to the democratic concept, the convention added a provision to prevent the president from perpetuating his power, the famous "no re-election" provision on which Madero had based so much of his political activities.

The delegation of powers to the states, fixed in the 1857 constitution, also was allowed to stand. But a critical provision was added to hold the states in check, a provision which allowed the federal senate to replace state administrations which "abused" their local powers.

The concept that the government should not be used to dispose economic favors was preserved by using the old Juárez provision on that point — a clause which forbids monopolies, special privileges, and tax exemptions. And the provisions for holding the Church in check also took their cue from the laws and constitutional proceedings of the Juárez era.

But the Juárez constitution offered no guide to ways of restraining the foreigner. Accordingly, drawing on bits and pieces of experience in Mexican history, the draftsmen devised some new constitutional restraints. For one thing, the president was empowered, in Article 33 of the 1917 constitution, to eject any foreigner from the country whose presence he judged "inconvenient." But much more significant in curbing the foreigner was a sweeping redefinition of private property. Purporting to return to the principles of Spanish law which had prevailed until the Porfirian era, the drafters of the constitution provided that the subsoil of Mexico belonged irrevocably to the nation and that private persons could acquire only such rights of use as the state assigned to them — in short, that the nation was the ultimate owner of Mexico's oil and minerals and that the companies engaged in exploiting these resources were doing so only on state sufferance. Besides, foreigners were prohibited from acquiring any surface or subsurface rights to Mexican land unless they gave up their claim to protection from their home governments. And foreigners were forbidden to acquire any rights whatever in border or seaside areas. These provisions were the opening gun in a campaign which, in the end, would significantly reduce the importance of foreign investment in Mexico's land and minerals.

The foreigner having been dealt with, the next problem was that of reducing the landholder's control in rural Mexico. For that purpose, a number of measures were adopted. In principle, the collective landholdings of the communal villages were to be reestablished as they had existed before Juárez' land law; landless villages were to receive expropriated land; and a program was to be developed for breaking up and redistributing the land of Mexico's large haciendas.

There was one new set of provisions in the constitution which could not easily have been predicted in advance — the clauses on labor. By 1917, the Mexican labor movement could claim to have had a long and eventful history.[3] But it could hardly make any pretense to being a significant economic or political power; perhaps its only major *coup* up to that time had been its raising of a ragtag civilian army in support of Carranza two years earlier. Labor's ability to draw concessions from the constitutional convention, therefore, seemed to rest not so much upon its political strength as upon the fact that the largest bodies of organized labor in the nation were working for foreign employers — for the oil companies, the mines, the public utilities, and larger industrial plants. The only major exceptions to this pattern were some of the railroad workers and textile workers. It was not difficult, therefore, for a few determined men to push through an extremely advanced concept of workers' rights.

The labor article of the constitution runs the gamut of modern-day concepts for the protection of labor. It covers hours of work, minimum wages, special protection for women and children, protection against layoffs and lockouts, and recognition of the right to organize and strike. Furthermore, it goes beyond these now-familiar provisions by establishing the principle of worker participation in the profits; by requiring large corporations to provide housing, schools, infirmaries, and other public services; and by requiring compulsory government arbitration in labor disputes. In fact, the paper rights of Mexico's labor unions are so broadly defined in the constitution that since 1917 the apparatus of the labor movement has been almost indistinguishable from the apparatus of government.[4] Though sporadic conflicts have occurred between some sectors of labor and government, it does not violate reality too much to think of Mexico's labor unions as an arm of government through which it seeks to affect the conduct of the private sector.

With the drafting of the 1917 constitution, Mexico had taken a major step. But it was only a beginning — the introduction to a period fraught with tension and crisis, the first stage of an era which, by the opening of the Second World War, could be said to have produced the modern Mexican state.

From 1917 to 1940, as shown in Table 5, Mexico had eight different administrations. Mexican history is so fascinating that one is tempted to review the major struggles of all eight. To understand something of the evolving relationships between the public

TABLE 5

Presidential Administrations in Mexico, 1915–1964

President	Dates of office
Venustiano Carranza	February 5, 1915, to May 21, 1920
Adolfo de la Huerta	May 22, 1920, to November 30, 1920
Alvaro Obregón	December 1, 1920, to November 30, 1924
Plutarco Elías Calles	December 1, 1924, to November 30, 1928
Emilio Portes Gil	December 1, 1928, to February 4, 1930
Pascual Ortiz Rubio	February 5, 1930, to September 1, 1932
Abelardo L. Rodríguez	September 2, 1932, to November 30, 1934
Lázaro Cárdenas	December 1, 1934, to November 30, 1940
Manuel Avila Camacho	December 1, 1940, to November 30, 1946
Miguel Alemán	December 1, 1946, to November 30, 1952
Adolfo Ruiz Cortines	December 1, 1952, to November 30, 1958
Adolfo López Mateos	December 1, 1958, to November 30, 1964

and the private sectors in this period, however, only certain issues need to be emphasized.

As far as Venustiano Carranza was concerned, the adoption of the constitution left his prime problem unaltered. During the years of revolution and counterrevolution between 1910 and 1920, while the national government was in suspension for much of the time as an effective administrative force, local generals were arising once more to gain control of Mexico's widely separated states. Local taxes and trading privileges, never altogether suppressed, were rapidly being re-established under the protective wing of local chiefs. Labor leaders, feeling their incipient power, were learning to play the game which was visible all around them; by force and extortion, they were extracting concessions wherever they could, sometimes for their unions, often for themselves.[5] The foreign oil companies, having as little faith in the national government as most Mexicans had, were recruiting local armies for defense, bribing local politicians for protection, and threatening to call in the Marines if they were not allowed to go their accustomed ways. The Church, seeing the opportunity to regain some of its lost power and land, was whipping up rural peasant groups into local terroristic uprisings.

In dealing with these sources of dissidence and opposition, Carranza had little room for maneuver. In the Mexico of his time, no president could risk opposition for long — for a very simple reason. There was no tradition in Mexico of a legal and orderly passage of power from any national group to its opposition. There was no expectation that such a transition could occur. Whatever a leader's aspiration might be for democratic rule, he had to assume that an opposition group would operate on the principle that the only way it could redress its grievances was by force. Hence, an opposition group could not be brooked.

Perhaps for this reason, Carranza and his immediate successors reverted to a political technique much like that of Porfirio Díaz. In a word, the policy toward every source of potential opposition was either to include it within the national government system or else to crush it. Constitution or no constitution, Carranza began by recognizing the power of the local generals who had physical control of the various sections of the country and by putting together a system of alliances among the military leaders. The operating method was fairly standardized. The local military leaders were turned into governors and were given enough privileges so that they would see advantages in remaining in the system. The men surrounding the president were allowed enough personal loot to make their continued adherence to the president worthwhile. But the subordinate whose power became so great that it began to threaten the security of the center or whose corruption became so obvious as to compromise the political machine was retired, deported, or assassinated. By 1920 it would have been hard for any observer to believe that Mexico was headed in any of the directions suggested by its 1917 constitution.

But Carranza had the railroad grid, the road system, and the telegraph on his side. Local leaders of Oaxaca and Sonora could not hope to be insulated from the power of the national government by time and distance, as they had fifty years earlier. Nor could such leaders generate local support quite as readily by promises of local privilege and monopoly; too many of the leading industrial and agricultural enterprises of Mexico were by now dependent on national markets.

Therefore, Mexico's outstanding leaders of the period — men like Venustiano Carranza, Plutarco Elías Calles, and Alvaro Obregón — could do many things to bring the local leaders to heel which would not have been possible in an earlier era. For one thing, the national government could not only impose national taxes, but to a degree could also enforce their collection. The levies of the national government, therefore, were carefully built up, while those of the state and local governments were held in check. Little by little, despite the constitutional theory of administrative decentralization, the states were obliged to look to the national government for revenues to build schools, dams, hospitals, and roads. Little by little, the agricultural reform program and the protection of labor — functions which the constitution envisaged as the responsibility of the states — were gathered up by the federal government. Step by step, the apparatus of a modern state emerged. The outlines of a modern civil service system began to be visible in the 1920's; a national public school system began to emerge at the same time; a central bank, the Banco de México, was created in 1925; and an agricultural credit bank appeared in 1926. Carranza and his successors had no hesitation in using the growing resources and powers of the federal government without restraint, in order to maintain their control over local groups.

The ability of the center to control the states was also helped by one of the constitutional innovations of 1917 — the provision which allowed the federal government to "vacate" a state government for abuse of power. Whenever the national government could not get rid of an unwanted state regime through informal pressures, or whenever the national government was particularly anxious to make a public example of a venal, inefficient, or disobedient state chief, the constitutional power was invoked to declare that the state government did not exist, and new local leaders were substituted for the old. That power was formally invoked twenty-four times between 1918 and 1927, and sixteen times between 1928 and 1937.[6] In addition, there were a number of cases in which the threat of using the power was sufficient to bring local leaders to heel.

The increasing strength of the central government was tested and proved not only by its capacity to control the states but also by its success in open warfare with the Catholic Church. In 1926, during the Calles regime, the Church republished its objections to the anticlerical provisions of the 1917 constitution. The struggle that followed saw the deportation of bishops and archbishop, lockouts by the clergy, and acts of terrorism by fanatical religious groups. But in the end, the Church sued for peace.[7]

Of course, there was nothing inevitable about the eventual triumph of the central government over forces such as the Church and the local generals. There was always the threat that some local military leader might abort the trend with a successful revolt from his local lair. Aware of the risk, Mexico's presidents slowly set about trying to convert Mexico's loose federation of local armies into a national institution.[8] Each step was a delicate, dangerous testing of power, punctuated with revolts. When, in the mid-1920's, generals were detached from their troops and rotated in assignments, the whole system seemed to teeter on edge.

Nonetheless, the growth in the strength of the central government was persistent from 1917 to 1934. The power of the president to control the state political machines, once that power became evident, fed upon itself. It meant that he could also control the nominations of the states to the national Congress. Hence, more and more, the Congressional representatives were handpicked at the center rather than by the local political chiefs. The movement in that direction began to be apparent in 1929. At that time, Calles — still operating behind the scenes as Mexico's political boss even though his presidential term had ended — invited all the local chieftains to affiliate their local political machines with a single national party, the forerunner of what would later become the Partido Revolucionario Institucional, the PRI. His invitation set off one local revolt, but it was quickly crushed. In the end, recognizing the growing power of the national center and calculating that they had more to gain by acquiescence than revolt, the generals and local civilian leaders responded to the call.

Of course, the local military and civilian politicians were not automatically removed as a threat to the national government merely by the creation of the party. Inside the party, the effort of the national government to control the local chieftains went on. Calles signaled the trend which that effort would take by his overhaul of the party in 1932. In that year, he introduced the concept that special-interest groups such as government employees and labor unions should have a formal role in the party structure and a formal right to participate in nominations. Every step in this direction diluted the power of the local chiefs a little further.

Thus the consummate skill and ruthlessness of Carranza, Obregón, and Calles removed one major barrier to the development of Mexico as a national entity. But the dilution of local rule was not the only power problem facing Mexico's presidents. In the early 1930's, the cluster of national interests upon which the stability of the national government depended was narrowly based and hence inherently instable. The young national army and the growing national bureaucracy were, in fact, the only organized groups of much significance which identified their interests with those of a strong national government. A Mexican president who lost the support of either group or who confronted a new major national group not in sympathy with his policies was in danger of losing his job.

Almost as soon as Lázaro Cárdenas took office in 1934, he began to display his sensitivity to the problem. Like Díaz or Carranza or Calles, he continued to see to it that no major group in the Mexican economy was disregarded or isolated. In addition, however, he set about ensuring that no national group would come to dominate the central government. Just as Calles had weakened the local chieftains by the counterpoise of the new national groups, now Cárdenas began to weaken the power of the first national groups by creating more national groups. For example, as Calles had created the beginnings of a national army, now Cárdenas tried to offset its power with a national militia of peasants and workers.

The Cárdenas touch in pursuing a diffuse-and-conquer strategy was particularly evident in his reorganizations of the internal structure of the PRI. As Calles had added the government employees to the national party structure, now Cárdenas began giving a voice to the labor unions, which Calles had put in temporary eclipse. Pursuing his strategy further, Cárdenas drew the organized agrarian groups out from under the domination of labor and set them up as a separate political force inside the party. Ultimately, he pushed the diffusion trend to its logical end — a new "popular sector" of the party was created which individuals were allowed to join in their personal capacities rather than as members of an organized group. Based originally upon the 250,000 unionized government employees, the popular sector ultimately acquired distinguished old Revolutionaries, prominent landowners, outstanding lawyers, and other men of substance.[9]

But it would be a mistake to think of Cárdenas' political activities exclusively in these terms. The proliferation of national forces in his regime was not only a response to his desire for political stability but also a reflection of a difference in perspective and in aspiration. Until the Cárdenas regime, Mexico's presidents had been so busy building the power of the center against the local chiefs that they seemed to have neither the time nor the inclination to do much more. At times, Presidents Obregón and Emilio Portes Gil showed an interest in pushing beyond the consolidation stage toward one of active development; but the interest, wherever it appeared, was soon aborted by some new political crisis. Indeed, there were times — such as the year 1930 when Plutarco Elías Calles was manipulating presidents from behind the scenes — when basic programs like agricultural reform seemed to have been irrevocably abandoned.

Cárdenas was the appropriate man available at the propitious time to change the emphasis from political consolidation to economic growth. An indication that the time was ripe had been provided in 1933, a full year before his inauguration, by the Revolutionary party's adoption of an elaborate Six-Year Plan, embracing many of the principles which Cárdenas was soon to push. His conception of how Mexico should grow, however, was not through close imitation of the industrialized societies, certainly not the capitalist industrial societies. Instead, he seems to have been attracted by the possibilities of various communal forms of social organization, forms which might combine the advantages of rural living with the advances of industrialization.[10] From time to time he exhibited considerable sympathy for socialist institutions and methods as the best means to achieve his ends. In response, many "popular front" organizations seemed to gain strength in Mexico, and various home-grown varieties of Marxist ideology were widely taught and espoused.

At the same time, Cárdenas began to expand the economic apparatus of the national government, creating new programs and new sources of credit as rapidly as they could be devised. The central banking powers of the Banco de México had been expanding a step at a time since its birth in 1925; now they were broadened a little further. Other public credit institutions were created or expanded — Nacional Financiera, Banco de Crédito Ejidal, Banco Nacional de Comercio Exterior, and various others. These were not revolutionary institutions by the standards of the 1960's; today, their counterparts will be found throughout most of the underdeveloped world. But, for their time, they represented daring experiments in the use of government credit to stimulate the national economy.

If any of Cárdenas' policies deserved to be called "revolutionary," they were his policies on land reform.[11] In their own way, they represented almost as great a turnover in Mexican landholdings as Porfirio Díaz had achieved in his time. In 1910, about half of Mexico's rural population lived on haciendas, typically working under a form of peonage which bound them to the land. The 1917 constitution promised great changes. But between 1917 and Cárdenas' assumption of office in 1934, only modest steps were taken to alter the landholding picture, the emphasis being primarily upon the restitution to villages of land which had been seized by force or fraud. Besides, the usual problem of corruption was making a travesty of much that was done under the heading of "reform." For every case in which the lands were "restored," one could find another in which the lands were transferred to a local leader as loot.

It was not until the Cárdenas regime that the land reform program became an instrument for revolutionary change in the landholding practices of Mexico. The hacienda system of landholding was marked for extinction. In its place a variety of communal landholding practices were substituted. In most cases, in accordance with the practice of earlier years, only the *title* to the expropriated land was communal; the actual working of the land was split up among the families of the village which held the title. But Cárdenas introduced a number of variants, combining communal and individual elements in the ownership and use of the land. In a few exceptional cases, trying to preserve the existing unity of an efficient large-scale agricultural operation, he instituted genuine collective farms. By 1940, the Cárdenas program had moved so far that the various communal units of one sort or another (the *ejidos*) had come to include about half the crop land and half the rural population of Mexico. Meanwhile the population on the haciendas had dropped from what may have been 3,000,000 in 1910 to only 800,000 in 1940.

Cárdenas' land reform program drastically altered the political power structure of Mexico's rural areas. By 1938, Cárdenas felt that his position was strong enough to revamp the national party structure on lines which reflected the diffusion of power. In the new structure, the power of the old-fashioned local political leader was diminished even more; each local political machine became a grouping of organizations, including those representing agriculture, labor, the army, and government employees. It was clear that the national government had begun to achieve real power through the multiplication of the groups which were entitled to have a voice in government.

But several major groups with potential power still lay outside the political system. One was the Catholic Church, subdued by its bitter encounter with Calles but far from tamed. Cárdenas, in his handling of the opposition, made minimum use of the technique of suppression and maximum use of the tactic of envelopment. Thus, even as Marxist doctrines were being dispensed in the public schools, the anticlerical laws were being relaxed a little. In one state, Cárdenas intervened to prevent too oppressive a limitation on the number of priests; in another state, the Supreme Court intervened to the same end. The Church responded to the overtures by recognizing that there were good features in the Revolution.[12]

In the same spirit Cárdenas sought to draw organized business into his system of government. One has to search very hard in the history of Mexico before Cárdenas to find any overt evidence that Mexican businessmen were taking much of a direct hand in the political affairs of the country. The era is replete, of course, with accounts of rather heavy-handed efforts on the part of foreign business groups to influence the political drift of successive Mexican administrations. Here and there, too, indirect evidence appears that domestic business interests must have been active behind the scenes in the preservation of their positions — witness the restrained and cautious way in which the powers of the Banco de México were defined during its early years. But until the Cárdenas era, the business community seemed to have had neither the disposition nor the organization for overt cooperation with or overt resistance to the growing power of the state. The principal tactic seemed to be that of maintaining personal contact with the leaders of each administration in order to obtain the contracts, the compromises, and the dispensations which made a profitable and expanding business community possible.

The strategy of Cárdenas, however, demanded that Mexico's

modern business be brought more fully into the public structure and the public process. Although the constitution of 1917 had taken cognizance of organized labor and organized agriculture as quasi-governmental instruments, business had been given no analogous role. As long as organized business consisted largely of foreign interests, this political isolation was tolerable. But by the 1930's the Mexican businessman was no longer a *rara avis*. The old commercial bankers and Monterrey's industrial interests, both predating the Revolution, were coming back in strength. In addition, other entrepreneurs were appearing — a few from the remnants of the old landed families, some from the progeny of the more acquisitive politicians, and some from immigrants and their children. To leave the growing business class out of the system would have been at variance with the strategy of giving a stake in the continuance of the system to every major source of power, in order to reduce the threat of subversion and revolt. Besides, once in the system, business could act as a useful counterfoil to labor and agriculture.

The beginning of the return of organized business into the power structure of Mexico was visible in 1931, when the Confederación Patronal de la República Mexicana (Employers' Confederation of Mexico) was given legal status under the federal labor code. When Cárdenas first came to power in 1934, the return of business into the fold seemed to suffer a temporary setback; as the friend of organized labor and the communal farmer, as the sponsor of public works and public credit, Cárdenas seemed the natural ideological enemy of private enterprise. Still, Cárdenas remained true to his basic political principle of maintaining contact. To that end, he required all enterprises above a minimum size to take membership in some designated chamber of a network of national trade associations. These associations were eventually organized into the two national groups mentioned in Chapter 1, the manufacturers' CONCAMIN and the merchants' CONCANACO, and were assigned the job of maintaining a bridge between government and business. In time, their representatives were placed on the board of the nationalized railway system, on the national commission concerned with securities markets, on the advisory committees concerned with public utility rates and tariffs, and on numerous other government bodies. Accordingly, though business was not invited into the official political party on a basis formally coequal with that of labor, agriculture, and bureaucracy, it acquired a direct stake in the machinery of government itself.

But the political problems of Mexico's presidents from Carranza to Cárdenas were not confined to harnessing internal threats. Another problem, as Mexico's presidents saw it, was to curb the threat offered by the foreign investors. By the early 1930's, foreign capital and foreign enterprise were not quite so prominent in the Mexican economy as they had been in the Porfirian era; but the foreigners' position was still a formidable one. The concept that foreign interests were a threat to the growth and stability of Mexico had been built into the viewpoint of Mexico's protesting intellectuals since the days of the Spanish Crown. The country's reaction to the Porfirian era gave that concept a new vitality, and, in Mexican eyes, events after 1910 seemed only to confirm it. The United States ambassador's role in Madero's overthrow and death in 1913, the landing of United States Marines at Veracruz in 1914, and the United States army's pursuit of Pancho Villa into Mexico in 1916 and 1917 — all these fixed "gringo" as a word of opprobrium in the Mexican vocabulary.

On top of all this, there were the increasing disputes between the Mexican government and the American oil companies in Mexico. Tomes have been written on the rights and wrongs of these disputes.[13] The basic point, however, is that the conflicts transcended questions of right and wrong. The struggles simply represented a clash between two different orders having different norms and different systems of values — a clash which would be repeated later in Venezuela, Iran, and Iraq.

The clash occurred in Mexico first because the old order passed earliest there. Oil exploration had begun in Mexico in the reign of Porfirio Díaz. The first major strike had been made in 1901.

In 1911, production passed 10 million barrels. In 1921 it was 193 million barrels; this figure, over one quarter of the world's production at the time, was the highest ever recorded in Mexico, before or since.

The oil companies had negotiated their major concessions under the rules of the Porfirian regime. At first, they had been subject to a levy of 10 per cent on their profits, a far cry from the 50–50, 60–40, and even 75–25 splits seen in other countries of the world in the 1960's. For a time, the largest producer of all even managed — quite legally — to be exempted from all taxes except some nominal stamp taxes. Under the Porfirian system, this division of profits was perfectly possible and altogether legal so long as the appropriate powers were appeased.

With the departure of Díaz, however, the Mexican political system was forever changed. The national government could no longer live with the terms of the agreements fixed earlier. The 1917 constitution fundamentally altered the rules of the game in ways already described. And each Mexican administration, in succession, tried to capture a share of the profits which oil exports were generating.

The oil companies fought back. Without the perspective and experience which the next thirty or forty years would bring, it was hard for them to realize the fundamental shift in the political forces arrayed against them. They battled every attempt of the Mexican government to modify their methods of operation or to take a larger share of their profits, using all the considerable diplomatic pressure from the United States and Great Britain that they could muster. They threatened some Mexican regimes and propitiated others, holding off the day of reckoning.

But in the end, a basic change in the relations between Mexico and the oil companies had to come. Under the Cárdenas regime, the labor unions with which the oil companies had to deal were merged until they represented a powerful national organization. Labor no longer consisted of isolated local organizations whose leaders could be bought off as needed; now it was playing for —

and was being used for — much larger stakes in national politics. Having gathered its strength, labor made its inevitable demands on the companies. The oil companies said no. In the subsequent compulsory arbitration proceeding, the oil companies inevitably lost. Even then, however, after all their judicial remedies had been exhausted, the oil companies pleaded poverty and refused to pay the judicial award. When the smoke cleared in 1938, the companies' property had been expropriated.

The battle over Mexican oil — the persistence and force with which the oil companies clung to their erstwhile rights — deepened the antiforeign feelings of the new groups in Mexico. Those feelings were an important element in the pattern of events which followed the regime of Lázaro Cárdenas. But in order to understand these later events more fully, it is well to look a little more closely at the economic and social performance of Mexico in the period from 1910 to 1940.

THE ECONOMIC PERFORMANCE

The striking feature of Mexico's economic performance in the decades which followed Porfirio Díaz' exit was the resumption, after a pause of eight or ten years, of the growth in the economy which had taken place in the Porfirian era. This was more than a simple extension of the growth of the Porfirian era, however. The physical and institutional barriers between the modern and the traditional worlds of divided Mexico were now being rapidly lowered, permitting an accelerated flow of labor and capital across the dividing wall. In addition, the public sector was gradually emerging from the relatively passive role which it had exercised before 1920 to one of aggressive participation in the growth process.

Among the many symptoms of economic change in Mexico between 1910 and 1940 was the continued drift of people into the big cities. Although the country's population as a whole was reported as growing only 30 per cent in the thirty-year period, the population of the urban areas went up by 56 per cent. Guadalajara doubled in the period, Monterrey more than doubled, and Mexico City actually tripled in population; in fact, the 1940 census indicated that nearly half the people then living in Mexico City had been born somewhere else. During this period "middle class" occupations — occupations like clerks, skilled workers, bank and government employees, professionals, and operators of small businesses — grew much faster than the population at large.[14] Illiteracy among the people over ten years old fell from about 70 per cent to about 50 per cent — a result directly related to the fact that the number of teachers in rural schools rose from practically zero in 1910 to nearly 20,000 in 1940. And the value of assets in manufacturing enterprises, measured in peso terms, grew several times over — considerably more than the general price level.

To get a good sense of what was going on during this thirty-year period, one has to look at the three decades of the period separately. From the available evidence, it appears that the ten years from 1910 to 1920 were lost years for Mexico, at least in terms of current growth. Nobody really knows what hapened in detail, but everyone suspects the worst. Official figures suggest — it is possible that they may be reflecting the facts — that although there was not much difference in total agricultural output between the beginning and the end of the decade, the production of corn declined about 40 per cent.[15] A barely credible index of manufacturing output suggests that this branch of economic activity may have declined by about a quarter during the decade.[16] The production of minerals, in general, was lower at the end of the decade than at the beginning. The only bright spot in Mexico's economic structure was oil. But the oil economy operated in such an isolated enclave with so limited a use of indigenous manpower and local services, comparatively speaking, that the activity could not have done much to buoy the rest of Mexico's economy. By the same token, when oil production fell dramatically after 1921, the decline probably did less harm to the rest of the economy than the figures might imply.

Between 1920 and 1930 came the first faint signs of economic resurgence. One element in the renewed growth, it is fairly clear, was the resumption of mineral exports as a major activity. Economic expansion in the United States and Western Europe during the 1920's caused an increasing demand for silver, lead, zinc, and copper, with beneficial effects for Mexico's mines. A world boom in henequen also was a factor in Mexico's revival. Besides, during the latter years of the decade there came a swift growth in Mexico's manufacturing industries.[17]

The reasons for the manufacturing spurt are less obvious than the reasons for increased exports. It may be that the modest growth in mining output, which in the aggregate accounted for about one third of Mexico's total output of goods, contributed to the strong upward trend in manufacturing. Again, part of the growth was probably due to nothing more than the re-establishment of security on the railroads. The group of young industrialists that had been brought into existence in the Porfirian period had simply drawn in their horns during the years of Revolutionary turmoil and waited again for the day when steel, glass, beer, textiles, and chemicals could be shipped with safety on Mexico's beleaguered railroad lines. When shipments of this sort grew safe in the 1920's, the industrial plants began again to find and exploit the waiting markets in distant parts of Mexico.[18] But the growth of Mexico's industrial production from 1920 to 1930 was not confined to the pre-Revolutionary industrial plants. Some other vital force seemed to be at work, pushing output upward. Any effort to identify that force is largely conjecture. One particularly plausible line of conjecture, however, relates to the effects of the land seizures and revolutions which went on after 1913. From that date on, there was a wholesale abandonment of haciendas in much of troubled Mexico, and a flight of both capital and labor out of Mexican agriculture.

The flight of capital out of agricultural production and out of rural trade produced the decline of agriculture on which we commented earlier. Of course, most of the capital devoted to agriculture had been frozen on the land in the form of buildings, fences, irrigation works, and other land improvements. But some assets were liquid or could be turned into liquid form, such as bank balances, gold plate, movable crops, trade inventories, and livestock. A part of these assets was exported to the United States and Europe; a part was plundered. But there were also cases here and there in which rural assets were successfully transferred into urban trade, real estate, and industry. As a result, as one traces the lineage of the great names in Mexican industry today, he occasionally comes upon a family whose prominence goes back to the landed estate and the early banking ventures of the Porfirian era.

Meanwhile, the decline of the hacienda system probably weakened the ties which were holding considerable amounts of underemployed agricultural labor on the land. Though the hacienda owner of the Porfirian era may have seen advantages in keeping his labor bound to the land, the incentive of the small private or communal farmer for supporting extra hands on his meager holdings was obviously much weaker. Though there were strong cultural pulls holding family groups together in some localities, the younger sons of many rural families nonetheless were allowed to drift off the land in search of higher pay and better opportunity.[19] The ties of the farmhands to the land were weakened further when hordes of peasant soldiers marched in and out of Mexico's major cities as recruits in the armies of Zapata, Villa, and Carranza. What economists like to call the "demonstration effect" must surely have begun to exert its force on the recruits.

So the big cities, we can assume, began to acquire idle capital and cheap labor during the 1920's. Some of the labor went into construction, just as some of the capital went into private dwellings and apartment houses. But some apparently went into manufacturing. It is hard to say what motivated this movement of capital and human enterprise into manufacturing so soon after the black days of civil war. Persons who lived through the period talk of an unbelievable euphoria which seized many Mexicans of intellect and energy at the time. According to their accounts, the wounds of the Revolution were just beginning to heal and stability was beginning to return to the countryside. José Vasconcelos' teaching missionaries were touring the hinterland; Diego Rivera was adorning Mexico's public buildings with his powerful murals of protest and promise; there was a sense of nation and destiny in the air which had not been felt in Mexico since 1857. A gamble on the concept that Mexico was just beginning to emerge as a modern country may not have been so difficult in such an atmosphere.

The fact that there was a fairly significant flow of investment into the manufacturing industries in the 1920's is suggested not only by the subsequent performance of this sector but also by the comparative importance of capital goods in the total supply of Mexico's goods during that period. According to figures laboriously developed by the Economic Commission for Latin America, capital goods accounted for 10 to 12 per cent of the total supply of goods in Mexico during the years from 1925 to 1930. And of these capital goods, the largest category by far was "machinery and general equipment," a term which excludes agricultural and transportation equipment, iron, steel, and cement.[20]

The process of financing the growth of Mexico's cities partly by draining capital and idle facilities off the land could not have gone on forever. The insufficient production of foodstuffs would in the end have proved a bottleneck to further industrial growth. We can see from Chart 1, however, that the 1930's provided the first feeble signs of regeneration in the agricultural sector — enough, at any rate, for food crops to grow once more roughly at the same rate as the population.[21] The reasons for the beginnings of regeneration seem fairly clear. The land programs of Calles, Portes Gil, Rodríguez, and Cárdenas — but especially Cárdenas — were beginning to reduce the uncertainties about agricultural land ownership all over Mexico. Squatters were beginning to get the assurances they needed about continued possession. Others who had not had the courage to seize some land forcibly were beginning to acquire the land by other means, principally through the expansion of the cooperative and semicooperative agricultural villages. Irrigation was gradually increasing; between 1926 and 1940, the acreage of irrigated land went up by 15 or 20 per cent. Despite the fact that the 1926 experiment in agricultural credit had been a fiasco, such credit by the 1930's finally began to get a little easier. Though

CHART 1

Output of Major Activities of the Mexican Economy
(Based on 1950 Prices), 1895–1910, 1921–1940

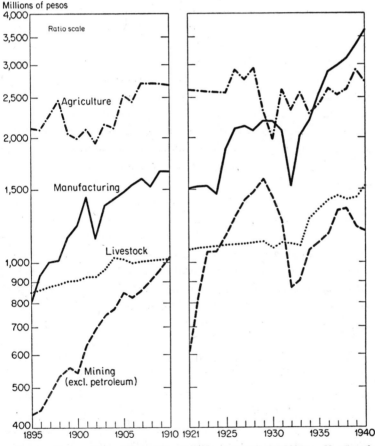

Source: Enrique Pérez López, "El producto nacional," in *México, 50 años de revolución: La economía* (Mexico, D.F.: Fondo de Cultura Económica, 1960), pp. 588–589.

many areas of agricultural Mexico were overlooked, and some even retrogressed in economic and social terms, the general direction for agricultural Mexico was upward.

Nonetheless, as Chart 1 indicates, manufacturing was the star performer in the Mexican economy during the decade of the 1930's. After a brief depression dip in the first years of the decade, manufacturing expanded at a swift rate.* The physical supply of Mexico's investment goods continued to grow, with a sustained heavy emphasis on "machinery and equipment." All types of products were considerably increased, not only such old stand-bys as textiles, beer, sugar, shoes, soap, and tobacco, but also newer products like cement and iron and steel.[22] Various related indexes grew rapidly as well. The use of energy rose steadily from 1925 to 1940, with gasoline and electric power leading the growth. Measured in kilowatt hour equivalents, the total use of energy rose from 6 billion to 11 billion units during the period. Railroad freight increased from three and a half billion ton-kilometers in 1925 to over five and a half billion in 1940.[23] Clearly, the Mexican economy had already begun to stir.

The basis for the growth of manufacturing was as much a matter for conjecture in the 1930's as it had been in the 1920's. Certainly it was not exports this time that provided the prime stimulus. Mexico's exports dropped off sharply from 1929 to 1933 as the world demand for metals declined. Despite Mexico's devaluation of the early 1930's, changing the peso's value from about 40 cents to about 28 cents in United States money, the quantity of Mexico's exports in 1940 was barely back to its 1930 level. Neither can

---

* The figures in Chart 1, which end in 1940, are considerably less reliable than those available for subsequent periods. For instance, though the index on which the chart is based shows roughly a 60 per cent increase in manufacturing output during the decade ending in 1940, other indexes suggest an increase of as much as 200 per cent. It is hard to say which may be closer to the facts. The index portrayed in Chart 1 seems to have been based upon component output series with invariant product coverage; thus, it omits new industries which appeared during the decade and fails to measure the effect of the more-than-average growth rates which are typical of such industries. On the other hand, the other indexes also suffer from major weaknesses.

one turn to foreign investment as a significant factor in the growth of manufacturing — at least not in this period. Foreign investment in manufacturing was beginning to grow a little, but the growth was still at a quite unimpressive rate, at less than half a million United States dollars a year.

It may be that the process of recovery for manufactures which began in 1933 was stimulated in the first instance by the increased price of imports, a consequence of the drastic devaluation of the peso. Later in the decade, the pick-up in the demand for metals and the unprecedented growth of spending from the public sector added to the expansive forces. Beginning in 1935, Cárdenas launched an extensive program of public works, with the usual demand-stimulating effects. By 1940, total investment in public works by the Cárdenas regime came to 1,018 million pesos. Budgetary deficits were recorded each year from 1936 on; and resort to central bank credit was heavy. Not only did this increased public spending stimulate internal demand in Mexico, but it also offered Mexico's comparatively timid young industrialists more frequent opportunities to earn a large riskless profit in the filling of public contracts, thereby stimulating investment in new ventures in the private sector.

But it also seems likely that something more than devaluation and public works spurred the process of growth. The continued trek to the cities, generated partly by the institutional loosening of ties to the land, almost certainly explains part of the process. There, one may conjecture, Mexico began to reorganize its human and capital resources in an environment which used both more effectively. The demand for shelter gave a great lift to the construction industry in the cities. Village handicrafters producing textiles or shoes were superseded by city factories; home-produced food and drink were replaced by the output of industrial plants. Human activity was brought together in clusters, sufficiently large to justify the installation of electric distribution systems, reliable water supply systems, maintenance and repair services, and trucking terminals. Self-financing from profits supplemented the finance capital which may previously have been drawn out of the agricultural sector. It may be that the new environment, taken as a whole, was more congenial to the exercise of latent entrepreneurial ability. The result was the changing pattern for Mexico's economic activity which is reflected in Chart 1.

GOVERNMENT AND BUSINESS

By the close of the 1930's the division of responsibilities between the public and the private sectors which characterizes modern-day Mexico had already been largely established. The government was gradually gaining control over the country's basic utilities, gradually learning how to break bottlenecks by providing needed facilities to agriculture and industry. At the same time, the government had planted its ideological banners in roughly the positions that they were to occupy in the two succeeding decades — positions which included an acknowledgment of governmental responsibility for the public welfare, an insistence on the government's right to invest and produce wherever private industry would not, an assertion of the government's duty to regulate the country's economic life to the extent that it felt the public interest would be served.

Meanwhile, although considerable tension existed between the government and many private groups, the private sector had also begun to assume the position which it would hold in the succeeding twenty years. In agriculture, private producers and communal farmers were finding their places in the national economy, with the former specializing in commercial crops and the latter tending to emphasize subsistence products — and with both using the credit and the irrigation water which the government was prepared to provide. In banking, the private institutions were just beginning to take cognizance of the regulatory presence of the Banco de México, while learning to use the supporting resources of the government institutions. In manufacturing, the preeminent position of the private sector was already well established; the principle that the private sector might call upon the government for help in the form of protection against imports or industrial credits had already been tested; and the possibility that the government might move into fields of production where the private sector was hesitant to go had already been aired.

Nonetheless, though all the elements of a *modus vivendi* between the private and the public sectors were in place by 1940, one would hardly have considered the Mexican structure a mature and seasoned system at that time. If one could believe the public press, the two competing economic ideologies inside the country were those of Karl Marx and Friedrich von Hayek. If one could credit the public stances of business groups and government officials, no common ideological ground existed between them.

To be sure, the underlying realities were probably not as grim as the surface struggle might suggest. Mexico's businessmen, with the pragmatism and single-mindedness which had always characterized their dealing with government, were managing to arrange their individual transactions with public bodies and to find their way through the labyrinthine regulations of the day. Still, it would have been a reckless seer who suggested in 1940 that the basic relations between the public and the private sectors would crystallize and stabilize in roughly the patterns which existed at that time.

Chapter 4

Economic Policies and
Performance since 1940

THE year 1940 is something of a benchmark in the developing relations between Mexico's public and private sectors. It is the year in which there appeared the first of a succession of presidents devoted to the proposition that industrial growth on the modern pattern was indispensable for Mexico. It is the year in which the impact of World War II began to make itself felt, giving Mexico a major opportunity to begin realizing its industrial possibilities. It also marked the opening of a period in which the public official and the private businessman — despite periodic "crises of confidence" — were obviously beginning to converse effectively across the ideological wall which once seemed to separate them.

Our analysis would be altogether in the Hollywood tradition if it could demonstrate that Mexico had found the philosopher's stone — that, by a process which first became evident in 1940, the public and the private sectors had at last been integrated into a harmonious national mechanism which today serves the interests of all segments of Mexico's life. This, however, is not to be the outcome of our analysis. Instead, we suggest that, despite the obvious advances since that benchmark year, Mexico is now approaching a new and difficult stage in the relations between its public and its private sectors, a stage both perilous and promising, a stage generated partly by the increasing political maturity of its people and partly by a growing dissatisfaction with the performance of the country's economy.

In order to develop this thesis, we shall focus first upon the evolution of the country's economy since 1940 as the political economist would see it. Following that, in Chapter 5, we propose to probe a good deal more deeply into the elements of constancy and of change in the public sector. Thereafter, in Chapter 6, we shall try to throw some light on the recent evolution of the private sector. In a final chapter we propose to speculate upon some future political and economic changes and what they may mean for relations between the public and the private sectors.*

TWO DECADES OF GROWTH

Whatever the problems of the future may be, the economic progress of the Mexican economy since 1940 has been impressive by any yardstick.[1] Chart 2 shows the trend in the physical output of goods and services. Output in Mexico went up between 1939 and 1960, according to published data, at an annual rate of slightly less than 6 per cent; unpublished figures circulating in government circles suggest a slightly higher growth rate, about 6.5 per cent. At the same time, the population seems to have grown at an annual rate of about 2.7 per cent. Nearly half of Mexico's growth, therefore, has gone to match the growth in people, while the rest has gone to raise per capita income.

There have been some variations, of course. Mining output has lagged considerably behind the rest of the economy throughout the two decades. But manufacturing, electrical energy output, and petroleum output have been star performers, more than tripling in real terms over twenty years. Commercial activities grew with

* The reader is warned, if warning is needed, that the account which follows in Chapters 4 through 7 often strays beyond a mere recounting of the surface facts and represents the writer's interpretation of these events. The interpretation has been derived from numerous sources, including current official and private periodicals and endless discussions with businessmen and government officials who lived through the period in greater or lesser positions of responsibility. I have used citations sparsely, however, because citations in support of conclusions of this sort would represent a kind of spurious scholarship; the interpretations are no less subjective for having had the concurrence of others.

great rapidity for a while, if one can believe the uncertain data for this particular sector of the Mexican economy, but then they appeared to slow down.[2] The physical output of crops intended primarily for export, such as coffee, cotton, and tomatoes, grew

CHART 2

Gross Domestic Product Components of Mexico, in Real Terms
(Based on 1950 Prices), 1939–1960

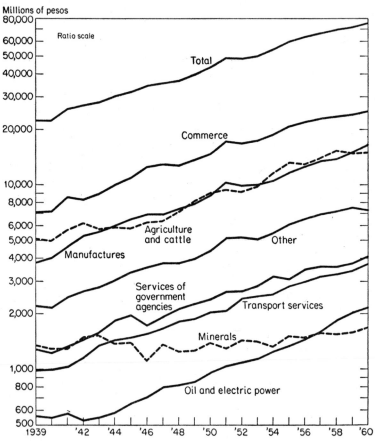

Note: The figures underlying this chart will be found in Appendix Table A-1. For qualifications especially applicable to the "commerce" data, see p. 207, note 2.

much more rapidly than the output of crops for the home market. But by and large, as the illustrative figures in Table 6 show, the growth has pervaded nearly every sector of the Mexican economy.

TABLE 6

Illustrative Measures of Growth in the Mexican Economy, 1940 and 1960

	1940	1960
Crude steel production (000 tons)	238	1,556
Cement production (000 tons)	485	3,086
Paved roads (000 miles)	4.8	25.6
Trucks operating (000 units)	42	301
Rail freight (billion ton-kilometers)	5.8	13.4
Land irrigated with government aid (000 hectares)	271	2,811
Installed electrical capacity (000 kilowatts)	681	2,740
Gross domestic product (billions of 1950 pesos)	20.7	67.0

Sources: Various official publications of the Mexican government.

In welfare terms, the growth of the Mexican economy has been almost as impressive. The diet of the Mexican people, once largely confined to corn, wheat, rice, and beans, now includes considerable quantities of eggs, poultry, meat, fish, green vegetables, and prepared foods. In the decade following 1950, for instance, meat consumption in Mexico seems to have doubled while the population increased by less than a third. At the same time, milk supplies began to reach an increasing proportion of the people. Despite the greater variety, per capita consumption of the old staples probably has also gone up, as suggested by Table 7.

For all the increases in these totals, Mexico has a long way to go before it will have provided basic food and shelter needs for most of its people. Nutritional diseases still account for a considerable part of the deaths of children of preschool age and are still encountered frequently in hospitals and clinics.[3] As for housing, although the available statistics on the subject are unreliable and contradictory, no one who has seen Mexico's cities and countryside needs to be told that there is still considerable human suffering for lack of adequate shelter.

TABLE 7

Apparent Annual Per Capita Consumption of Selected Foods in Mexico
(in kilograms)

	1937–1944	1957–1960
Corn	138.1	164.7
Rice	4.8	7.7
Wheat	21.1	39.2
Beans	5.4	15.6
Potatoes	3.0	7.0
Tomatoes	3.1	7.1

Source: Computed by the author from official production and trade data. These figures require numerous qualifications. There is some evidence of underestimation of agricultural output in the earlier years, on a scale larger than in later years. Changes in consumption by farmers and in the end-use of some basic foodstuffs, such as the diversion of corn to the feeding of livestock and to industrial uses, also affect the interpretation of the data. For useful comments on the adequacy of Mexico's agricultural data, see Edmundo Flores, *Tratado de economía agrícola* (Mexico, D.F.: Fondo de Cultura Económica, 1961).

Partly as a result of the obvious unfilled needs of Mexico, the country has been rocked with continual controversy over the question: Who has benefited from the improvement so far? The issue has been raised by all sectors of Mexico's political life, from the Sinarquista on the right to the Marxists on the left. It has colored the political and economic policies of the country to such a degree that it is important to have some inkling of the facts.

In the course of Mexico's growth, there was no consistent plan either to redistribute the productivity gains to broad sectors of the economy or to withhold the gains for some favored group. From time to time, in response to pressure from rural or urban interests, one Mexican president or another threw added support to the agricultural sector or expanded some feature of the social security system. At other times, Mexican presidents pursued policies which increased industrial production, added to industrial jobs, and provided higher profits for investors and business groups. At still other times, the control of inflation encouraged or prevented shifts in income distribution. But these were the consequences of spot pressures, not the manifestation of a grand macroeconomic plan.

Partly as a result of these variations in emphasis and partly as a result of the economic circumstances surrounding Mexico, the improvement of Mexican living standards during the two-decade period has been neither continuous nor all-embracing. In much of the 1940's, living costs rose so rapidly that they appeared to outdistance wages,[4] and it was only in the latter 1940's and the 1950's that wage increases began to pull ahead of price rises.[5]

Nonetheless, a very considerable proportion of the Mexican public seemed to increase its living standards by a substantial margin during the twenty-year period. Shoes appeared on the feet of the urban poor and in the countryside. Bicycles became a commonplace in rural areas where they had been a rarity. The variety of goods in humble rural and urban neighborhood stores expanded considerably. Whatever the uncertain and conflicting statistics could be made to say in one direction or another, the evidence of the eye suggested a broad improvement in living standards.

This improvement occurred through at least two different routes. The number of jobs in Mexico rose in relation to the number of people; and the kind of jobs available to Mexican workers was progressively upgraded. The increase in the number of jobs came about partly through the expansion in jobs for women, especially in business and government offices. Between 1940 and 1950, women increased from 8 per cent to 13 per cent of the total labor force, then rose to nearly 17 per cent in 1960.[6] The total labor force went up from 53 per cent of Mexico's adult population in 1940 to 59 per cent in 1950, and to about 62 per cent in 1960. Meanwhile, the general shift out of low-paying jobs into higher-paying ones was evidenced in a number of ways. For instance, the comparatively low-paid agricultural workers, who represented 64 per cent of the nation's labor force in 1940 and 58 per cent in 1950, were down to about 52 per cent in 1960. Concurrently, there was a corresponding rise in the comparative importance of workers in the higher-paying activities, such as manufacturing and the generation of electricity. At the same time, there was a general upgrading of jobs inside many industries. In most manufacturing groups for which data exist, the relative importance of salaried workers — as distinguished from workers compensated on a time or piecework basis — went up significantly.[7]

Of course, giant discrepancies in income persisted in Mexico, not only among the different income classes of the nation[8] but also from one geographical area to the next.[9] But no solid support exists for the suspicion that Mexico's growth was largely a case of the rich growing richer while the real income of the poor declined.[10] The rise of foodstuff consumption and decline of the infant death rate since 1940 suggest the opposite conclusion. So does the visible expansion in free public facilities for supplying education, medical help, and various other services. The tendency for the income levels of different areas to converge a little during the twenty-year period also affords a shred of evidence in the same direction.[11]

Still, Mexico was far from being a tranquil and contented country at the close of two decades of growth. Indeed, the soul-searching, the doubts, and the tensions of the country were as high as they had ever been since the era of Cárdenas. In both the public and private sectors, there was the worry that the economic system of the country, which seemed to have performed adequately for two decades or more, might be faltering. To understand some of the economic reasons for this concern, it will help to look a little more closely at Mexico's economic evolution.

ECONOMIC IMPACT OF THE WAR

When Avila Camacho took office in 1940, he fell heir to an economic situation dramatically different from that of his predecessor. Whereas Cárdenas had operated in an international setting which was not especially conducive to swift industrialization, World War II provided a considerable stimulus. As the new administration began to recognize the opportunities of the time, it placed more and more emphasis on the need to industrialize. By the time Avila Camacho left office late in 1946, the Cárdenas image of Mexico based upon a contented, semi-industrial, semicommercial peasantry had been obscured by a new image of Mexico — an image of the modern industrial state.

The war created a new external demand for Mexico's exports, doubling the total between 1939 and 1945. The demand for manufactures was especially strong.[12] Textile products, which had been less than 1 per cent of Mexico's exports in 1939, were up to 20 per cent by 1945. Exports of manufactured food, drink, tobacco, and chemicals, also insignificant in 1939, made up another 8 per cent in 1945. At the same time, the war held down Mexico's supply of manufactured imports. Though imports as a whole expanded rather considerably during the war, imports of textiles, chemicals, and vehicles lagged behind, generating internal shortages.

The demand for manufactured exports and the shortage of manufactured imports presented an opportunity which Mexico's private entrepreneurs could not resist. Though the scarcity of industrial machinery prevented any large investments in equipment, it was still possible to improvise in many ways. Textile plants throughout the country went from a one-shift to a three-shift basis. Simple distilleries were set up to draw alcohol from sugar. Ingeniously devised machines produced various items for everyday household needs.

The strength of Mexico's response to the opportunities of the war was probably increased by the continued trickle into Mexico of refugees in the early 1940's. Some of them had capital; practically all had a measure of professional skill or business training. A large number gravitated to Mexico City and exerted their influence on developments there. In addition to the arrival of potential entrepreneurs with funds, there was also both an overt and a stealthy flow of unaccompanied foreign capital into the country, amounting to several hundred million dollars during the course of the war.[13]

Nevertheless, without belittling the influence of the war, we may take it as probable that the sufficient conditions for Mexico's growth in the early 1940's were forces within Mexico's borders rather than external factors. As the war generated opportunities for manufacturing, the entrepreneurs who stepped forth to seize them were without much question mainly native-born. To be sure, many displayed some recent European influence in their family backgrounds. But, if we are not being misled by the scraps of information we have on the subject, the new entrepreneurs were drawn to a considerable degree from the incipient Mexican middle class. It is doubtful that the group would have been as large but for the major developments between 1920 and 1940 — the trek to the city, the rise of city literacy and education, and the demonstration effects of a growing Mexican industry.

Another factor which probably deserves credit in explaining Mexico's growth in the war period was the continuing impact of Cárdenas' land reform program of the 1930's. In any earlier era, a Mexican businessman who was exploiting a wartime bonanza through the manufacture of textiles or simple chemicals would have been likely to invest his profits in a ranch or hacienda, sinking his funds into new houses and barns, new fences, and good horses. In the early 1940's, however, only a very ignorant or a very courageous investor would have made large-scale investments in rural land. High living, foreign securities, and urban real estate provided alternatives, to be sure. But the decline of agricultural opportunities had also increased the attractiveness of reinvesting in productive trade and industry.

Still, Avila Camacho could not confine his role altogether to that of handmaiden to private enterprise. Operating in the shadow of the Cárdenas legend, he continued to invest considerable sums in the public sector. Chart 3 (later in this chapter) shows that from 1940 to 1945, public investment just about kept pace with a rapidly increasing gross domestic product. During this period, the government put large amounts into its recently nationalized oil properties and even larger amounts into the overburdened railway system. This was the era, too, in which the government began to make its first tentative investments in manufacturing enterprises. In 1942, Nacional Financiera took a minority interest in Altos Hornos de México, S.A., destined to be Mexico's largest steel company. This was a case of a sort which would be repeated several times in later years — a case in which private investors developed the initial concept of the operation, and then, frightened off by the size of the commitment and the technical uncertainties that they faced, welcomed government participation as a form of risk insurance.

There was a limit, however, to the amount which the government could invest in industry, particularly in the early years of the war when industrial equipment was in such scarce supply. The government, therefore, had not only the disposition but also the means to continue the Cárdenas policy of making heavy investments in the rural development of Mexico. Thus, in the Avila Camacho era, 1940–1946, the all-weather road system was doubled and the lands serviced by government-financed irrigation were nearly tripled.*

The period, therefore, abounded in almost riskless opportunities for business: opportunities to produce for a goods-hungry domestic or world market, and opportunities to produce for the government on terms which almost invariably afforded high profits and few worries.

But Avila Camacho could not neglect the problems of the urban poor. And his efforts to discharge that responsibility provided one significant test of how far Mexico's public sector had progressed. Like every other wartime economy, Mexico was faced with major inflationary pressures. As the deposits of the private banking sector swelled because of the inflow of foreign funds, the stage was set for a large expansion in domestic credit.[14] At the same time, the shortage of goods for export from the United States was being felt throughout Mexico. These two factors alone might have been

* See Appendix Table A-2 for data on government investment, by categories, from 1940 to date. The more specific measures of accomplishment in the public sector referred to in this chapter, such as the length of roads constructed, irrigation works completed, electric power installed, and so on, are taken from many sources, principally from the various chapters of *México, 50 años de revolución: La economía* (Mexico, D.F.: Fondo de Cultura Económica, 1960) and from the *Anuarios estadísticos* issued by the Secretaría de Industria y Comercio.

enough to produce a sharp rise in prices; but the tendency was aggravated still further by the pervasive existence of monopolies and restrictions in the Mexican distribution system and the deep-seated habit of commodity speculation among the country's commercial class. Prices in Mexico approximately doubled during the war period.

Given the place and the times, the controls which the administration tried to apply at this stage were remarkably advanced and sophisticated. In fact, the monetary and fiscal policies of the Mexican government during this period of inflation, if gauged by Latin American standards, could almost be labeled as restraining and austere.[15]

To be sure, a considerable fraction of the funds used for public investment was obtained by inflationary techniques — by the sale of government bonds to the Banco de México. But about three quarters of the public sector's investments was matched by the public sector's savings during the war period, that is, by public revenue left over after all current expenditures had been met. (The data will be found in Appendix Table A-3.)

In addition, as the deposits of the private banking sector increased, the government's brilliant minister of finance, Eduardo Suárez, broke new ground by instituting a program for the regulation of credit. In 1941, the powers of the Banco de México were broadened from those of a mere central bank of issue to those of a government institution theoretically capable of enforcing some sort of monetary policy. In the next few years the Banco de México experimented with the whole range of monetary devices which today are the standard apparatus of a modern state. In order to hold down the total volume of credit being extended by private banks, it applied reserve requirements against the deposits of the banks, then stiffened them as credit persistently expanded. In order to curb speculation in commodities, it refused rediscount privileges for certain types of paper. And as a means of diverting funds to industry, it bought the securities of industrial issuers. As the government pursued these policies, it periodically bemoaned the absence of a broadly based securities market in which open-market operations might be more effectively conducted.[16]

None of these measures, it is true, was sufficient to prevent a considerable increase in the loans and investments of the Mexican banking system or to stop the swiftly rising prices of wartime Mexico. One result of the sharp increase in prices was that living standards for most Mexicans rose very little during the first half of the 1940's. Of course, a strong argument can be made for the view that, at this stage in Mexico's economic development, the noticeable lag in industrial wages — engendered partly by the overhang of an endless supply of unskilled labor and partly by a captive and compliant labor organization — was a boon to Mexico's growth.[17] For the moment, the rate of investment did not depend upon the expansion of total domestic demand; the need to substitute for imports and the opportunity to supply export markets were strong enough at the time to put to work any capital which chose to venture into the industrial field. The more important problem, it may well be, was to overcome the reluctance of many Mexicans to invest in Mexican industry. Long strides were made in this direction as new fortunes were made from trade and manufacturing. But the issue of income distribution would return again and again to bedevil the governments which followed Avila Camacho.

THE ERA OF ALEMÁN

All the presidents of Mexico are sons of the Revolution by political necessity, but some are less Revolutionary than others. Miguel Alemán's advent to power late in 1946 represented an even greater de-emphasis of the policies and objectives of Lázaro Cárdenas. The shift from Avila Camacho to Alemán was not dramatic; the policies of the two administrations bore more signs of continuity than of change. Alemán had no more hesitation in using the economic powers of government than did his predecessor. His arrival, therefore, did not bring a reduction of the Mexican government's economic powers and activities. Rather, it brought a somewhat greater willingness to use those powers in tandem with the rising business class.

In 1946, it was easy to see the signs of trouble ahead for Mexico's economy. Economic growth had slowed a little. The war-

CHART 3

Gross Fixed Public and Private Investment in Mexico as a Proportion of Gross Domestic Product, 1940–1960

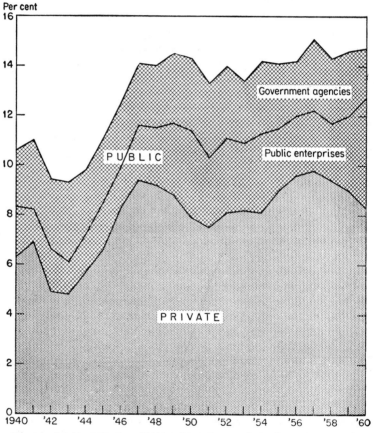

Sources: *Combined Mexican Working Party Report of the International Bank for Reconstruction and Development* (Baltimore: Johns Hopkins Press, 1953); and Nacional Financiera annual reports.

stimulated industries were on the verge of losing their overseas markets and of facing their first dose of hard competition at home. Some of the refugee capital which had taken haven in Mexico during the war was departing. Various pent-up demands for foreign goods which could not be satisfied in earlier years — some for capital goods, some for consumer goods — were being filled at a rapid rate. To add to these difficulties, Mexico's upper-income groups, which as a rule had a high propensity for foreign consumer goods or for the purchase of foreign securities, were bulging with liquid funds.

Alemán proceeded upon the principle which Avila Camacho himself had seemed more and more disposed to adopt — the principle that what was good for Mexican business was probably good for Mexico. As capital was drained out of Mexico, he permitted some easing of the credit restrictions which the Banco de México had heretofore been applying to the private sector. Following up the tentative lead of Avila Camacho, he instituted a considerable increase in the tariff structure, giving a fresh dose of protection to Mexico's industry.[18] At the same time, however, he was careful not to place burdensome restrictions on the capital goods or industrial materials which Mexico's industries were importing from abroad.

With the decline in credit restraints, the increase in protection, and the reappearance of capital goods in international markets, investment by Mexico's private sector shot up to new heights. As Chart 3 indicates, the year 1947 registered a new peak in the relation of fixed private investment to gross domestic product, a high which would not be reached again until 1956.*

* The figures used for Chart 3 are based on current peso expenditures, without adjustments for relative price changes. An unpublished study by the U.N. Economic Commission for Latin America suggests that if adjustments for price changes are made, the ratio of private investment to gross domestic product was higher in 1947 than it has ever been before or since — indeed that an almost continuous decline in the ratio set in after that date. However, the problems associated with this sort of calculation are most formidable both conceptually and statistically; and they are especially difficult when the effort is applied to a rapidly changing mix of goods over a long period.

The Alemán policy of increased protection and the growing confidence of the private sector had one effect which could readily be foreseen. Already in the Avila Camacho era, foreign investors had begun to acquire a small foothold in Mexico's new industries. With the increased friendliness of the Alemán administration, a number of foreign enterprises which previously had been selling considerable amounts of consumer goods in the Mexican market began thinking about setting up production facilities — or at least assembly and final processing facilities — inside Mexico's borders. By this time, recollections of the acerbity of the Cárdenas administration had been dimmed a little. In addition, the internal Mexican market had by now grown large enough to support some assembly and processing plants of an efficient size. Accordingly, the trickle of United States investors in Mexico began to grow.

This was a somewhat different type of foreign investor from the kind that had previously appeared in Mexico. In earlier times, the foreign investors had consisted largely of two kinds: the gullible buyer of railroad, utility, or government bonds, unaware of the risks of the investment and responsive to the pressures of his investment banker; and the enterprise in search of raw materials for export, anxious to maintain as little contact with the Mexican economy as was consistent with extracting the raw materials. The group which began to appear in Mexico in the middle and late 1940's hoped to sell their goods in the Mexican market. Accordingly, their success — as many of them were aware — depended upon the continued growth of the Mexican economy and upon the continued willingness of the Mexican government to suffer their presence. This basic change was reflected in their public relations, in their labor policies, and in their dealings with the Mexican government.

But Alemán, no less than Avila Camacho, also had to consider the welfare of rural Mexico. Among other things, he had to continue the pattern of heavy investments in agriculture. True to his role, Alemán pumped large amounts into rural roads and irrigation works. Indeed, during the six years of the Alemán regime, the expansion in irrigated land was larger than that in the Cárdenas and Avila Camacho regimes combined.[19]

Alemán demonstrated, however, that symbols could be one thing and substance another. For most Mexicans, projects in agriculture conjured images of the lowly Indian, tilling his primitive acres of poor corn, and living on the edge of the monetary economy. For Alemán, projects in agriculture meant principally huge dams and other public works concentrated in the north of the Republic, that is, in the areas near the United States border where commercial rather than subsistence agriculture was the rule. Under the impetus of this public investment, Mexican private investors, a number of whom had made their fortunes in wartime commerce or manufacturing, lost their fear of agricultural ventures and turned to these northern areas as outlets for their funds. President Alemán, to speed the trend and reduce the risks of expropriation for such investors, altered the land-reform provisions of the constitution, giving increased protection to private holders of agricultural land. As a consequence, though the acreage under cultivation for practically every major Mexican crop expanded considerably in the Alemán regime, the acreage for cotton expanded much more rapidly than the rest. One of the results was a swift rise in Mexico's cotton exports during the Alemán regime.

Alemán did not confine his public investment to the agricultural sphere. In the later years of his era, investment in Mexico's public enterprises increased considerably. Large amounts were directed into the railroads, Pemex, and the federal electricity commission. Nacional Financiera, drawing on credit from the United States Export-Import Bank and on the proceeds from certificates sold to the Mexican banking system, sharply increased its participation in various new enterprises.

Some of Mexico's private entrepreneurs registered concern over the increase in state activity, particularly those whose fortunes were not directly helped by it. These, on the whole, tended to be the older industrialists and the older private banking interests — groups which had adequate internal credit sources of their own and which had confidence in their ability to prosper without state help.

But the newer industrialists, multiplied and strengthened by the war and by the protectionist policy of Alemán, seemed to welcome the growth of government activity. For many of these, the expansion of public investment in energy sources and in transportation meant greater profits from their construction and supply contracts with the government; in fact, rumors about widespread bribery, unconscionable profits, and raids on the public treasury in connection with such contracts were daily fare during this period. Whether or not bribery and high profits were more common during these years, the burst of public spending provided industry as a whole with better "overhead" facilities for their operations. The increase in Nacional Financiera's activity meant easier access to credit and improved assurances of a bail-out by government if the going got rough. The fact that Alemán sometimes took steps contrary to private interests, such as introducing an excess profits tax on business profits, was no more than a minor irritant in a generally benign environment. For the newer industrialists, therefore, the era of Alemán was much more an opportunity than a threat.

So the Alemán regime afforded a demonstration of the enduring power of the symbols of the Revolution; of the use of these symbols to expand the opportunities of the private sector; and of the impulse toward growth which this blending of forces produced. But it also provided a dramatic illustration of the extent to which external equilibrium problems have recurred to hold down the freedom of action of Mexico's presidents. For the easing of controls that characterized the closing months of the Avila Camacho era, plus Alemán's expansive policies in the early part of his regime, provoked one of those external financial crises which have punctuated Mexican growth since the 1930's. In 1946 and 1947, just before and after Alemán took office, the internal expansion in the country plus the catch-up in demands which could not be fully satisfied during the war led to a sharp increase in imports, as shown in Table 8. Indeed, Mexico's reliance on imports became so heavy that in those two years the quantity of imported goods

TABLE 8

Significant Items in Mexico's Balance of Payments, 1939–1961

(in millions of U.S. dollars; "plus" means net receipts, and "minus" means net payments)

Calendar year	Total merchandise imports	Total merchandise exports[a]	Exports of: Cotton and coffee	Exports of: Copper, lead, and zinc	Net tourist and border trade	Net change in reserves of Banco de México
1939	128.0	155.7	8.0	35.8	+21.7	+0.1
1940	131.9	147.1	5.4	30.4	+22.3	+24.2
1941	199.2	148.7	9.8	32.8	+31.5	−1.3
1942	172.1	195.0	8.1	39.6	+23.4	+44.8
1943	212.1	239.6	14.1	44.8	+35.3	+140.3
1944	310.8	238.2	24.4	44.6	+42.5	+40.3
1945	372.3	280.1	21.9	51.5	+50.9	+80.4
1946	600.1	344.8	40.4	48.8	+87.3	−121.7
1947	719.2	472.8	74.2	97.9	+82.7	−122.0
1948	597.4	464.1	46.9	126.6	+104.0	−68.8
1949	519.9	436.4	97.4	118.2	+132.3	+29.3
1950	597.3	533.2	187.4	120.0	+156.1	+172.1
1951	889.2	629.4	209.2	150.2	+175.2	−1.0
1952	830.9	676.7	243.5	168.1	+164.7	+2.9
1953	807.5	610.8	232.3	122.8	+162.2	−26.4
1954	788.7	660.0	252.2	126.8	+163.6	−35.1
1955	883.6	808.5	334.0	152.4	+200.2	+200.1
1956	1,071.6	849.9	368.1	170.5	+292.7	+60.5
1957	1,155.1	758.0	279.1	131.2	+348.3	−27.8
1958	1,128.6	760.3	266.3	85.0	+304.0	−85.1
1959	1,006.6	756.1	268.3	88.5	+342.4	+51.8
1960	1,186.4	786.8	231.8	88.9	+373.0	−8.6
1961	1,138.6	842.9	236.3	83.4	+385.4	−21.5

[a] Including production of all nonindustrial gold and silver.
Sources: *Combined Mexican Working Party Report of the International Bank for Reconstruction and Development* (Baltimore: Johns Hopkins Press, 1953); and Banco de México annual reports.

rose to about one third of the goods produced in the country, though the typical relationship in other years was one fourth or one fifth.

The usual consequences followed. Foreign and domestic investors in Mexico, seeing the peso under pressure, added to the stress with a flight of capital from the country. For a time, Alemán tried to hold the value of the peso by borrowing from the International Monetary Fund and the United States Treasury. But in July 1948, as Mexico's foreign-exchange reserves began to get dangerously low, the peso was cut loose from its pegged rate of about 21 cents in United States currency and was allowed to drift downward for nearly a year; then it was pegged again at a new low level of 11½ cents. As devaluation pushed the price of imported goods upward, there were large price rises throughout Mexico's economy and large wage increases as well.

During the process of devaluation, Mexico's imports were squeezed back. Meanwhile the foreign exchange earned by her exports and her swiftly expanding tourist trade and "border trade," * more than held their own; by 1950, in fact, exports were rapidly on the rise again. Mexico's economists are still debating whether this reaction was due to the devaluation, to a concurrent pick-up in United States business conditions, or to the outbreak of hostilities in Korea; whatever the cause, it added to Mexico's strength. In 1950 also, the capital which had previously fled from Mexico returned to realize the profit accruing to it from its timely flight. The Banco de México's external assets were given a needed boost. For a year or two thereafter Mexico had the appearance of external stability.

---

* Mexico's "border trade" consists principally of the purchase of goods and services in Mexico's free-trade zones by United States residents, and imports from the United States by Mexicans living in these zones. Some of the purchases by United States residents are really a part of the tourist trade, and some are indistinguishable from commercial exports. As for the purchase of U.S. goods by Mexicans living in the free-trade zones, the suspicion is widespread that some part of this traffic is the first stage in the contraband import of goods destined for the Mexican interior.

The policies of Miguel Alemán are among the most contentious in Mexican economic history. That his early expansionist policies gave a fillip to Mexico's growth no one doubts; in this respect they satisfied one major drive in the Mexican national psyche. But, for a Mexico which still recalls the dubious political and welfare consequences of the expansionist patterns of the Porfirian era, questions of politics and welfare continue to be at least as important as the question of growth itself. The war years, with their galloping inflation, had seemed to postpone the day when some of the benefits of Mexico's development would be spread to the ordinary worker in Mexico's modern sector. By the end of the Alemán regime in 1952, a considerable segment of Mexican public opinion was asserting that the benefits to the workers still seemed quite remote.[20]

Exactly how well the low-income groups of Mexico really fared under Alemán is not at all clear. The administration, like that of Avila Camacho, from time to time acknowledged its role as protector of the urban poor by undertaking various measures to alleviate the effects of the increase in prices. Export taxes were applied, for instance, to discourage the outflow of sugar and other scarce foods and to hold down the domestic price of cotton. The import of wheat and edible oils was subsidized for a time to muffle the price effects of the devaluation. In addition, price ceilings were instituted for foodstuffs. All these measures and others, though often ineptly applied and poorly enforced, apparently had some effect. Per capita food consumption, which had barely risen during the war years of the Avila Camacho era, increased by 1950 to a level 30 per cent higher than that of 1939.

THE PERIOD OF ECONOMIC RESTRAINT

By the close of the Alemán period in 1952, Mexico had acquired a habit pattern in its private and public investment. For all the worries and doubts afoot in the country, twelve years or more of prosperity had conditioned the private sector to more of the same. And a similar period of expanding public activity had riveted certain patterns into the plans and attitudes of public officials.

Nonetheless, the revulsion against the high, wide, and handsome strategy of the Alemán era colored the administration of Adolfo Ruiz Cortines from its inception. Ruiz Cortines was unwilling to be quite so uninhibited in his use of the Alemán strategy — the strategy of giving the private sector its head while using the state as a partner and expediter whenever bottlenecks were to be broken or excessive risks reduced. His attitude toward the private sector was distant and "correct." Time and again, he emphasized the need for probity in government affairs. For a time, too, he was not willing to extend the welcome mat to foreign capital with the unrestrained enthusiasm of his predecessor. The new administration's ties to the private sector, therefore, seemed less intimate than those of Alemán.

At the same time, though Ruiz Cortines drew back a little from the private sector, one could hardly say that the direction of his administration was to the left. On the contrary, it blended its roles of agricultural revolutionary and protector of the urban poor into a mixture which, in the end, proved more conservative in some respects than that of Alemán. The restraint of the Ruiz administration was apparent not only in the field of public investment but also in its monetary and fiscal policies. In general, there was far less dash and somewhat more order and control than had prevailed in the era of Alemán. As Chart 2 indicated, the net consequence of all the circumstances of the Ruiz administration was to produce a rate of growth which — in the official statistics — appeared a little slower toward the close of the six-year period than the average growth rate since 1940.[21]

To appreciate how the characteristics of orderliness and conservatism came to be emphasized in Ruiz Cortines' administration, one had to begin by recalling that he took office under economic circumstances that were in some respects similar to those which had confronted the Alemán administration in its early years.

This time, Mexico was trying to absorb the shock of the slump in demand that followed the 1950–51 boom period of the Korean war, rather than the after-effects of World War II. Though Mexico's foreign-exchange reserves were reasonably high and though internal prices were more stable than they had been in a long time, the country's domestic output had practically stopped growing.

The government looked hard for some set of policies which would stimulate growth. The policies it chose at first were not unlike those which Alemán had favored in similar circumstances. The restrictions on private credit which had been put in effect during the Korean boom period were relaxed. At the same time, public credit institutions were allowed to have easier access to the resources of the Banco de México. As a result, public investment was stepped up considerably, partly through the use of domestic resources and partly through borrowing from the United States Export-Import Bank and the World Bank.

Having followed some of the expansionist aspects of the early Alemán pattern up to this point, Ruiz Cortines also encountered some of the restraints which had curbed the Alemán pattern toward the end. Early in 1954, signs of weakness in the external-payments position of Mexico began to appear. This time, however, the Mexican government seemed determined to act long before a crisis arrived. Mexico's foreign-exchange reserves were not yet seriously depleted. Yet the parity of the peso was changed in April 1954 from about 11½ cents in United States currency to 8 cents.

After the devaluation there was a swift resumption in the growth of the Mexican economy. The cause of the spurt is a matter of debate. Some ascribe it to the stimulus of the devaluation, others to the fortuitous resumption of growth in the United States economy late in 1954, which generated an expansion in Mexico's tourism and in coffee and cotton exports. Whatever the cause, Mexico expanded 9 per cent in 1954, when measured in real gross-product terms, and 11 per cent in 1955. At the same time, a step-up in capital inflow and in tourism boosted Mexico's foreign-exchange reserves to 410 millions of United States dollars, close to their all-time high.

From one viewpoint, however, the results of the devaluation were nearly disastrous. Prices inside Mexico, which had not gone up markedly for two or three years, began mounting swiftly again. From January 1954 to November 1955, wholesale prices rose about 30 per cent, canceling out much of the price advantage which the devaluation had achieved for Mexico's foreign trade. There was widespread protest throughout the country, and the seeming placidity of Mexico's political structure was shaken in a way which had few precedents since the 1930's.[22]

The lesson of the 1954 devaluation was one which neither Ruiz Cortines nor his successor would forget. From then on, the style of the Ruiz Cortines regime was one of cautiously treading on half-cracked eggs. Throughout the policies and pronouncements of the regime, thereafter, there ran the twin themes of avoiding inflation and increasing the purchasing power of the Mexican worker. As Chart 3 showed, public investment was held in check to such an extent that in three of the four years following 1954, the public sector's investment activities gradually declined in relation to those of the private.

Nevertheless, though Ruiz Cortines could hold down public investment in some degree, his position as heir to the Revolutionary tradition prevented him from holding it down very tightly. After the fiasco of rising prices attending the devaluation, the need to demonstrate to the people that the government was solicitous of their welfare pushed him into a number of significant expansions in the social service programs of the nation. With Mexico's educational and other services still grossly inadequate, the pressure of deferred demand simply had to be recognized in some degree.

The main thrust of Ruiz Cortines' public investment program, however, was not in the cities but in the rural areas. With the loyalties of the urban poor in question because of the higher cost of living, Ruiz Cortines set about trying to ensure that he could at least count upon the continued support of the agricultural sectors. With judiciously placed investments, he achieved some extraordinary breakthroughs both in the extent of irrigated land and in the total volume of land under cultivation. Part of this growth represented the late fruition of some of the grandiose agricultural schemes of Miguel Alemán, who had often been accused of producing dams without distribution systems and roads that led nowhere. As a consequence, the total volume of land under cultivation in Mexico went up over 40 per cent. Since the largest increases, both in relative and in absolute terms, were registered in the corn, wheat, and bean crops, the welfare implications of the expansion were striking.[23]

Ruiz Cortines also put much emphasis on investment in the three other fields which, with agriculture, were the hallmarks of the Revolutionary tradition. One, of course, was the railroads, where increasing traffic had led to a near-crisis because of an acute shortage of equipment and persistent undermaintenance. In a classic illustration of the "bottleneck-breaking" approach to economic development, the government threw large doses of capital investment into the rehabilitation of the rights-of-way and the construction of new equipment. Venturing on new ground, the government financed Mexico's first plant for the construction of rail cars. The second field was that of electric power; there, largely as a result of public financing, the installed capacity for public use went up about 80 per cent in six years. And the third area was Pemex, which aggressively pushed its refining capacity up about 50 per cent during the presidential term.

The government's innate caution, however, prevented it from financing its added public investments through large increases in taxes. Perhaps this caution was the result of a desire to avoid any added political disturbances, or perhaps it was due to the assumption that increased taxes in Mexico's imperfect markets might be inflationary rather than otherwise. Whatever the reason, Mexico's federal, state, and local governments continued to hold their receipts down to about 10 per cent of national income, a strikingly low proportion when compared with that of most governments of the world.

Placed in a squeeze by limited tax revenues, Ruiz Cortines was forced to look outside Mexico for some of the resources to finance the public sector — resources principally in the form of added loans from the Export-Import Bank and the World Bank. Even though public investment was not quite keeping pace with the growth of the country, an increasing proportion of this investment found its financing abroad.

Given the inherently cautious character of the Ruiz Cortines administration, its growing reliance on external resources to finance the public investment program must have been a source of considerable perturbation. The continued ability of Mexico to borrow abroad depended in part upon its being able to maintain its balance-of-payments position on an even keel. And this equilibrium was being threatened from various directions. One threat was the continued adverse movement of Mexico's terms of trade. After the 1954 devaluation and until the end of the Ruiz Cortines administration in 1958, international prices persisted in moving against Mexico; in the four years after 1954, for instance, Mexico's export prices fell about 11 per cent, while import prices rose about 10 per cent.[24]

Of course, there were growing strengths in Mexico's external position as well. As one can see by turning back to Table 8, the balance earned by Mexico from tourist trade and border traffic began to reach extraordinary heights. In fact, by 1958, foreign expenditures in these categories were coming very close to the nation's ordinary merchandise exports.

In general, however, Mexico was still uneasy about its balance-of-payments position. Accordingly, as foreign investors expanded their interests in Mexico's growing economy, Ruiz Cortines laid aside his earlier expressions of cautious hostility and turned a benign eye to the proposals of the foreigner. For a time, the administrative machinery of the government dealt kindly with foreigners' investment proposals. This policy, coupled with Mexico's internal growth, produced the results shown in Table 9. In each of the four years from 1955 through 1958, foreign private direct investments grew by over 100 million United States dollars.

TABLE 9

Long-Term Capital Account Items in Mexico's Balance of Payments, 1952–1961
(in millions of U.S. dollars)

Year	Net private foreign direct investment[a]	Public foreign loans		
		Received	Repaid	Net
1952	+68.2	55.3	33.8	+21.5
1953	+41.8	31.6	31.2	+0.4
1954	+93.2	63.5	48.0	+15.5
1955	+105.4	102.7	64.5	+38.2
1956	+126.4	114.7	79.3	+35.4
1957	+131.6	158.2	82.3	+75.9
1958	+100.3	238.9	137.9	+101.0
1959	+81.1	221.0	158.4	+62.6
1960	−38.1[b]	332.8	167.3	+165.5[b]
1961	+93.0	345.9	179.2	+166.7

[a] This column includes not only net fresh capital sent into Mexico from abroad but also reinvestments of profits by foreign firms established in Mexico. The Banco de México's practice is to record all profits of foreign-owned enterprises, whether or not remitted, as current account debits while recording all reinvestments as capital account credits.
[b] Reflects 116.5 millions of disinvestment by foreign electric power companies resulting from the government's purchase on credit of the equity interest of the companies.
Source: Banco de México. Figures on public foreign loans published by Nacional Financiera are slightly different from those shown here, apparently because of slight differences in definition between the two sources.

As a result of the continued inflow of foreign investment, the question of controlling the foreigners' role in the Mexican economy once more was elevated to an issue of major proportions in Mexican political circles. It was not so much that foreign ownership was widespread; to the extent that the figures can be believed, they indicate that about one sixth of the output of Mexican manufacturing enterprises in 1957 was in United States-controlled companies.[25] But the tendency for United States companies to appear large and aggressive by comparison with their Mexican competition had the effect of magnifying the impact of the investment in the Mexican economy. Besides, even where ownership did not exist, foreign licensing arrangements and technical assistance contracts seemed to give an even broader reach to foreign influence.[26]

By 1957 or 1958, many of Mexico's industrialists were beginning to see some advantages in limiting this inflow of foreign capital. At the same time, the *técnicos* in the Mexican government (to be discussed more fully in the next chapter) were feeling an increasing concern over the long-run increase in foreign remittances which each investment was generating and over the long-run impediments which foreign companies might present as the Mexican economy pushed toward greater import replacement of manufactured goods. It should be recalled that the first postwar wave of foreign investment in Mexico — the wave attracted in the era of Miguel Alemán — had consisted largely of assembly and processing plants. Such plants characteristically had continued to rely upon foreign sources for their intermediate products and machinery; indeed, as subsidiaries of United States parents, they often represented nothing more than the final stage of a production process begun in the parent establishment. By the time the Ruiz Cortines administration was well along, the *técnicos* were realizing that the rate of Mexican industrialization was dependent in part on how far and how fast Mexico's assembly and processing plants could be persuaded to shift from foreign to domestic sources for their intermediate materials. As a group, these plants had already gone quite far in this direction,[27] but there were notable exceptions, such as the automobile assembly plants. The *técnicos,* looking for new fields in which industrial investment might be expanded in Mexico, championed various measures to complete the "integration" process.

Though Ruiz Cortines resisted this internal drive to curb the foreign investor, it would be an overstatement to say that he paid it no heed at all. Since his Revolutionary role required him to respond in some degree, he re-emphasized the view that foreigners who came to Mexico to invest would do well to find Mexican partners for their ventures. This pattern had already begun to be applied in Mexico, but after the mid-1950's it became somewhat general.[28] Furthermore, there were some respects in which the politicians went much further in acceding to the proposals of the *técnicos*. In 1955, Mexico's laws exempting "new and necessary industries" from various taxes were made to apply only to those manufactured products which had a stated minimum proportion of "Mexican" content.[29] Though the *técnicos* had already been laying down conditions of this sort through the exercise of their administrative discretion, the codification of these conditions was an important concession to their point of view. This kind of pressure, because it represented the carrot rather than the stick, could be applied with minimum risk of frightening off coy foreign capital.

At the same time, the administrative style of the Mexican government began to acquire certain new accents. In the first place, the apparatus for national planning began to appear bit by bit. By 1952, a coordinating office had already been created in the finance ministry with the purpose of controlling and meshing the investment activities of the multiplicity of public entities. Two years later it was elevated to the status of an independent organization, attached to the president's office. Meanwhile, inside the principal economic agencies, a little greater stress began to be placed on general economic research of the Mexican economy.

Other manifestations of the *técnicos'* influence also were visible in the latter years of the Ruiz Cortines administration. The government's surveillance and regulation of the activities of the private sector became more and more systematic and professional. Its industrial studies became more technical; its familiarity with the details of the private sector's operations broadened; and its economic controls over the private sector became more particularistic. Accordingly, one began to see even more selective methods of credit control than in earlier administrations; more discriminating applications of the tax-exemption provisions for "new and necessary" industries; more detailed demands on enterprises to adhere to price ceilings; more explicit limitations on the size and nature of foreign ownership in individual investment projects.

This is not to say that the *técnicos* assumed control of government policy — far from it. Access by any vested interest to the ear of a minister continued to be a more effective means for the shaping of governmental decisions than the support of the technicians. However, the flow of proposals originating from below and the implementation of the policies transmitted from above both took on a more particularistic as well as a more professional tone. As far as the apparatus of government was concerned, the stage was set for what the Mexicans were already beginning to call a mixed economy — an *economía mixta*.

THE THREAT OF STAGNATION

About the time that Adolfo López Mateos took office in 1958, one could sense a major shift in the outlook of Mexican businessmen and officials regarding the long-run future of the Mexican economy. The bonanza of World War II had buoyed up the regime of Avila Camacho until 1946. Postwar shortages, import protection, and free public spending had kept Mexico growing through the years of Alemán. In the period of Ruiz Cortines, even though the pace of growth seemed to be slackening a little, the continued process of substituting domestic production for imports, coupled with an accelerated flow of tourist earnings and foreign investment, had managed to generate a fairly satisfactory performance for the country. In the late 1950's, however, Mexicans were beginning to wonder where the next impetus to growth would be coming from.

By this time, as Table 8 showed, some of Mexico's staple exports — cotton, coffee, and nonferrous metals — had registered a year or two of shrinking sales. And there were no signs of an improving outlook. At this stage, few Mexicans believed that their manufactured products could find extensive export markets. First of all, Mexican businessmen and officials were accustomed to thinking of themselves as high-cost producers. Secondly, many of them had acquired a firm conviction, despite evidence to the contrary, that the advanced countries would never permit the large-scale importation of manufactured products from less-developed countries.

By the late 1950's, too, the easy opportunities for domestic investment in import-substituting manufactures seemed to be reaching an end. Consumer goods were no longer being imported into Mexico in very large amounts; less than one fifth of all Mexican imports fell in the consumer category. Substitution from this point forward would have to take place mostly in intermediate goods — in steel instead of bed springs, in aluminum instead of kitchen pans, in engine blocks instead of assembled cars, and so on. Such substitution usually involved larger investment, more difficult technology, and a more difficult market structure; from all points of view, therefore, it represented much more forbidding terrain.

Only the foreign tourists and the foreign private investors seemed good prospects for providing an increased stimulus to Mexico's growth during this period. But these sources of stimulus were accepted by many Mexicans with decided reservations — tourism because it did not seem to add directly to the industrialization of the country, and foreign private investment for a variety of familiar reasons already mentioned.

Besides, Mexicans concerned with the continued growth of their economy were beginning to sense that they could not turn to the public sector quite as readily as in the past to provide the necessary fillip to Mexican growth. For one thing, the astonishing increases in Mexican population, amounting to about 3 per cent a year, were beginning to make their inexorable demands on government revenues in the form of "nonproductive" expenditures — expenditures on schools, health facilities, even housing. For another, the government was growing more chary than ever of deliberately resorting to deficit financing as a means of providing funds for the public sector. The disconcerting internal consequences of the 1954 devaluation had turned Mexico's central bankers into conservative hoarders of credit, determined to avoid inflationary tendencies at all costs. Besides, if Mexico was to continue to rely upon external public financing, as Ruiz Cortines had done, this meant that she would have to measure up to the standards of fiscal orthodoxy upon which international agencies were wont to insist. In economic terms, Mexico was being boxed in.

Nonetheless, the first reaction of the Mexican government to the change in regimes in December 1958 was to register a sharp spurt in public spending. This early increase does not seem to have been the result of conscious administration policy. On the contrary, it seems to have been due to nothing more than the presidency's temporary loss of control over the diffused and complex agencies of the Mexican government. For four years or more, the *técnicos* in the various agencies had been under wraps; public capital expenditures which the various agencies considered indispensable had been carefully controlled; restrictions and regulations which the bureaucracy hoped would speed the rate of "productive" private capital formation or reduce the scope of foreign participation had been systematically watered down. The inauguration of López Mateos seemed a signal for every Mexican agency to exercise its autonomy to the full. The tight rein which the president's office and the finance ministry had characteristically exercised over economic policies suddenly seemed to go slack. There seemed to be more room for free-wheeling by the government bureaus and more opportunity for the *técnicos* of one agency or another to push the lines of policy which Ruiz Cortines had held in check.

The president's office, of course, was aware of the sudden slack inside the governmental apparatus, and valiant efforts were made to reassert some discipline from the center. In order to bring the free-spending government enterprises and decentralized agencies back under control, various measures were taken. In 1959, a Comité de Importaciones del Sector Público was created whose purpose was to control the importations of the governmental entities. In 1960, a Comisión Asesora Permanente was created to look into their basic plans and programs. And in 1961, the finance ministry's control over the foreign borrowing of the decentralized agencies of the government was perceptibly tightened.[30]

These countermeasures did not prevent — very likely they were not intended altogether to prevent — a large rise in public investment. As shown in Chart 3 earlier in this chapter, the years 1959 and 1960 brought a substantial increase in the amount of public investment relative to gross product. The increase was not only relative but also in absolute terms.[31] Part of it was due to a rush of investment by the familiar trinity — the railroad commission, the electricity commission, and Pemex.* But part of it was also due to the added stress on social services and education which had begun to appear under Ruiz Cortines.

If the *técnicos* in the public sector saw the advent of López Mateos as an opportunity to increase investment, the investors in the private sector had no such reaction. Private investment in the years immediately following the close of the Ruiz Cortines regime did not manage to keep up with the growth of Mexico's output. And, in 1960, a succession of growing uncertainties and unsettling events so disturbed the private sector as to create the beginnings of a major crisis for the Mexican economy.

Even before those events had begun to pile up, there were indications that the private sector was in a mood to be shaken. For the reasons already discussed, business had been sluggish for two or three years and was showing no real signs of rapid pick-up; even the extraordinarily high level of public investment in 1959 and 1960 was failing to produce its expected results. On top of that, Castro's seeming successes in Cuba had done nothing to increase the attractiveness of investment in Mexico. Finally, the government was in process of implementing some very modest, albeit quite unprecedented, changes in Mexico's tax laws which

---

* Signs of the slack rein at the center were evident from the fact that by the spring of 1961, Pemex seems to have become badly overextended. Supplier contracts were being canceled wholesale; United States credit sources were drawing back from further commitments; and the director of the company was shopping in Europe for new sources of credit. It took nearly a year to bring the Pemex finances back under control, partly through a funding of short-term liabilities.

would introduce a certain measure of progressiveness in the personal income tax.

These considerations alone might have been enough to generate an outflow of capital from Mexico, in search of safer opportunities abroad. But the strain was intensified by the fact that López Mateos, presumably reacting to the Cuban successes, felt the need to make some moves as concessions to the left. One was an ill-timed statement to the effect that his administration's policy was to follow a path "on the extreme left within the constitution." Another was the apparent decision to cut back energetically the role of foreign direct investment in Mexico — a decision that was implemented in a variety of ways.[32]

First of all, the government began to buy a number of private enterprises in which foreigners had a heavy interest. These included the two remaining foreign-owned electric power companies, at a cost of slightly over 100 million United States dollars; two chains of movie theaters — more precisely, the exhibition contracts owned by the two chains — in which a former United States citizen had a heavy interest; and the United States-held controlling interest in a major Mexican steel company, La Consolidada. Coincidentally with these purchases, the Mexican government was borrowing heavy sums from abroad (see Table 9, earlier in chapter), including sums from private banks and insurance companies. By 1961, one would have been justified in concluding that the administration had begun substituting foreign public credits for foreign private investments on a fairly large scale.

The practice of selectively buying out foreign interests was supplemented by a policy of pressing foreign investors, much more strenuously than Ruiz Cortines had done, to surrender majority control to Mexican private or public holders. Pressure was applied in various ways. In mining, where a few United States companies still dominated the field as carry-overs from the Porfirian era, a new principle of discriminatory taxation was adopted, favoring mining companies with majority Mexican ownership. In the award of government contracts, the pressure was exerted simply by refusing to buy the products or services of foreign-controlled Mexican enterprises, irrespective of price. When foreign investors sounded out the Mexican government on its willingness to let them establish new facilities, they were advised that the necessary permits to do business in Mexico were in general more likely to be granted to facilities controlled by Mexicans than to foreign-controlled operations.[33]

The position of the foreigner was altered in still another respect. Attempts to force the rate of import replacement became much more vigorous, even though such replacement, by this time, involved cutting off imports of intermediate products and machinery for Mexico's industries.

To speed the rate of import replacement, the government brought into play the same battery of weapons it was using to encourage joint enterprises. The withholding of import licenses was, of course, one obvious means. This technique was used most spectacularly in the case of the automobile assembly industry, which was still organized on a basis of importing about 80 per cent of the value of the assembled vehicle. Partly as a way of making sure that the import licenses were dispensed with the appropriate degree of closefistedness, the Mexican government for the first time introduced the concept of an annual import budget. Another means of hurrying the import-replacement process was a more stringent application of Mexico's tax-exemption law. Because, even before the López Mateos era, the benefits of this law had been available only to industries whose products incorporated certain minimum proportions of Mexican goods and services, only a tightening of the administrative practices was needed.

In import replacement, as in reducing foreign control, the government's informal clearance process for new investment was highly important. As foreign investors tested the receptivity of the Mexican government to their various proposals, they soon learned that projects which involved principally the assembly or final processing of goods — and therefore required heavy imports — would face a maze of added governmental restraints.

Many of Mexico's domestic businessmen, unnerved by sluggish business trends and by the thunder on the left, decided to interpret López Mateos' actions as an attack not upon foreign business but upon business in general. Capital flight accelerated in 1960 and 1961, manifesting itself not only in the capital accounts of the country's balance-of-payments records, but also in a huge negative "errors and omissions" figure — just under 200 million United States dollars in 1961 alone. Only heavy fresh credits from the Export-Import Bank and other public sources saved the Mexican peso from crisis.

Then ensued an extraordinary effort on the part of the Mexican government to demonstrate its continued esteem for, and appreciation of, the critical role of business in Mexico's economic life. In a series of major speeches through 1961 and 1962 the president and his principal lieutenants repeatedly emphasized the loyalty, respect, and support which the government was prepared to offer to Mexico's domestic businessmen.[34] The efforts seemed to work. By 1962, the standard image of all the Mexican regimes since 1940 had been re-established — an image of reserve toward foreign private capital but of a readiness to deal with domestic private capital on a friendly, empirical, and pragmatic basis. The one worrisome fact that remained was the lack of rapid growth in the national economy.

Chapter 5

The *Políticos* and the *Técnicos* since 1940

To develop some sense of the future interplay between the public and private sectors, it is obviously not enough merely to review events. One has to know something about the motives and values of the actors which lay behind the events. In the Mexico of the early 1960's, the need to understand the actors in order to predict their future responses was especially strong. For it was not only Mexico's problems that were changing rapidly; so were the values and attitudes of the public and private leaders who were to guide the two sectors of the Mexican economy. These changes in public and private viewpoints opened up vistas of new departures and new solutions for the problems of the Mexican economy.

THE ECONOMICS OF THE *POLÍTICOS*

Ask any Mexican intellectual when the Revolution of 1910 came to an end and the chances are very high that he will say 1940.[1] And it is true, of course, that something seemed to stop in that year, some yeast or ferment that had existed through the epoch of Lázaro Cárdenas.

This is not to say that progress stopped in 1940; on the contrary, we have already shown that the growth of the economy after that year was impressive. But the differences from one administration to the next after that benchmark year were less those of purpose than of style. Manuel Avila Camacho, coming to power immediately on the heels of Lázaro Cárdenas, seems small and impotent in retrospect, appearing to give only feeble direction to Mexico through the parlous war years. The name of Miguel Alemán, on the other hand, conjures up images of vigor, flamboyance, and corruption in the typical Mexican memory. The administration of Adolfo Ruiz Cortines, by contrast, is usually described as cautious, upright, and industrious; and that of Adolfo López Mateos tends to evoke such adjectives as vacillating, compromising, and confused.

For all the differences of style, the asserted goals and claimed priorities of all four presidents have been strikingly similar. Each of the four has taken economic growth as a prime objective. Each has sought in one way or another to have himself identified as an agrarian revolutionary. Each has tried to register his concern for the plight of the urban poor. Each has maintained a flow of investment to the nationalized industries of the country. And each, within the limits of Mexico's needs for external resources and markets, has made one gesture or another to prove his independence from the foreign investor. Yet all of them have exhibited a certain restraint in their actions, reflecting a respect for the going system and a desire not to disturb any of its basic characteristics too greatly.

The agrarian programs of all these presidents since Cárdenas had three main elements: the expansion of credit to agriculture; the distribution of land to the landless rural families; and the improvement of the rural infrastructure, especially the supply of roads, dams, and schools. All these programs have been marked by vigorous action, punctuated by frequent charges of corruption. Agricultural credit has been rapidly expanded, reaching parts of the population which otherwise would have lacked the financial resources for production. At the same time, if the stream of charges and exposés can be believed, considerable amounts have been diverted into the pockets of government servants and their friends. In land-distribution activities, though all the presidents have shown real vigor, none has managed to match the Cárdenas program, which involved 18 million hectares of land — nearly one tenth of Mexico's land surface — but each of the four has distributed at least 3 or 4 million hectares.[2] In this case, too, extensive public corruption has often perverted the intent of the land-distribution program.[3] Various devices, for instance, have been permitted to develop in the meantime, to circumvent the intent of the landholding laws and to permit individuals to control parcels of land well in excess of the legal maximums.[4] Nevertheless, the programs of agricultural credit and land redistribution remain an indispensable requirement for presidential legitimacy and still continue to have political and economic impact.

The other main parts of the agrarian reform program, consisting of investments in dams and roads, have also been pursued assiduously by all four of the post-Cárdenas presidents. As a result, the national road system went up from 9,900 kilometers to 21,400 kilometers between 1940 and 1950, then reached 40,800 by 1960; and lands serviced by government-financed irrigation, which amounted to 267,000 hectares in 1940, rose to 1,187,000 hectares in 1950, and reached 2,811,000 hectares by 1960. Other aspects of rural development, such as rural education, lagged pitifully, but the more spectacular and more directly productive symbols of Revolutionary progress were appropriately observed.[5]

Once again, of course, it is well to distinguish substance from spirit. There were times in the years after Cárdenas when it was hard to know what the dominant purpose of these government-financed public works might be, whether to increase the well-being of agriculture or to increase the opportunities for industry to sell contracting services and materials to the government. In the period of Alemán, for instance, the ambiguity — perhaps it would be better to say, the multiplicity — of the objectives in the government-financed irrigation programs became especially marked. And all the other administrations, from time to time, showed signs of this same ambiguity.

The concern expressed for the lot of the urban poor, as we observed, has also been a common thread linking the style of every president since Cárdenas. Avila Camacho, operating in an inflationary wartime economy, apparently was aware that he could not do very much on this score. Even he, however, tried to stimulate agricultural production, to restrain bank credit used for commodity speculation, and to increase the number of jobs in industry for urban workers. Miguel Alemán kept up the manifestations of this concern by maintaining a feeble system of price ceilings on a number of staple commodities, by subsidizing the import of wheat and edible oils, and by discouraging the outflow of sugar and other scarce foods. Ruiz Cortines pushed much more aggressively and probably with more genuine purpose in the same direction. Various measures to subsidize the distribution of staple commodities in the cities were tried, albeit with indifferent success. At the same time, Mexico's social security system, almost entirely urban in its coverage, took a huge surge forward; by the end of the Ruiz Cortines era, the system's coverage had nearly tripled so that it embraced perhaps one fifth of Mexico's urban population. Free medical services, an important part of the system, were provided for over 12,000,000 cases in 1958. López Mateos, proceeding in the same tradition, rapidly extended the coverage of the system even further. Meanwhile, he used even more daring means to hold down prices for the urban poor, including the development of government-owned itinerant markets, mounted on trucks, which sold staples at prices well below prevailing levels.

The distinction between form and substance needs to be emphasized once more, however. Both have been important to Mexico's governments, which, when they could not retain the substance of a measure to protect the urban poor, still tried valiantly to maintain the form. Illustrative of the distinction was the practice followed in the fixing of the ceilings on drug prices. There is not much doubt that these ceilings have held down drug prices in Mexico during recent years, especially in the capital city. From time to time, however, the drug companies have been able to make a case for increasing the price of one drug or another because of mounting costs. In those instances, the government has not always found it politically wise to raise the ceiling; instead, it has quietly advised the drug companies that if they violated the law, the infraction would be ignored. This device has been used more than once in governmental regulation in politically sensitive areas.

Not much need be said about the continuing tradition of maintaining heavy investments in the nationalized industries. As usual, Cárdenas had set the pattern by his efforts to improve the government-owned railway system, to extend the government-owned portion of the electric power industry, and to improve and expand the oil industry after it came into government hands. Once again, every president after Cárdenas emulated him; in each administration, government-financed investments in the nationally owned railway system, in the federal electricity authority, and Pemex were at the top of the list of public capital investments. In fact, the process of investment and the expectation of continued investment in these sectors were so thoroughly institutionalized that presidents who sought from time to time to retrench in these fields were not always successful in their efforts. The momentum of the bureaucracy in these decentralized activities was sometimes so strong that directives from the center were not sufficient to stem the continued flow of capital funds.[6]

Finally, Cárdenas' successors have felt obliged to make obeisance to the idea of independence from foreign interests. No president has failed to use one or more major occasions to address himself to the question of foreign investment; and, in one version or another, every president at some time in his administration has taken the position that although foreign enterprises were welcome in Mexico, the welcome was extended only so long as the foreigners accepted the obligations of Mexican nationals and only so long as the enterprises served the interests of Mexico.

Concerning foreign investment there have been changes in the climate from time to time. Some presidents have felt the need to go further than mere speechmaking in order to evidence their independence from foreign interests. As the interest of United States investors in the Mexican economy revived during the later stages of World War II, the Avila Camacho regime promulgated an emergency decree, which later became permanent law, authorizing the designation of certain industries in which foreigners could only hold minority interests in Mexico. Miguel Alemán, less careful than his fellow executives in his observance of the inviolable principles of the Revolutionary president, later aborted the effect of the law by limiting its application to a brief list of oddly assorted industries, including such diverse activities as radio broadcasting and the bottling of orange drinks.[7] Ruiz Cortines continued to deal with the problem ambiguously, torn between the desire to attract foreign capital and the need to prove his right to the Revolutionary role; even so, he revived and reiterated the view that foreigners who came to Mexico would do well to find Mexican partners for their ventures. López Mateos seized the nettle more firmly for a time, applying a forthright policy of restraint to foreign private investment. But all four presidents, despite the variations in their behavior, sought to maintain the public stance of protectors of the Mexican economy against the threat of foreign invasion.

In stressing the similarities of the four regimes, however, we must not overlook the differences. Trends there were — significant trends which, as we propose to show, are rapidly bringing Mexico to the threshold of hard choices and possible changes. Underlying these trends, and basic to an understanding of the changing ties between the public and private sectors, were the changes which took place in Mexico's political organizations.

THE PARTIES AND THE PRESIDENTS

No one can doubt that part of the explanation for Mexico's apparent stability since 1940 has been the political system which has gradually evolved under the banner of the Partido Revolucionario Institucional, the PRI.[8] No one will question that the stability derives from some process other than pure suppression and physical force. What, then, is the magic formula?

In our discussion of the Revolution we indicated how a series of Mexican presidents began the long process which brought the appearance of political stability to Mexico. Until the latter 1920's, the prime political objective of the federal government had been to overcome the regionalism of Mexico and to create a powerful force at the center. With Cárdenas, that goal was practically achieved. Only one major difficulty now remained: the vulnerability of the government because of its dependence upon the loyalty of a few-score key organizations and individuals. At that point, therefore, the instinct of Mexican presidents was to multiply and to diffuse the number of sources of national power on which they depended. By the era of Adolfo López Mateos, that goal had been fairly well achieved. Today, one would have considerable difficulty in pinpointing any small group of individuals or organizations whose continued loyalty was indispensable to the government's stability.

Perhaps this growing diffusion was a natural and inevitable by-product of Mexico's economic growth — a reflection of the fact that the Mexican economy was becoming more complex and more specialized. But the process was speeded up by a number of deliberate changes in the PRI organization. We have already alluded to some of the changes which were instituted in the Cárdenas regime. In that era, the government party was organized on a sectoral basis. That is to say, the building blocks of the party consisted of a national labor sector, an agricultural sector, a government sector, and a military sector, each with its complement of state and local units. Every sector was allotted a given number of selected public offices in the state and national governments; and each sector provided the requisite candidates to "stand for election" to its offices. Later in the Cárdenas administration the military sector was dropped as an entity, a sign of the fact that the free-wheeling generals had finally been tamed. Then a new "popular sector" was created, attracting a considerable number of aggressive individuals outside labor, agriculture, or the government service who were anxious to have a hand in politics and who heretofore had been blocked from participation by the nature of the party structure.

As the administration of Lázaro Cárdenas came to an end in 1940 and the presidency passed to Manuel Avila Camacho, the new popular sector continued to grow swiftly into a position of dominance in the national party. Its lawyers, intellectuals, independent farmers, and aging military heroes of the Revolution proved a difficult aggregation to beat. By 1943, the popular sector had acquired an effective national organization of its own — the Confederación Nacional de Organizaciones Populares — through which it exercised a voice in party councils. In the election of that year, the popular sector contributed 78 of the 147 members of the national Chamber of Deputies. Meanwhile, the labor sector and the farm sector settled for 23 members and 46 members, respectively, despite the fact they claimed a combined membership twice as large as that of the popular group.[9] In the elections of the 1940's and 1950's, the popular sector continued to dominate the Chamber and the PRI itself, even though its military men by this time were dropping out of active political life and the public limelight.

In addition to the growth of the relatively individualistic popular sector, there were other signs inside the government party of the diffusion of political power. In 1946, the whole concept of the sectoral structure of the government party was deliberately weakened. The sectors were deprived of the right to designate the party candidates for certain stipulated offices, and the nominating function was turned back to nominating conventions. In theory, all that the sectors were expected to do at this stage was to provide some agreed number of delegates to the conventions.

As the years have gone on, the PRI has made repeated efforts to generate grass-roots participation, or the appearance of grass-roots participation, in the designation of party candidates. At various times, innovations in the nominating procedure have been tried, and municipal and regional committees of the party have been exhorted to enter into the nominating process. Although these efforts have been greeted with widespread skepticism or indifference, the nominating conventions themselves have begun to show signs of the weakening of control by a limited clique. In many parts of the country, the ability of some local individual or two simply to dictate the slates to be adopted by each local convention has become a thing of the past. Procedures for submission of nominees to the convention floor have become liberalized. In fact, sensitivity to public opinion has now grown sufficiently great that regional units of the government party from time to time have dropped a duly nominated "official" candidate when he demonstrated an outstanding capacity to repel public support.

Despite the changes, the office of the presidency itself has been exempted from the democratizing process. In this respect, the oligarchical procedures of the last twenty years seem to have changed very little. A small clique, presided over by the outgoing president and including the living ex-presidents, chooses a successor. After the designation has been made, there are heroic efforts to rally popular interest in the official choice. Half the stone walls of Mexico are painted with giant signs of public support; all the mass media are alive with eulogies. But at this stage the die is already cast.

The political change in Mexico can be summarized, therefore, as that of a series of oligarchs gradually trying to free themselves of their one-time reliance on a few critical organizations and individuals and gradually trying to create a broad popular basis for their administration. In doing so, however, they have only given up one set of masters to serve another set. To get broad popular support in Mexico, the presidents have had to maintain the Cárdenas policy of keeping their lines of communication open to dissidents, large and small. They have not dared to suppress discontent and opposition; neither have they felt secure enough to disregard it. Instead, they have tried to assuage and envelop it. As more and more sources of pressure have been generated, the political structure has become increasingly eclectic, increasingly malleable, hence increasingly without doctrine or direction.

The government's effort to create the appearance of increased tolerance and nonsuppression has had its effects beyond the PRI itself. Almost unavoidably, it has meant a growing acceptance of nonconforming groups outside the PRI. The trend has been apparent in various ways. Although the government has extensive powers to outlaw opposition parties and has used these powers from time to time, its general tendency has been to acknowledge the proper role of such parties and to credit them with at least a minimum showing at the polls. For instance, although the opposition parties held no seats in the Chamber of Deputies in 1943, they were assigned six to ten seats in the various chambers after that date.

Even the office of the presidency has been acknowledged as being subject to contest. In 1940, electoral officials reported that the opposition parties collectively had garnered only 7 per cent of the popular vote for the presidency. In the sexennial election of 1946, however, the government was prepared to admit that 21 per cent of the votes had been cast against its presidential nominee, and in 1952 it was 26 per cent. On the other hand, the election of 1958 brought a reported landslide for López Mateos, with over 90 per cent of the popular vote recorded in his favor.

Under the shelter of official tolerance, various political parties have appeared, flourished briefly, and died. One, however, has managed to hang on through the years, the Partido de Acción Nacional, or PAN. Before 1934 it would have been close to inconceivable for such a party to be openly permitted in the Mexico of the Revolution. But by 1939 it was possible for PAN to organize legitimately and, without serious personal risk to its leaders, to begin a career of open attacks upon government policy.

In the parliamentary structure of Western Europe, PAN would occupy a position immediately to the right of center — a position identified with classical liberalism and religious sympathies. Its platform contains the usual elements of any such group when occupying a minority position. Like the government itself, the opposition party supports increased security for individuals, greater industrialization, and economic improvement in the countryside. Like any realistic conservative party of the 1960's, it is prepared within limits to accept such concepts as social security programs, collective bargaining, and cooperative housing. But PAN sees corruption, bureaucracy, and excessive centralism in government as interfering with national goals. Its aim is to reduce the role of the national government, and to increase the scope and freedom of private enterprise and state governments. At the same time, PAN is against the extensive constitutional restraints placed upon the Catholic Church, especially the restraints against religious education.

The fact that the Mexican government permits the existence of opposition parties does not, of course, demonstrate the existence of a policy of genuine political tolerance; by itself, it need mean no more than that the government is desirous for the *appearance* of legitimacy. But in an open society such as Mexico — a society in which the apparatus of a police state is happily lacking and in which there is easy access to the press of other countries — a desire for the appearance of legitimacy cannot fail to involve genuine concessions to the opposition.

Some concessions have been undeniable. Though the government controls the supply of newsprint, for instance, it has permitted the circulation of newspapers and periodicals which follow a line of frank hostility to government policy. On the right, the near-fanatical Sinarquista party has been permitted regularly to publish its diatribes against godlessness, corruption, communism, and liberalism in the government apparatus. On the left, the Soviet-sympathizing magazine *Política* has been suffered to berate the government as a supine tool of the gringo capitalist interests. Between the extremes, every shade of political conviction can be found in the public press.*

Perhaps the best measure of the government's tendency to

---

* One can easily get lost in a fog of semantics if he asks whether the Mexican press is "free" or "controlled." Two assumptions about the Mexican press, however, are almost universally accepted in Mexico: first, the assumption that a considerable portion of the press is prepared to accept secret subsidies from one political source or another; second, the assumption that most members of the press are chary about straining the tolerance of the government too far. The sanctions of the government are sufficiently strong to constitute a threat to any totally uninhibited periodical. Accordingly, though criticism of government policy is not uncommon, criticism of the president himself is almost unheard of.

brook the reappearance of potential opposition has been its tolerance of the increasing activities of the Catholic Church. The constitution prohibits any church from owning property or administer-
ing charitable or research institutions; forbids church officers from
mixing in politics, holding public office, or criticizing "fundamental
laws"; prohibits the wearing of ecclesiastical garb in public; and
even provides for limiting the number of priests in each state. It
will be recalled that Calles was in open warfare with the Church
throughout the latter 1920's. The turning point came in the 1930's
when Cárdenas made conciliatory gestures. By 1940, Avila Camacho was publicly describing himself as a "believer." And by
1962, López Mateos was permitting the open disregard of most of
the constitutional prohibitions. Political action groups, concerned
about the rise of Castroism, were being formed with the open support of the Church; ecclesiastical garb was being worn in public;
fairly extensive properties were once more owned *de facto* by the
Church.

It is not at all clear that the Church, if it were relieved of all
its constitutional restraints, would be found in sharp opposition to
the economic and social policies of existing Mexican governments.
Until the 1930's, it is true, the Church had been one of the traditional enemies of Mexico's Revolutionaries. In present-day
Mexico, however, the direction of Church policy cannot be so
simply defined. Although large segments of the Church are tied
to the conservative liberalism of PAN, and although some clerics
— a clear minority — are associated with the fanaticism of the
militant Sinarquistas, significant groups inside the Church hierarchy
are identified with aims and means which to the outsider seem
scarcely distinguishable from those of the Revolutionary presidents.

Whether or not the Church represents a rival philosophy, however, there is no doubt that, from the PRI point of view, it constitutes a rival source of power. In 1951, Catholic organizations
could claim to have 4,500,000 members out of a total Mexican
population of 27,500,000; and by the 1960's the Church's influence
was unquestionably even more widespread. These increasing activities are one more sign of the diffusion of political power in Mexico.

The significance of this trend toward diffusion should not be missed. It has introduced an increasing measure of caution in the style of recent presidents. Temperamental differences may account in part for the seeming caution and indecision of the two most recent presidents as compared with their many decisive and vigorous predecessors; but the differences in the times and in the situation have also played their part.

One must bear in mind that there has not yet been an instance in the history of modern Mexico in which the "outs" have succeeded the "ins" by legitimate means; hence, no president of modern Mexico can fail to be uneasy in the face of opposition. One must also realize that practically the whole political experience of Mexico's recent presidents has been inside the structure of PRI and its predecessors. The shattering of the PRI, the termination of its hegemony over Mexico, would be the total and final judgment of failure in the eyes of any president unlucky enough to be in office at the time. But how can any president maintain solidarity inside the PRI and neutralize the hostile forces outside PRI, if at the same time he is obliged to seem tolerant of opposition and to eschew acts of outright political suppression?

The only formula which López Mateos has been able to find has been the time-tested technique reminiscent of Díaz, Carranza, Obregón, Calles, and Cárdenas — the formula based upon the principle that the squeaking wheel must never be denied at least a little grease. So the political course of López Mateos has been a continual zigzag between the screeching right and the squealing left. One week he has been "on the extreme left within the constitution"; the next, he has been the unfailing friend of private enterprise. Subsequently, apparently frustrated for the moment by his inability to placate either the right or the left, he has insisted that he would thenceforth follow only one line of policy — the policy of moving straight down the middle.*

* See the López Mateos speech of June 7, 1961, in celebration of the Day of the Freedom of the Press, reproduced in *Siempre,* July 5, 1961, p. 124. The tone of the speech is reflected in the following translated frag-

López Mateos' apparent political frustration need not reflect either less ability or less purpose as compared with his distinguished predecessors. His problems in many ways have been more difficult. The complex machinery of modern Mexico contains more wheels than the Mexico of past decades. The inhibitions against using overt measures of force and repression, blatant bribery, and other time-honored techniques for achieving political unity are considerably greater. The president's elbow room, therefore, is gradually shrinking. And there is nothing to indicate that, under the general form of Mexico's one-party system as we know it today, the president's ability to act decisively in any direction will grow again.

THE *TÉCNICOS* IN THEORY AND PRACTICE

In the development of nations, the economic technician is rapidly coming to be thought of as the indispensable man. By general agreement, such subjects as exchange-rate policy, fiscal and monetary policy, investment and saving policy, and similar esoteric matters can no longer be left entirely to the rough-and-ready ministrations of the politician. For one thing, the economic techniques have grown so complex that they are beyond the easy understanding of the amateurs; for another, the increasing flow of communications between nations and with international agencies on these subjects has demanded that every country develop a class of responsible officials which is capable of holding up its end in the interchange. In Mexico the economic technician has become an integral element in the decision-making process on issues affecting Mexico's development.

In many advanced countries, the distinction between the technician and the politician has come to be blurred and indistinct. Inside the Mexican government, however, there is still a reasonably

---

ment: "Therefore, my government will curb the excesses of demagogic persons or groups of the right or the left who, outside the framework of the constitution, try to destroy the national way of life or to violate the constitutional order . . ."

clear line between the *técnicos* and the *políticos*. There have been times, of course, when a technician has jumped the fence into the higher and lusher pastures of the politicians, and these cases promise to be more common in the years ahead. But on the whole the division between the two groups is fairly well maintained.

This does not mean that all Mexican technicians tend to think alike on economic issues. There are some considerable doctrinal distinctions among them. A tiny minority, as nearly as any outside observer can tell, are doctrinaire Marxists; a much larger number are inclined to a mixed economy, with increased emphasis on the importance of the public sector. Within the latter group there are large differences over appropriate public policies. Some of the technicians connected with the Banco de México, for instance, tend to look on monetary and fiscal restraints as an indispensable instrument in ensuring a steady process of growth, while those in the investing and spending agencies tend to see such restraints as a handicap to growth. Economists in the industrializing agencies, such as Nacional Financiera, tend to put a high priority on steel mills, while economists in the agricultural services place greater emphasis on irrigation and farm-to-market roads.

Nevertheless, as seen through the eyes of an outside observer, the similarities in viewpoint among Mexico's economic technicians, whatever their function in government may be, are more striking than the differences. They have a common ideology which, harnessed to the government apparatus, constitutes a strong force in shaping the behavior of the public sector in Mexico. True, at this stage in Mexico's governmental development, there is still only a limited amount of the relatively easy interchange between the official and the civil service levels that one finds in Canada, the United States, or Britain.[10] Accordingly, the strength of the technicians lies not so much in their powers to shape policy directly as in their capacity to choose the technical alternatives which are presented to their political masters. But this is a very potent force in itself. And when the instructions from above are ambiguous or when the situation calls for technical action in the absence of instructions, the power of the technician is enhanced even further.

In looking for the roots of the Mexican *técnicos'* ideology on economic issues, one need go back no further than the great depression of the 1930's. Its effects on Latin America are familiar enough but they will bear the briefest recounting. The depression affected all Latin American nations in some considerable measure, though Mexico less than most. The countries whose exports were concentrated in the fewest products were especially vulnerable to the swift declines in demand and the sharp drops in price which were typical of the period. The price declines were all the more pronounced, of course, because the exporters of many raw materials could not cut back on output with the same celerity as could be done with manufactured goods. As export proceeds declined, so did imports. With the shrinkage of foreign trade, government revenues also shrank, since these depended in good measure upon export and import taxes.

The contraction process did not stop there, however. Because the fall in export proceeds characteristically was greater than the fall in imports, most countries in Latin America found themselves rapidly losing foreign exchange. The loss was aggravated by the fact that the decline of their export markets was accompanied by a decline in the inflow of foreign investment. The two phenomena were linked, of course, by the fact that the development of many of the export products was achieved through foreign capital. In the rudimentary banking systems which were characteristic of Latin American countries, the supply of foreign exchange was one of the most important determinants of the volume of money and credit available in the country. As a result, domestic credit contracted as exports fell off, dealing a double-barreled blow to the unfortunate Latin American economies.

World War II reversed the experience of the 1930's, especially for Mexico. For a time, the problem was too much exports and too little imports. Though the added foreign exchange was welcome, there were not enough goods to spend it on. As money poured into the exporting countries of Latin America, there was no effective way to prevent the flood from causing price inflation; so the pot of gold at the end of the rainbow was no closer, after all. Later, when goods became available again in international markets, imports increased so fast as to outdistance exports, and Latin America lapsed back into balance-of-payments difficulties.

During the years immediately after World War II, the United States and the United Kingdom showed themselves quite insensitive to the experiences and viewpoints of the less-developed countries. Displaying an extraordinary measure of ethnocentricity, they framed the principal economic goals of the postwar world in terms which reflected their own special problems: the elimination of excessive and discriminatory trade barriers; the avoidance of competitive exchange depreciation and discriminatory financial restrictions; the development of an international apparatus to give temporary assistance to currencies under pressure; and the provision of modest amounts of foreign public capital, first for reconstruction and later for development. These were the emphases embodied in the early drafts of the charters of the International Trade Organization, the International Monetary Fund, and the International Bank for Reconstruction and Development.

In the eyes of Latin Americans concerned with the development of their respective economies, the ethnocentric emphases of these proposals could only be interpreted as a form of neocolonialism, an effort to hold the Latin world to its prewar role as a supplier of raw materials and an importer of manufactured goods, with all the uncertainties of outlook and second-class status that such a role implied.

The suspicion of conspiracy was heightened by another fact. The international trade doctrine which had greatest currency in the advanced countries at the time was that of comparative advantage and international specialization. For the reader trained in economics, the implications of any simplistic application of this doctrine to Latin America will be evident. For other readers, it is enough to say that the simpler versions of the doctrine do not concern themselves with the problems which arise from cyclical instability or from governmental efforts to speed economic growth. They merely preach the wisdom of having each country continue to do more of what it does well. Though the hard facts of the depression and the timely teachings of Lord Keynes had greatly modified similar doctrines as they applied to the domestic affairs of the advanced nations, there had not yet been much explicit application of the Keynesian concepts to the domestic and international position of underdeveloped countries.

To the Latin countries, it seemed clear that a program of trade-barrier reduction was not their most pressing need in the postwar period. Accordingly, when the United States proposed its so-called "Economic Charter of the Americas" at Chapultepec in 1945, Mexico along with most other Latin American countries demurred. Later still, when the United States sought the adoption of the charter of the International Trade Organization (ITO), Latin Americans fought a very successful rear-guard action.

The strength of their forces accelerated the dawning appreciation of economists in other countries that new programs and new principles were needed to deal with the problems of economic development. As a result, the ITO charter emerged from its gestation period with considerable revisions in emphasis and approach. The idea that there might be virtue in commodity price stabilization received explicit recognition. The principle of infant-industry protection was elevated to an international tenet. The right of countries in balance-of-payments difficulties to do pretty nearly whatever they chose to safeguard their scarce foreign-exchange reserves was acknowledged. And the responsibilities as well as the rights of foreign investors were given considerable emphasis.

For all practical purposes, Mexico had won its point. Though the ITO charter never came into effect, the agreement which succeeded it in 1948 — the General Agreement on Tariffs and Trade — embodied most of the new emphases in trade policy which the charter had incorporated. In its later revisions in the mid-1950's, the General Agreement went even further in the direction signaled by the revolt of the less-developed countries.

Mexico's *técnicos,* however, could not shake off their belief in the conspiracy theory. For the few who were Marxist in orientation, the conspiracy theory came naturally. For the others, the credibility of the theory was fortified by an important coincidence — the fact that the official in the U.S. Department of State whose name was most closely associated with the ITO charter was also the senior officer of an international commodity firm which marketed large quantities of cotton in Mexico. Incongruous as it may seem to those who knew his purposes at the time, the name of Will Clayton became the symbol of neocolonial oppression in Mexico. In the end, therefore, Mexico refused to join the General Agreement on Tariffs and Trade and renounced her bilateral trade agreement with the United States. From that time forward, Mexico's *técnicos* took the view that Mexican trade policy was not a subject for discussion or negotiation with the developed countries, certainly not with the United States.*

Where strongly held convictions exist, they are not long in generating their supporting theories. In the years following the 1945 revolt of the Latin Americans at Chapultepec, a set of theories defining the nature of Latin America's development needs began to emerge. Although the theories are largely associated with the name of Raúl Prebisch, executive secretary of the Economic Commission for Latin America, they have many other sources of intellectual support, not only from other Latin American economists, but also from economists in the advanced countries.[11] Collectively, they form a body of doctrine to which, with one variant or another, Mexico's *técnicos* are inclined to subscribe.[12]

Many thousands of pages have been published in recent years on this body of theory on economic development. No recapitulation in the compass of a few pages could possibly capture its nuances or present its justification, and no one version of these

---

* The fact that United States foreign aid went principally to Europe in the late 1940's and early 1950's added grist to the mill. The suspicion was rife in Latin America that this priority was influenced in part by a desire on the part of the United States to force Latin America to accept foreign private investment.

theories can give appropriate recognition to the esoteric doctrinal struggles among the experts. Still, by the time the complex and qualified principles have been applied by the *técnicos* on the firing line, they unavoidably emerge as bold and unsubtle postulates to be boldly and unsubtly applied. For our purposes it is perhaps more important to be familiar with these operating versions than with the theoretical constructs on which they are based.*

One fundamental conclusion of the *técnicos,* of course, is that Mexico must rapidly reduce her reliance on the exports of raw materials and on imports of manufactured products. There are various strands in the argument. Apart from the problems of the cyclical instability of demand, there is also the so-called "terms-of-trade" argument — the argument that nations reliant on exports of raw materials are forced over the long run to lower the prices of their exports in relation to the prices of their imports. On this assumption, if 500 pounds of copper ore could buy a refrigerator in 1940, it might take 700 or 800 pounds to buy the refrigerator in 1960.

The reasons for the assumption are various. In the long run, according to the argument, raw materials such as iron ore tend to be displaced by synthetic substitutes; this fact alone gives more buoyancy to the price of manufactured products than of raw materials. Besides, new exporters of raw materials tend to come into existence more readily than new producers of manufactured products, as each developing country expands its production first

---

* It is with a certain sense of uneasiness that I present these arguments without evaluation. In my view, some are clearly valid; but some are overdrawn, some are incomplete, and some invite effective rejoinders. Nonetheless, I have resolutely determined to resist the temptation to offer a critique on these pages. The purpose of this presentation is simply to describe a body of doctrine on which the *técnicos* operate, and nothing more. For those who are interested in a critical evaluation of some of these propositions, see Werner Baer, "The Economics of Prebisch and ECLA," *Economic Development and Cultural Change,* January 1962, pp. 169–182; Gottfried Haberler, *International Trade and Economic Development* (Cairo: National Bank of Cairo, 1959); Charles P. Kindleberger, "The Terms of Trade and Economic Development," *Review of Economics and Statistics,* Supplement: February 1958, pp. 72–90.

in the areas that are easiest. Beyond this, when labor-saving innovations occur in the production of raw materials for export, the
reduction in cost usually gets passed on to the buyer in the form
of reduced prices. The heavy competition among the unskilled
laborers and the suppliers in the exporting countries means that
the exporting economies are in no position to hold back a share of
increased productivity in the form of higher wages or higher profits.
As a result, increases in efficiency in the exporting countries simply
lead to fewer jobs and greater unemployment, rather than to
higher pay. Contrariwise, in the developed countries, according to
the argument, labor unions and monopolies tend to hold on to the
fruits of their cost reductions, either in shorter working hours,
increased wages, or increased profits. The net effect of these
tendencies is to raise the price of manufactured imports relative to
raw material exports over the long run.

Apart from this so-called "terms-of-trade" argument, Mexico's
técnicos assert other advantages in industrialization, advantages
which will be familiar to any student of development theory. The
técnicos maintain that increased industrialization leads to a more
rapid increase in output per unit of manpower and capital than
does the increased production of raw materials. This is due partly
to the fact that, as factory installations grow in scale, their efficiency
increases rapidly, more rapidly than the increase in efficiency of a
growing mine or a growing farm. Besides, "*external* economies of
scale" are more important in an industrial complex than in a ma-
terials-producing economy; the growth of a chemical industry, for
instance, supports the expansion of an efficient electric generating
system which then makes an efficient aluminum plant possible.

The argument goes further still. Industrialization, in which the
worker learns new skills and disciplines, tends to upgrade the
human resources of a nation in a way which mining and agriculture
do not. Industrialization also tends to alter the distribution of income, so that it is easier to generate an increase in savings and
investment; either the industrialist himself makes the increased
savings and investment, or the state does the added savings and

investment through increased taxation and public spending. Industrialization tends to relocate the population in compact centers so that it is easier and less costly to provide such public services as health and education — unless, of course, the population becomes too concentrated at one given point, such as Mexico City, in which case a certain rediffusion of population is called for. And so on.

Of late, the industrialization argument has grown a little more complex. In recent years, particularly in Mexico, there has been added emphasis on the point that, in the headlong rush to industrialize, agriculture should not be neglected. For, if agriculture is neglected, the price of foodstuffs remains high and the quantity of foodstuffs is limited. As a result, the industrial worker is forced to pay dearly for his subsistence and is forever being cheated of the advantages of his increased industrial productivity. Besides, agricultural workers represent over half of the labor force of Mexico. Unless they can increase their output per man, these workers will not be able to absorb the growing volume of industrial goods pouring out of Mexico's factories. Mexico's industrial sector, with half of its potential market stagnant, will be doomed to a stunted growth. So some sort of balance is the key. Agriculture must be stimulated — but primarily for the domestic market, and only secondarily for export.

The *técnico* is not only in wholehearted support of industrialization; he also is in favor of achieving that industrialization through the maximum use of domestic capital rather than foreign capital. There are many advantages to the use of domestic private capital, as he sees it. One such advantage is that the country's skills and manpower are upgraded faster; foreign firms, it is assumed, tend to hold the top management jobs for their own nationals, out of distrust for the ability or the "loyalty" of their indigenous employees. Foreign capital also drains a country's foreign-exchange reserves, it is argued; for though the inflow of capital may add to these reserves when the investment is first made, the remittances of company profits and foreign employee savings to the home country soon wipe out the temporary gain from the initial capital inflow.

Foreign investment involves other disabilities to the host country. If the investment is in manufacturing, it often represents the final stage in an assembly or processing operation. (For Mexico, of course, the classic case is its automobile assembly plants.) For various good and sufficient reasons, the foreign-owned subsidiary will be especially loath to buy its machinery and its intermediate products inside the host country; so there will be special resistances to completing the process of industrialization. If the foreign investment is in raw-material production, especially production for export, the problems will be even worse. Investments of this sort are usually made by firms which have a number of alternative sources of their materials. On any decline in world demand for the product, the foreigner will be free to decide which source of supply he wishes to shut off, thus leaving the domestic economy at the mercy of his decision.

Nor are these the only difficulties which face the host country. Foreign installations, according to the argument, represent a type of "unfair" competition to the incipient domestic competitor. The foreigner can fall back on his access to technology, his easier credit, and his management experience to crush domestic competition. Quite apart from the equity considerations which apply in such a situation, there are also the problems of generating monopolies inside the country and of slowing up the emergence of an indigenous entrepreneurial class.

The *técnicos* also have some fairly explicit ideas on the relative places of the public and the private sectors in domestic capital formation. First, of course, they ratify the idea, by now quite widely accepted, that certain types of investment cannot realistically be left to the private sector: projects whose financial needs are so large that they exceed the resources of any private group; projects whose financial outcome is subject to such uncertainty that they exceed the risk-taking propensities of any private group;

and projects which, for welfare reasons, cannot pay out financially. Examples are a first experimental fertilizer plant, a school, a highway.

The *técnicos,* however, are inclined to go somewhat further in defining the appropriate role of the public sector. They begin by pointing to certain major reservations about the effectiveness of the price system in allocating resources. Take the division between investment in industry and investment in basic foodstuffs production; here, they are inclined to assume, monopoly pricing by the wholesale food merchants keeps agricultural profits so low that farm savings are held down and investment is discouraged. Accordingly, public investment in irrigation works, public assistance through easy credit, and public subsidies in the form of cheap fertilizer are seen as indispensable offsets to the effects of monopoly pricing.

The fertilizer case suggests another principle which most *técnicos* hold dear. According to their view, the achievement of the most rapid rate of development and of the most desirable distribution of income sometimes argues for the use of prices which are at variance with open-market prices. There are times when transport, power, or other basic products and services should be subsidized because of the stimulus which the lower rates will give to other branches of production or because of the effects of such subsidies on income distribution. The social gain to be derived from the altered rates is the real test, rather than the gain to the selling enterprise itself. In circumstances of this sort, public investment is sometimes the only possibility.

Still another element figures in the technicians' views regarding the relative places of private and public capital investment. The technicians tend to share an ideological conception that capital formation in an unregulated private economy proceeds from trial and error. Monopolists in control of the market, so the argument runs, are not concerned with making a careful study of demand and of industrial locations. And where competition exists in the market, there is too much ignorance, haste, or ease of entry to make any careful study useful or possible. Where private investment decision-making prevails, therefore, extensive error is certain — error whose costs are borne by society through bankruptcy, high monopoly costs and prices, or chronic idle capacity.

By contrast, the *técnicos* think of public investment as proceeding from reason and study; and they assert that the reason and study are all the more likely to produce adequate results because in theory they can be integrated with all of the planning that goes on in other parts of the public sector. The *técnicos* are prepared to agree, indeed to insist, that the intervention of the *políticos* is sometimes a fly in the ointment of rational decision-making; but they see this as an imperfection, not as a fatal flaw, in the system.

These views of the Mexican technicians stem not only from their theoretical assumptions about the nature of the private economy in general but also from their evaluation of the attitudes and training of Mexican businessmen in particular. The *técnicos,* in general, have been drawn from schools of economics. To the extent that the businessmen are associated with any particular branch of professional training, it is with law or accounting. Though many of the *técnicos* are quick to agree that Mexico's schools of economics are far from providing an ideal training ground for market analysis, locational studies, and capital budgeting at the level of the individual firm, they tend to see themselves as well ahead of the private decision-maker in their training and preparation for activities involving industrial investment and management.

The programs and attitudes of the Mexican economic technicians are explained not only by their basic views but also by their current concerns about the nature of the roadblocks in Mexico's economic development. One of the worst, according to their view, is the nonegalitarian income distribution of the Mexican people. As they see it, this distribution prevents the development of mass demands for manufactured goods inside Mexico and prevents the growth of large-scale industry. The *técnicos,* therefore, tend to be strong supporters of measures which could lead to the redistribution of income. Some favor tax measures; some insist that wage boosts are the key; some concentrate on improvements in the pricing and marketing system of Mexico.

Because of their concern for the development of larger internal markets, practically all *técnicos* also tend to endorse the Latin American Free Trade Association, in hopes that the enlarged markets toward which the Association should lead over the next decade — though not necessarily altering the Mexican distribution of income — will offer Mexico some of the opportunities for large-scale production which its own internal markets do not. To charges that they may be attempting to exploit the less-developed countries of Latin America, using the very techniques that they impute to the foreign investors of the United States and Europe, they point to the provisions of the Association's treaty which seek to protect the laggard countries from the dominance of the senior partners in the Association.

A last point or two. Mexico's economic technicians are inclined to believe that Mexico has now developed its human resources and has now achieved a potential for domestic savings and investment to the point at which close contact with the more advanced countries is no longer indispensable to its growth; or, to put the case more modestly, that Mexico's remaining needs for foreign technology and capital are sufficiently limited that it can afford to bargain hard on the terms on which these needs should be provided. The ideal channel by which foreign technology should be brought into the country, in their view, is not through direct investment but through licensing agreements. And the ideal means by which foreign capital should be introduced into Mexico is likewise not through direct investment but through public loans in general support of Mexico's balance-of-payments position.

Most of the *técnicos* do not draw back from the implications of their particularistic approach to economic development. They do not flinch from the task of deciding in detail which investment should be made with public funds and which not, which product should be imported and which exported, which items should be relieved of taxes and which actually subsidized. For them, the word *dirigiste* has none of the invidious connotation which it usually carries in the French tongue. The *economía mixta,* according to their view, is the swiftest way to growth and social justice in the Mexican setting.

The views of the *técnicos* have had important implications for the policy lines to be followed by the Mexican government. In the range of proposals which the *técnicos* have formulated for the consideration of the *políticos,* it is unlikely that they have very often suggested a major relaxation of controls over the private sector; this possibility, we are safe in assuming, has not been a serious starter in the race among competing ideas within government councils.* It is equally improbable, however, that extremely ambitious proposals in the opposite direction, such as proposals for a swift and drastic extension of government powers and government investment, have been pushed upward by the *técnico* group. Though an exceptional case occurs from time to time, it is not in the nature of most government technicians knowingly to propose a line of action which they believe the *políticos* are unlikely to accept.[13] The *técnicos,* therefore, while tending to urge the continued extension of governmental powers in discrete and limited fashion, have not been a sufficient force to joggle the *políticos* off the "middle position" to which Mexican politics have slowly bound them.

CONFLICT OF INTEREST IN THE PUBLIC SECTOR

In gauging the likely behavior of the public sector, one more factor has to be taken into account. Many of Mexico's key public officials have significant interests not only in their careers as public officials but also in "outside" private business activities.

The fact that responsible people in the public sector retain a major stake in the private sector is nothing strange; the situation exists in practically every country that has a private sector. Dif-

---

* One major exception is the field of monetary policy, where one sees the beginnings of a move from particularistic to general controls. As of the end of 1962, however, there were no signs that the approach was spreading to other fields of control.

ferences of degree exist from one country to another, of course. The executive and judicial arms of the national governments of many Western European countries and of the United States have come a far way since the moonlighting days of Samuel Pepys and the spoils system of Andrew Jackson. Even in these countries, however, egregious conflicts of interest and gross corruption still come to light from time to time.

No one has systematically catalogued the private interests of Mexico's public servants. Nonetheless, when the catalogue is finally developed, there is not much doubt about what some of its principal headings will be.

The most common way in which individuals divide their interests between the two sectors is multiple jobholding. Though the official hours of work differ somewhat from one Mexican government agency to the next, a typical pattern is to have the day begin at 8:30 a.m. and end at 3 p.m. without a luncheon break. In those circumstances, it is not at all unusual for a person to arrive a little later and leave a little earlier than the official hours, devoting the rest of his energies to other jobs.

In most cases, the dual positions on the public and the private payroll would no doubt prove to be innocent and uncomplicated, signifying only that skilled men are scarce and government salaries are not very high. In some instances, the private or quasi-private posts held by officials are simply by-products of their public duties. For example, the Mexican government holds large equity interests in several score industrial enterprises, entitling the government to a seat on the board of directors. The men who occupy the seats, like other directors in Mexican enterprises, receive a fee which is much more than nominal. These fees represent a fairly significant source of income for key *técnicos*.

Then there is that curious grey area, the nemesis of all governments under the sun, in which knowledge acquired in a public capacity can be applied for private gain. For the Mexican government, this problem is especially great because of the particularistic nature of its regulation. Consider the range of Mexico's governmental activities as they apply to individual firms. Nacional Financiera stabilizes the open market in the securities of private firms and makes loans to private firms for their growth and expansion. The Secretaría de Industria y Comercio licenses the imports of selected products and sets price ceilings on others. The Secretaría de Hacienda grants tax exemptions to individual plants. The Banco de México designates specified firms or groups of firms as borrowers who are to receive privileged access to loans from commercial banks. And so on. These are activities pursued not in the heat of some national emergency but year in, year out, as a normal function of government. In a setting such as this, only mortal fear or an extraordinary *élan* could restrain some public officials from developing their liaisons with the private sector and exploiting their information.

Then, of course, there is the problem of undiluted, unambiguous corruption. The literature of Mexico, like that of many other countries, is punctured with allegations of graft and malfeasance in public life.[14] From time to time, one even hears the Mexican government characterized by serious observers as representing a conspiracy by a small clique of private interests to use government powers as a means of exploiting Mexico.

Like most simple theories of complex institutions, the notion of total conspiracy is a misleading parody of the facts. The corruption that is encountered in the Mexican government is less systematic than such a theory would suggest. Sometimes the initiative in cases of corruption comes from the private sector, as it seeks to avoid a penalty or to capture a privilege or an exemption — the right to import, the agency for export, the contract to supply a government bureau. Sometimes it comes from the public official who has the power of decision. Always, as one discusses the course of any major transaction between the public and private sectors of Mexico, question and innuendo on the tactics and interests of the parties to the transaction flit in and out of the discussion. One is unable to say whether the corruption itself is widespread, but it can be said with certainty that the assumption of the pervasive existence of corruption is nearly universal.

This is not a problem to which Mexicans react indifferently. The desire for open nondiscriminatory treatment by government is a Holy Grail whose quest began with Mexico's War of Independence in 1810. It sparked Juárez and Madero, and it warmed the deliberations of the 1917 constitutional convention. Nonetheless, the sporadic bursts of passion in support of an incorruptible government simply punctuate a more enduring Mexican attitude of resignation and cynicism on the subject of corruption. Nondiscriminatory government, like so many other constitutional goals, is an ideal devoutly to be sought, but not a concrete objective likely to be achieved. It falls in a class with honest elections, an incorruptible press, and an unreachable judiciary. Businessmen continue to see the role of government as that of the dispenser of privilege or exemption, while a considerable part of the government sees itself in the same light.

Two trends in Mexican public life, it is often suggested, may be weakening this aspect of the relations between the public and private sectors. One such trend is the increasing professionalization of the Mexican technician. A tax collector without much professional training, technical standards, or supervision, it is assumed, is inherently more corruptible than one who is part of a professional system; the training, the standards, and the supervision are each a factor reducing the likelihood of corruption, according to the argument. The other trend is the increasing volume of business done by the Mexican government. According to this view, a large volume of business at any government post — at a tax office or a border point — breeds the use of standardized methods; and standardized methods are more corruption-proof than those which are applied to the handling of an occasional transaction. So it is said that routine business, at least, is likely to be handled more and more on an impersonal, nondiscriminatory basis as its volume grows.

For our present purposes, however, the critical points are these: Extensive ties between public officials and private interests are part and parcel of Mexican life. Venality and corruption draw bitter public reaction, from time to time, but the reaction is only transitory. And the "conflict-of-interest" problem in its more subtle forms is not a real issue and does not even draw an initial reaction. Any major shift in the existing relations between the private and the public sectors could well disturb the characteristically profitable ties which key public officials have managed to develop with the private sector. This has probably constituted an added factor which has slowed the process of change in the orientation of the two sectors to one another.

Chapter 6

Leadership Ideology in the Private Sector since 1940

FOR a political structure such as Mexico has managed to achieve, the familiar iceberg analogy has special relevance. Most of the struggle between the private and public sectors over the subject of government policy goes on *sub rosa,* beyond the ken of newspapers and the public. Only a little bit of the process is visible to the naked eye.

This is especially true of the demands of labor and agriculture, demands which for the most part are muffled in the inner councils of the PRI. All that an outsider can hope to see of the struggle is its outcome. Sometimes the outcome is embodied in such grand initiatives of the government as the fixing of foodstuff prices, the provision of crop insurance, or the widening of social security coverage. Sometimes it appears in such local measures as the seizure and distribution of a large estate, the easing of agricultural credit in a distressed area, or the sudden extension of an all-weather road. If there are major ideological issues involved in this continual process of lubricating the body politic, they are issues which were resolved some decades ago, when the government began expressly to affirm its responsibility for the well-being of agriculture and labor and its intention to discharge that responsibility by active measures. Given the ideological framework, the choice and timing of the measures seem often to represent nothing more than the *ad hoc* exercise of government powers, designed to keep a going political machine at full strength.

In the government's dealings with commerce, finance, and industry, however, the signs of a struggle are easier to see. And if the words of the antagonists are to be taken at face value, the struggle seems at times to involve large questions of ideology.

Of course, the bulk of the day-to-day dealings between government on the one side and commerce, finance, and industry on the other can hardly be called a struggle between conflicting ideologies. Most of it involves the humdrum efforts of single enterprises and small groups of companies — operating within an existing framework of laws, regulations, contacts, and friendships — to obtain government credit, tariff protection, sales contracts, tax exemptions, import licenses, and the like. But we cannot make much sense out of the meaning of this daily struggle without exploring larger issues. We need to know, among other things, the background, values, and ideology which motivate the private sector and the direction in which they are changing.

MEXICO'S MODERN BUSINESS LEADERS

It is not easy to make any simple generalizations about the modern business leadership of Mexico. The modern business sector, at the present stage of its development, is far from being a homogeneous and concentrated society. The country's banking interests have a history quite distinct from that of industry; the life and traditions of its textile industry are sharply different from the background of its chemical sector; and the industrialists of Monterrey seem to have little in common with those of Puebla.

Studies of entrepreneurship in other developing countries have frequently drawn attention to the importance of foreigners — or more generally of groups lacking in status and security — as the major source of entrepreneurs in the early stages of development. The Jews and Moors in Spain, the Indians in East Africa, the Chinese in Southeast Asia, the Lebanese in West Africa, and the Germans and Italians in Brazil are classic illustrations of the pattern. In Mexico, too, one sees distinct traces of the fact that a disproportionate contribution to the early entrepreneurship of the country was made by immigrants. It would be hard to say whether the entrepreneurship was a consequence of the search for status and security on the part of the immigrants or whether it was due to the advantages of greater education and wealth, as compared with Mexicans of longer standing. Both factors no doubt exerted some influence.

Whatever the reasons, the immigrant acquired special prominence in the industrial and banking community which was being created in Mexico during the late nineteenth century and early twentieth century. In these early stages, it was the European immigrant who seemed to be the principal innovator — the French and British in textiles, banking, paper, and cement, the Germans in beer, and so on. This foreign influence was strengthened by two or three immigrant waves after the Revolution, such as the refugees from Franco and Hitler in the late 1930's and early 1940's. Nonetheless, in the course of time, the institutions generated by the immigrants and their children rapidly began to lose their foreignness and to acquire Mexican identity.

The biographical information that one is able to obtain about the background of Mexico's present-day business leaders is altogether in accord with the historical evidence. Though most of the leaders of Mexico's business world were born in Mexico, an unusually high proportion have at least one European grandparent. Out of a group of 109 business executives who were canvassed in 1957, 26 reported that their paternal grandfathers were born outside Mexico; and in a more select subgroup, consisting of a blue-ribbon crop of 32 outstanding business leaders in Mexico, 14 reported a foreign paternal grandfather.* These are extraordinarily high pro-

---

* The sample of 109 men referred to in this and the next two paragraphs consisted of 17 chief executives or principal owners of large businesses, 20 vice-presidents or general managers, and 72 others at high management levels. The study was designed and carried out by James C. Abegglan and William R. Holland as part of a larger survey of entrepreneurship conducted by Everett E. Hagen under the auspices of the Center for International Studies of the Massachusetts Institute of Technology. I am grateful for their generosity in giving me access to these materials and for their permission to publish the data.

portions in a country whose immigrant population has rarely been more than a tiny fraction of its total numbers.[1]

Despite the foreign influence among Mexico's business executives, it has been assumed at times that the recent upsurge in the Mexican entrepreneurial class has been a movement based on the pattern which Horatio Alger made famous — that Mexican entrepreneurs characteristically leaped in a single generation out of humble beginnings on farms and in villages to the leadership of national industry. The facts, however, seem to suggest a rather different pattern. In the sample of 109, no less than 86 claim to have been born in large towns or cities — this, in a country whose population was at least three quarters rural at the time these men were born. Of the 109 nearly three quarters described their fathers as being in white-collar, managerial, large-proprietor, professional, or military occupations. Finally, as further evidence of the atypicality of the group in terms of Mexican norms, 58 had gone beyond preparatory school to a university and 32 of these had acquired a graduate degree — this, in a country in which nearly nine out of ten adults have not gone beyond the sixth grade.

It would be a mistake to infer from these figures that Mexico's business leaders are drawn from an unchanging elite and that upward mobility is absent in modern-day Mexico. On the contrary, 19 of the group of 109 reported their initial occupation as "laborer," and 36 reported humble occupations for their fathers. But, in general, we have no right to think of Mexico's business executives of today as being typically a rags-to-riches group. Cases of this sort exist, to be sure. But the group as a whole can best be thought of as one which acquired its status by accretions — in capital, education, and position — over more than a single generation.[2]

What kind of values do men of this sort possess in modern-day Mexico? The typical description of this group, when made by Mexican intellectuals, charges them with being ruthless, money-grubbing opportunists, utterly devoid of social consciousness, without culture or refinement, imitating the worst in North American society, extravagant without limit.[3]

This viewpoint is of considerable importance, not because it invariably corresponds with the facts, but because it is so widely believed, particularly by the literate and educated intellectuals of Mexico. This simple and pervasive image painted by the Mexican intellectual conditions the strategies which the business groups feel obliged to use in dealing with the government, and it conditions the public responses which the government feels obliged to make to any overtures by the group. Though the image does not prevent the Mexican government from dealing intimately and continually with individual leaders of the business world, it does require that governmental negotiations with the business class as a whole should be publicly cloaked with a certain reserve.

Is the Mexican businessman truly the extraordinarily repulsive creature painted by Mexican intellectuals? It is not difficult to find individual cases which conform nicely to the description. But neither is it difficult to find individual cases of cynicism, corruption, egocentricity, and extravagance in any walk of Mexican life — in the private sector, in labor organizations, in government, and even among the intellectuals themselves. Individual cases of outstanding creativeness, frugality, dedication, and probity also are to be found — though they are less widely advertised — scattered haphazardly through the various sectors of Mexico's economy.

Still, it does not do to assume that Mexico's leading businessmen carry the same set of values and reactions as European, North American, Middle Eastern, or African businessmen. All of these national groups, reacting to elements in their national culture, reflect somewhat different priorities and goals in their behavior patterns. And Mexican businessmen, despite the cosmopolitan influences in their background, are still very much a part of the Mexican culture.

Indeed, as one tries to describe the principal characteristics and values of Mexico's business leaders, he finds that the same characteristics and values seem to apply to Mexican leadership in general, whether that leadership appears in business, in politics, or in other areas. And it is the history and culture of Mexico itself that provides the richest clues to an understanding of these leadership characteristics and values.[4]

According to seasoned observers of Mexican culture, many of the characteristics of the Mexico of the nineteenth century have apparently survived into the middle of the twentieth, though somewhat altered in form and emphasis. It will be recalled that the Mexican of the early nineteenth century faced a hostile environment, in which fundamental guarantees were weak and the protection of basic rights was uncertain. The search for some form of social structure which would provide security led to a structure of follow-the-leader; the man who could offer protection could count on acquiring a following.[5] *Caciquismo,* bossism, became a fixed feature of the Mexican social structure, permeating business, politics, and social relations. So did a corollary phenomenon — that of paternalism. The strong leader accepted the fealty of his followers but also accepted a certain responsibility for their well-being.

Today, according to many observers, the tendency toward *caciquismo* and paternalism is a great deal weaker. But it still lingers. The strong individual, posing as the father image and spreading his figurative mantle of protection, still occupies an extraordinarily prominent place in the structure of Mexican society. Demanding unquestioning loyalty, he also undertakes to provide assistance and protection to those who follow his lead.

Another facet of paternalistic bossism is the importance ascribed to *machismo* in Mexican leaders. Mexicans, like any other people, are made up of a wide range of temperaments, outlooks, and subcultures. Still, considerable emphasis is placed by most observers on the role of *machismo* in the Mexican culture. Described in different ways by different writers, the concept almost invariably projects the picture of the aggressive male protagonist, alone and withdrawn — constantly preoccupied with the image he is conveying, constantly concerned to create the impression of masculinity and courage, invulnerability and indifference to the attacks of others.[6]

It may be, however, that the paternalism, loneliness, and aggressiveness which seem to characterize Mexican business leaders are
not so much a consequence of Mexican history and culture as of the
social strains which any industrializing nation seems obliged to
undergo.[7] Certainly, the syndrome smacks a little of England's
industrial class of 1810, Pittsburgh's moguls of 1890, and some
of the Texas millionaires of the past decade or two. If these characteristics are partly a reflection of the stage of Mexican development and not solely a function of its distinct culture, one should
expect to see change in the values and attitudes of Mexico's business class as the Mexican economy evolves.

And, as a matter of fact, some observers do claim to see considerable change in Mexican business values. Professor W. Paul
Strassman, for instance, reports the impact which Mexico's business
class had upon him in 1960, after ten years' absence from the
country. "The change," says he, "was as conspicuous as that in a
girl of nine, not seen again until she reaches nineteen." On the
basis of some extensive interviewing in Mexico in 1960, Strassman observed that two types had come to dominate among Mexican businessmen. One is the now-familiar *macho* type, who sees
himself as engaged in a secretive contest aimed at besting the government, the consumer, and the competitor. Deception, manipula-
tion, influence, and secrecy are his tools. The other group — newer
in origin, younger in age — consists of the trained, "scientific" business executives, chafing under the restraints of their elders, im-
patiently looking for opportunities to apply their "rational" tools
of analysis to business problems.[8]

The appearance of the second group is certainly a consequence,
in part, of Mexico's political stability in recent decades and of the
prospect that more years of stability may lie ahead; for long-run
planning does not play much of a role in a country torn by revolutions, and short-run planning demands *machismo* more than it
demands mathematics. But the rise of the trained businessmen,
though a consequence of stability, may in time also become a

cause of stability. A group oriented to "rational" calculations tends to place more stress on the possibility of long-run returns and tends to be less exclusively preoccupied with the possibility of short-run killings. Such a group considers the possibility that large volumes may be more profitable than large mark-ups; that low labor costs per unit may be inconsistent with low wages; and that, in the law, predictability may be more useful than flexibility.[9]

It is comforting to make these observations about the implications of the rise of the rational businessman, but it would be the height of ethnocentric folly for a North American economist to assume that the private-public relationships which would emerge would duplicate those of the United States. Predictability does not necessarily demand that the government reduce the scope of its intervention in business life; in fact, the predictability of business life can be increased, not diminished, if the intervention takes the form of guaranties and subventions. Nor is predictability incompatible with discrimination, provided the discrimination is suitably institutionalized. We ought not to exclude the possibility, therefore, that the drive of the rational businessman of Mexico will be to institutionalize the favored treatment that he seeks — to take that treatment out of the discretion of ministers and bureaucrats and to anchor it more solidly into law and administrative procedure.

The probability that the new group will see its future relations to the government in these terms is particularly great because of the base from which Mexican business starts. The original precepts of Benito Juárez, it is clear, simply are not a part of the psyche of economic Mexico. Except for a few old faithfuls, there are no serious protagonists in Mexico for the pristine concept of classical free enterprise. One has only to review the typical flow of proposals out of the business sector to observe how deeply ingrained are the expectations of government intervention.

One fruitful source in which these proposals are collected — a little dated by now, to be sure, but still typical enough — is the report of the round tables conducted by Miguel Alemán during his "presidential campaign" in the period from August 1945 to June 1946.[10] Among the many suggestions from responsible business groups during the conferences were the following:

— from the sugar refining industry, that additional mills should be prohibited by the government and the existing ones subsidized;

— from the cotton growers and traders, that new gins should be prohibited from locating elsewhere than near the cotton crops, and that the price of cotton should be guaranteed;

— from the chemical industry, that the government should guarantee a 7 per cent yield on investment, should provide free electricity to the industry, and should promote a system of monopoly partnerships between Pemex and existing chemical plants;

— from the electrical equipment industry, that the government should guarantee the purchase of fixed quantities of certain types of motors of agreed design;

— from the machinery industry, that imports of surplus machinery should be embargoed;

— from the fruit industry, that restaurants should be required to list fresh fruit on their menus, that bakers should be required to mix a stated percentage of casava and banana flour in all bread, and that the industry should be relieved of its existing debt obligations to the government;

— from the chicle industry, that the use of the chicle tree in construction or agriculture should be prohibited;

— and from practically all industries, that more protection should be granted against foreign imports.

Although no similar compendium has been compiled for more recent periods, the tenor of these proposals is altogether in accord with the suggestions made by business groups in later administrations. From a base of expectations such as these, there is no reason to assume that Mexico's future businessmen would see a system of laissez-faire as the right and natural objective of their existence.

MEXICO'S BUSINESS IDEOLOGY

In looking for the business leaders' ideology and in trying to detect its trends, one does not have to rely altogether on the sort of inference just employed. Mexico's complex system of trade associations exists largely as the mouthpiece of Mexican business; indeed, as explained earlier, the law expressly lays this task on CONCAMIN and CONCANACO and upon their constituent chambers. The public record of these associations, therefore, offers a spoor to the businessmen's ideology in Mexico.

To be sure, one must follow this seeming trail with caution. If there is anything to the analyses of the Mexican male which have just been cited, we must expect the pronouncements of the trade associations to represent weapons of combat rather more than confessions of faith. In other cultures, special-interest groups are sometimes trapped by their own ideologies and even feel compelled at times to support a course of action plainly not in their own interests; but we must assume that the special-interest groups of Mexico are somewhat less vulnerable to traps of this sort.

Besides, the voice of a trade association, as anyone will attest who knows trade associations well, is no infallible indicator of the temper of its membership in given circumstances. At times, trade associations are used by their members as stalking horses; the job of the association is to take an extreme position, well beyond the ideological limits of the rank and file of its members, in order to pave the way for smaller concessions from the powers-that-be.[11] At times, too, trade associations are captured by a few energetic and extreme leaders who use the docile or indifferent membership to widen the broadcasting range of their own ideological messages. And finally, there is the familiar situation of the association whose membership is in such internal conflict that the association is unable to present any adequate public picture of its interests, and feels obliged to confine its propaganda to a few time-worn platitudes. All of these situations seem to have existed from time to time in the major trade associations of Mexico.

Nonetheless, there is something to be learned from the associations' public statements.

Distinctions and conflicts

In the years immediately prior to 1940, most national business groups were active in voicing their discontent with the principal economic measures of the Cárdenas regime, emphasizing especially the government's nurturing of labor groups and the government's deficit financing policies.[12] At the same time, there was widespread uneasiness over the government's nationalization of the railroads, an uneasiness which found expression in complaints about the way in which the railroads were run.[13] There is every reason to assume that these complaints reflected a real unhappiness over Cárdenas' policies and a genuine concern that the government might prove to be a menace to business.

The trepidation of the business groups persisted through most of the regime of Avila Camacho, as the governmental machinery sought feebly and experimentally to cope with wartime inflation. Business groups felt especially resentful of the administration's efforts at direct intrusion in the marketplace — the establishment of a committee to propose measures for the application of price ceilings, the creation of government monopolies to control the trade in rice, corn, and beans, and so on. Though the commercial groups took the lead in voicing these complaints, they seem to have had the full support of the bankers as well.[14]

At this stage in the interplay between the Mexican government and the business groups, however, one could discern two distinctly different ideological platforms from which Mexican businessmen were launching their protests at the government.

One was the ideology of late nineteenth-century political liberalism. This was a philosophy which, in general, espoused freedom of action for private enterprise. But it was not to be confused with the classical liberalism of Adam Smith and Benito Juárez; for the classical liberals were passionately against monopoly in any form, but the political liberals confined their fire to economic power exercised by the state. According to this view, all government interference in the activities of private interests was objectionable and destructive, whatever its intent. So CONCANACO repeatedly attacked "economic totalitarianism" and offered its support of "any declaration stressing the importance of free enterprise over state socialism." [15]

While CONCANACO and its allies were assuming the position of the political liberal, a second business group calling itself the Confederación Patronal de la República Mexicana was articulating a basically different philosophy, a "new" philosophy which it commended to all businessmen. Using concepts and phrases which seem to have drawn much of their inspiration from the corporative and cooperative economic philosophy of the Catholic Church, the Patronal group in 1945 and 1946 was taking its philosophical stance on something like the following lines:

Cooperation between capital and labor ought to be based upon the mutual discharge of their social obligations. The workers should have the right to work in dignity and to receive a just wage, consistent with the capacities of their employers. Private property is not a means of exploiting man nor of unjustly acquiring wealth but a natural means for the achievement of man's well-being.

Liberal doctrines which flatly prohibit state intervention in economic affairs are false doctrines, which tend to create social injustice. Equally false are the doctrines which demand the totalitarian intervention of the state. The state has the right to intervene in the relations between capital and labor, always respecting the rights of private property, the human dignity and rights of free association of the worker, and the appropriate role of labor unions. The purpose of the state in such intervention should be the dispensation of genuine justice and concern for the public interest as a whole, rather than concern to improve its political position with particular groups, such as labor groups.

The faults of liberal capitalism must be eliminated; private enterprise must perform its social function and operate in a manner consistent with the common good; it must serve the material interests of man, but not his appetite for profit; it must not look on labor as a commodity subject to the laws of supply and demand. With principles such as these, free enterprise will make its contribution to the dignity of man and the just development of society.[16]

For a small group of Mexican businessmen, the distinction between political liberalism and Catholic "socialism" was a burning issue.[17] The likelihood is, however, that the issue commanded the interest of only a faithful few; to most businessmen and in the public mind, CONCANACO and Patronal were simply two organizations largely devoted to the common objective of attacking government policy.

From one point of view, the failure to distinguish between the politics of different business organizations was perfectly justified. Until the end of World War II, it would have been difficult to see any major distinctions in the recommendations of the various national business groups regarding large issues of policy. It was not until the late 1940's and early 1950's that the Mexican government's policy of inducing industrialization had begun to make enough progress to generate distinctions among the interests of the business groups. These emerging distinctions were between commercial interests and industrial interests.

The commercial group, CONCANACO, continued to hammer away at the government's intervention in the country's markets. As the domestic economy expanded and more of the country's internal trade became organized and monetized, CONCANACO seemed to become less concerned with import restrictions and more concerned with governmental interference in domestic markets.[18] In time, CONCANACO's *bête noir,* the epitome of unjustified state intervention, came to be the particular government corporation devoted to the buying and selling of staple foodstuffs — an organization which in the early 1950's was operating under the name of Compañía Exportadora e Importadora Mexicana S.A. (CEIMSA).[19]

Meanwhile, the worries of CONCANACO's sister organization, CONCAMIN, were concentrated on getting import protection and credits where they were needed by manufacturers, while keeping the government out of the field of direct production. Accordingly, CONCAMIN's affirmations of faith typically took the following form:

. . . the development of the country's industrialization is a function exclusively of private enterprise . . . The State is obligated to intervene when individual industrialists or national chambers of industry request protection and justified assistance, but such intervention may be considered legitimate and appropriate only when it is in accord with what the industrialists have asked for . . .[20]

As time went on, CONCAMIN was found requesting more protection for industry, more tax exemptions for new lines of production, a system of export subsidies for manufactures, and various other standard forms of government assistance to industry.

In addition to the distinctions between commerce and industry, a marked difference in orientation developed between the well-established industrialists and those who were struggling for a foothold in the Mexican economy. To a greater degree than the larger and older industrialists, the new group assayed the role of government pragmatically, uninhibited by the tensions of prior years or by identification with earlier ideologies. This difference between the new group of manufacturers and the old tended to find its focus in the split between the top command of the CONCAMIN and the leaders of one of its constituent bodies, the Cámara Nacional de la Industria de Transformación (CNIT). The CNIT group, composed of 15,000 comparatively small manufacturing companies, became the sponsor of a dynamic campaign whose principal points consisted of supporting government intervention in industry and assailing the role of foreign capital in the Mexican economy. At the same time the group upheld the claims of workers for higher wages and more social security, and the demands of farmer groups for more land and more credit.

The interests of Mexico's smaller firms in a larger measure of government intervention in the late 1940's and early 1950's were perfectly clear. As for domestic credit controls, almost any rationing system would treat the small firm more kindly than an unregulated market would, in view of the close connections between large Mexican manufacturing firms and the major Mexican banks. As for the control of foreign investment in Mexico, practically any restraints would also help the small firm in its competition with the large, in view of the easier access of the large firm to international capital sources. The control of foreign technicians would have a similar effect in favor of small firms, for similar reasons. Increased import restrictions, it is true, might pinch some small firms badly; but a government friendly to the objective could tailor its restrictions in such a way as to compel the larger firms to turn to small domestic manufacturers for products they might otherwise buy abroad, such as automobile parts or electronic components.

How to ensure that the government would in fact be friendly to the smaller firms? The probability would be increased, it was clear, if the group allied itself with the whole government program, demonstrating its own worthiness by its support of government policies in the fields of labor, agriculture, and social programs as well as in industry. So CNIT took its stand as an enthusiastic supporter of accelerated land reform, more extensive social security, and stronger labor unions. In fact, CNIT even went so far as to support direct government participation in some industries — provided, of course, that the participation was "supplementary" or "marginal," or was in industries in which small firms could hardly be expected to operate, such as petroleum.

Whatever may have motivated the CNIT leadership in developing its platform, there is hardly a serious possibility that the program, despite all its avowed concern for labor, farmer, and the urban poor, represented a new wave of support among Mexico's small businessmen for a "revolutionary" ideology.[21] Whatever can be said as a general description of the Mexican adult character, it does not include an easy identification with the interests and well-being of other social groups. This identification may yet develop, if *machismo* diminishes and the rational approach becomes ascendant; indeed, by the early 1960's (if my own extensive interviews are at all typical), some businessmen were evidencing a considerable sensitivity to the relations between a thriving agricultural and labor class and a thriving national economy. But the sense of interrelatedness seemed in evidence principally among larger industrialists, and was surely not widespread among the small Mexican businessmen of the late 1940's and early 1950's.

Convergence and reconciliation

After the mid-1950's, one could detect a blurring and softening in the sharp ideological distinctions voiced by the leadership of the various business groups of Mexico. To be sure, some differences still remained acute enough; even in the early 1960's the propaganda of the Patronal and the bankers could hardly be confused with that of the CNIT. And one must expect these distinctions to remain, if only for the reason that the leadership of any organization cannot hope to maintain its strength when its intellectual product becomes indistinguishable from that of rival groups.

Nonetheless, a convergence in viewpoints, modest though it was, seemed to be drawing the business groups toward common ground which they shared not only with one another but also in some respects with the Mexican government. The trend, of course, was not invariant. For instance, one found CONCANACO in 1957 still quoting with approval some of its more intransigent statements of 1952. Nonetheless, the general tone of the CONCANACO pronouncements was obviously shifting during the 1950's. For one thing, the undiluted free-trade approach of the merchants — a basic tenet of CONCANACO's existence up to 1954 — succumbed dramatically in that year in favor of a much more qualified view. In "an important declaration," CONCANACO announced its full support of the government's increased import restrictions, taken in the interest of the industrialization of Mexico and the restoration of equilibrium in Mexico's balance of payments.[22] From time to time, too, CONCANACO went out of its way during the latter 1950's to congratulate the government on its efforts to clean up tax collections, to expand the nation's infrastructure, and to encourage exports. Both in tone and content, CONCANACO's pronouncements on these points would have been out of the question in the 1940's.

The real measure of CONCANACO's shift, however, was its decision to cooperate with the government experimentally in its programs to distribute basic commodities at fixed prices — in short, to bury the hatchet with its enemy, the government corporation CEIMSA. The decision to cooperate with CEIMSA did not come totally without some advance indications. Already in 1956, CONCANACO was grudgingly acceding to CEIMSA a "marginal" and "supplementary" — albeit a "transitory" — function.[23] In August 1960, through a formal agreement between CEIMSA and CONCANACO, the government agreed to make certain stated quantities of beans, rice, and eggs available to the CONCANACO members who were in the food distribution business, provided they agreed to resell the products at certain fixed prices. After that first experimental period, the framework of the agreement remained in force, to be activated from time to time as circumstances required. By 1961, the state of mind of the CONCANACO leadership had moved so far that one of its principal spokesmen was saying: "Either we voluntarily spend a part of our time and our resources to raise the standard of living of those who live in ignorance and misery, or else we continue an attitude of disbelief and apathy, risking the loss of everything, perhaps even violently and irreversibly."[24]

Meanwhile the other major employers' organizations were moving in the same direction. With good reason, industrial-minded CONCAMIN had been adopting some of the government's positions on various major issues somewhat earlier, ever since official support for the industrialization of Mexico had begun to be translated into action. By 1961, CONCAMIN's leaders were emphasizing such themes as these: that the right of the government to intervene in economic affairs was no longer a subject for debate — only the forms and limits of such intervention; and that the objective of private enterprise must be the elevation of the living standards of the workers.

Even the staid and sober Asociación de Banqueros was bending with the times by the year 1962. Its propaganda in that year emphasized the need of its members to cooperate with the government in solving Mexico's economic problems. At the same time, the Banco Nacional de México, the country's leading private bank, was making numerous pronouncements that bankers used to consider heretical, such as the view that there was a need for higher prices to the farmer and for a reduction in luxury spending in the nation.[25]

The shrinkage in the differences among the business groups is best illustrated perhaps by the attitudes which they assumed toward foreign investment in Mexico. Enough has already been said about foreign investment to indicate the sensitivity of the issue in Mexican political life. As foreign enterprises, especially United States enterprises, began to develop a renewed interest in the Mexican economy during the late 1940's and the 1950's the issue resumed its historical prominence in the public press.

The facts, as usual, were not very clear. Investment in foreign-controlled manufacturing firms may perhaps have come to one fifth or so of total private investment in the Mexican manufacturing sector by 1960, but no one could be altogether sure. At any rate, as "Ford," "Coca-Cola," and "General Electric" blossomed out on the billboards and were mouthed on the radio, almost any account of the extent of foreign control of Mexican industry was given a respectful hearing. Many literate and educated Mexicans were even willing to take seriously the assertions of a Mexican investigator that about two thirds of Mexico's major manufacturing companies are United States-controlled, and, further, that four United States "supergroups" — to wit, the Morgans, the Rockefellers, the du Ponts, and the First National City group — form the hard core of the domination.[26]

The evolution in attitudes of the various business groups toward foreign investment faithfully mirrored their changing interests. CONCANACO, originally a staunch defender of freedom of investment, had begun overtly to show uneasiness over its free-investment position in the early 1950's, as Sears Roebuck & Company and other United States firms extended their activities in the

Mexican economy. By 1955, CONCANACO's uneasiness was crystallized into flat opposition to foreign direct investment in commercial activities.[27] Foreign investment might be helpful to Mexican development if it was in industrial projects, according to the CONCANACO view, particularly if it was in the form of mixed Mexican-foreign companies; but foreign investment in commerce was decidedly another matter.[28] As the years went on, such support as CONCANACO was still willing to extend to foreign investment grew more and more qualified.

By the early 1960's, it was hard to distinguish the position of the various business groups in Mexico on the subject of foreign investment. By that time, CONCAMIN and CNIT were both insisting upon two things: (1) that private foreign investment could be of help to Mexican development, provided it was supplementary or "auxiliary" to Mexican investment; but (2) that such investment would be harmful to the Mexican economy if control of the enterprise remained abroad.[29] The only remaining differences between CONCANACO and CONCAMIN on the one hand, and CNIT on the other, were differences of tone. Whereas the older organizations offered their new positions with a certain self-consciousness and restraint and even with an occasional backsliding, CNIT's spokesmen continued to attack foreign interests as if they were secret enemies of the Mexican republic.* But the ends of all these groups were no longer in dispute.

There is no simple one-factor explanation to be found for the tendency toward the convergence of the many views described above — of commerce and industry, big producers and small producers, business and government.

The bridge between commerce and industry may not be so difficult to explain, perhaps. The divergencies of the 1940's were nat-

---

* About this time, CNIT's principal spokesman, José Domingo Lavín, slipped from grace a little in the eyes of Mexico's intellectuals by selling a major interest in his Mexican chemical company to the Dow Chemical Company. This, of course, tended to limit the position he felt free to take; but not very much, as witness the tone of his weekly articles in *Siempre*.

ural enough when one group was still largely in commerce, the other still primarily in industry. But the Mexican economy, as we saw in Chapter 1, has grown considerably more complex since that date, tending to group itself into a series of nuclei each of which contains industrial, commercial, and banking interests. So, today, men like Carlos Trouyet, Luis Legorreta, Antonio Sacristán, and other key figures in the nuclei might have some difficulty in saying exactly where their principal interests lay, whether in production, distribution, or finance. At the same time, with the organized internal markets of Mexico probably growing faster than the foreign trade of the country, this tendency has given the industrialists and the merchants of Mexico a common interest in protection.[30]

The basis for the signs of common ground between big business and CNIT, at least as far as foreign investment is concerned, has also been reasonably clear. In bluntest terms, the time when foreign investors offered their capital and their skills in a seller's market has rapidly been passing in Mexico. For one thing, many Mexican businessmen themselves now have considerable financial and technical resources of their own. For another, the number of United States and European investors who have been looking actively for opportunities to invest in foreign countries — especially in so relatively "advanced" a country as Mexico — has been increasing over the long run. It has become a commonplace for foreign investors to bid competitively for the opportunity to go into partnership with a Mexican businessman, and a commonplace, too, for a foreign investor to be more optimistic about the prospects of Mexico's future growth than his domestic counterpart. In circumstances of this sort, Mexican businessmen have been more nearly unanimous in their readiness to limit the hand of the foreigner and to insist on conditions which a decade ago seemed out of the question.

At the same time, some of the small businessmen who not so long ago were hostile to all foreign capital — because it was so inaccessible — have been coming of age. Here and there, they have begun to see the possibilities of achieving a successful partnership with foreigners, provided they could negotiate from strength. So the distinction between large manufacturers and small has lost a little of its cutting edge since the time in the mid-forties when CNIT first declared war upon its older and larger rivals.

The reasons for the apparent convergence of views between business and government are more subtle and more complex. In the first place, one could not say that the tendency was so advanced that it had put an end to Mexican businessmen's fear and suspicion concerning the trend of political events in Mexico. On the contrary, the revolution in Cuba, coupled with the unhappy timing of López Mateos' various efforts to draw Mexico's left into PRI's enveloping fold again, had revived the talk about the "Communists" in the Mexican government and about the threat of violence from the Cárdenas wing. But it is important that the response of business leaders to their fears was not one of withdrawal; it consisted of a major effort to reassure the government of the continuing loyalty of business. And the response of the government was to seek to convince the business world of the government's continued esteem for and appreciation of the critical role of business in the country's development.

We have already discussed the government's motives in this urgent effort at reassurance — the government's continued attempts to walk the tightrope which Mexico's political system has imposed upon its presidents. As for business, its motives, too, seem evident. For all the stresses and strains, the present Mexican system has not dealt unkindly with business interests. Though by the early 1960's there were misgivings about the future rate of growth of Mexico's economy, these misgivings had not yet led to despair about the country's economic future nor to a violent demand for new and different policies. On the contrary, almost any major political change that Mexico's business groups could foresee in 1962 seemed to offer greater hazards than the *status quo*. Castroism in particular concerned them; and Castroism, to many of them, seemed the most likely alternative to the *status quo*. So the strategy of businessmen, like the strategy of government, was to join the chorus of mutual reassurance — that all soon would be well in what would surely be close to the best of all possible worlds.

Chapter 7

The Mexican Dilemma

THERE are very few periods in the history of any nation when continued economic growth can be taken as a matter of course. Though the obstacles may change as nations pass through different stages of development, there is rarely a long stretch of clear road ahead.

Nevertheless, historians will probably record that in the last twenty or thirty years, Mexico was traveling on a comparatively clear and open stretch in her upward course. World conditions during much of the period were not unfavorable to Mexico's growth. The political machinery of the country had matured to a point at which it could provide the necessary services and security. The public and private sectors had developed enough capabilities and sufficient rapport to be able jointly to exploit and enlarge the opportunities that world conditions had created.

In the early 1960's, however, Mexico's economy seemed to be approaching a new series of roadblocks. The country's growth appeared to be slowing a little and the prospects for some new impetus to growth seemed uncertain. If the economy were allowed to drift for very long, the loss of momentum might expose the country to serious political risks and economic losses. On the other hand, practically every major change in policy that offered some promise of stimulating the country's development also seemed to involve a considerable measure of political risk. The problem for Mexico's leaders was to find a way out of the dilemma — to seize the horn on which the country was least likely to be impaled.

THE ECONOMIC PROSPECTS

Mexico's economic development over the last seventy years has been a process of continuous evolution. On first glance, the elements of continuity may not seem dominant. Mexico's history is marked with traumatic interruptions — with bloody revolutions and *coups d'état,* with the impact of war and depression. On a more careful reading of her history, however, the interruptions seem less important than the connecting links that bind together the various stages of Mexico's growth. One sees an expansion of infrastructure, a maturing of institutions, and an upgrading of the human resources, continuing through the crises and the succession of regimes which cover the seventy-year period.

In the era of Porfirio Díaz, the state shaped its policy on the assumption that the only productive force available in the private sector was the foreign investors. The state allied itself with that force, changing the laws and enforcing the peace in ways calculated to give the foreigner maximum security and freedom of opportunity.

The Porfirian era, ending with the Revolution, left three legacies to Mexico: a network of railroads; a small urban middle class; and a tiny nucleus of half-Mexicanized entrepreneurs. These legacies afforded a means of mobility, an apparatus for focusing discontent, and some of the necessary preconditions for an expanding society.

After the destructive portion of the Revolution a number of different forces offered Mexico the opportunity for growth. In the 1920's, the flight of capital and labor from the land to the cities was probably one such force; so was the mounting demand in Europe and the United States for some of Mexico's raw materials. In the latter 1930's, the deficit-financed public works activities of Cárdenas were a key element in the resumption of Mexico's growth.

Between 1920 and 1940 the role of Mexico's governments was largely to promote and enlarge the opportunities of the modern private sector. As the government developed more effective mechanisms of administration, these proved more of an aid than a threat to the Mexican industrialists and to the growing urban middle class. As a public school system developed, as transportation and communication facilities were improved, as public credit sources emerged, their existence on the whole made life simpler for the modern private sector. Institutions such as the Banco de México and Nacional Financiera, though welcomed with no particular enthusiasm by the business groups, proved more allies than competitors.

Sketched in greater detail, of course, the picture was not that simple. Foreign interests were placed in a special category, to be carefully distinguished from domestic interests and to be dealt with in accordance with a different set of rules. Sometimes this treatment seemed to give foreigners special advantages; more often it seemed to expose them to special risks. In addition, in the relations between the private Mexican businessman and the public sector, the prevalence of favoritism and graft meant that some members of the private sector were advantaged over others. Moreover, whether because of indifference or inadequacy in the public sector, there was retrogression in the lot of some members of the Mexican public and some sections of the Mexican nation. But on the whole, the Mexican governments responded in ways which were relevant to the needs of the Mexican people and in ways which supplemented the activities of the private sector instead of conflicting with them.

By 1940, the machinery of Mexican government was beginning to develop the capabilities for a more active role in Mexico's economic life. For the first time, Mexico's administrative machinery became able to have a genuine monetary and credit policy. Selective import protection and selective tax credits became an administrative commonplace. The ability to administer public programs of short-term and long-term credits began to be in evidence. The capacity to plan, engineer, and build dams and roads became a part of the Mexican government's everyday skills. Despite its heightened level of ability, the Mexican government still showed little disposition to play the role of active competitor or active antagonist in its relations with the modern private sector. In general, it concentrated on improving the power, transportation, and communication network, providing land, water, and credit to the agricultural sector, and building up the urban school system.

Accordingly, when World War II gave Mexico an unrivaled chance to expand its domestic economy, the public sector's activities were a help more often than a hindrance to the private sector. It is true, of course, that the expanding government apparatus was often venal or stupid or inefficient; it is true, too, that the very pervasiveness of the regulatory apparatus was a nuisance of the first order to businessmen interested in getting on with their affairs. But the governmental apparatus was not officially hostile to the private sector. And the contracts, the infrastructure, and the credit that the government provided to the private sector were vital to many of the new ventures of World War II.

After the war, Mexico's economy continued to expand, bolstered by a thriving tourism, a conscious program of import replacement, and a flow of foreign capital and technical support. In this period, the Mexican government began even more overtly to accept the responsibility for rationing scarce credit and scarce foreign exchange. It became more aggressive in marshaling foreign credits. And its development of power, transportation, and communication facilities for the use of agriculture and industry became even more extensive. At the same time, the modern private sector also was developing rapidly and many of Mexico's indigenous entrepreneurs were acquiring experience, capital, and self-confidence. Though many of them were in partnership with foreign investors, the sense of being junior partners in these alliances and of bargaining from weakness was diminishing.

The increasing maturity of the Mexican entrepreneur could be seen also in his changing relations with the government. Several decades of prosperity and growth were beginning to relax the suspicion and hostility which an expanding government apparatus had once generated in the minds of businessmen. Events such as the Cuban revolution and the nationalization of some foreign-held properties in Mexico created occasional flurries of anxiety and alarm among the business groups. But such flurries were short-lived on the whole and the reconciliations that followed served to emphasize the strength of the mutual desire in the public and private sectors to work in tandem.

In the early 1960's, the Mexican success story seemed marred in only one respect: the rate of growth of Mexico's economy seemed to be slowing down and the economic outlook seemed far from promising. The obvious sources of Mexico's growth were becoming weaker, not stronger, with the passage of time.

The expansion of Mexico's merchandise exports, for instance, had once been a major factor in spurring the country's development. But the international market for exports of copper, lead, and zinc — about 10 per cent of Mexico's exports — had been distressingly weak since the end of the Korean war. And the markets for cotton and coffee — about 30 per cent of the country's exports — had turned soft a few years after that. To be sure, Mexico's rich variety of climates, soils, and natural resources, coupled with her proximity to the United States and her comparatively low labor costs, continued to attract new ventures in production for export. Sulfur became a new major export item in the 1950's, and by 1960 it had come to make up 4 per cent of Mexico's exports and showed signs of further sustained growth. A large export market for cattle and for shrimp began to appear — another 9 per cent of Mexico's exports. Sugar and tomatoes also developed major export markets. But all told, despite those bright spots in Mexico's export patterns, the value of the country's merchandise exports slumped after 1956; and the exports of that year, amounting to 850 millions of United States dollars, had not been matched again by 1962.

Projections of the future markets for Latin American exports offered no basis for anticipating that Mexico's economy would be greatly buoyed by exports in the early future. Western Europe, which is one of Mexico's major markets for cotton, was expected to increase its total imports of the product at the rate of only 0.5 per cent a year in the ten or twelve years ahead, according to one estimate.[1] Another estimate projected the annual growth rate in the demand for Latin American exports of cotton at 0.1 per cent until 1975.[2]

The projections for coffee, fruits, and vegetables were no more encouraging. The estimates for exports to the United States varied from a slight negative figure in the case of coffee[3] to various small positive figures on the order of 2 or 3 per cent in the case of fruits and vegetables.[4] Only the export markets for ferrous and nonferrous metal ores showed promise of much growth, according to the projections: anticipated growth rates of 5 or 6 per cent were typical for such products.[5] And by 1962, it began to appear that the metal ore projections might be too optimistic. In any case, even if the metal ore exports were eventually to grow, the increase would not be sufficient to offset the anticipated sluggishness in the exports of agricultural products.

None of these projections, of course, needs to be taken at face value. Indeed, one can safely assume that they are hopelessly error-prone for any period more than four or five years hence. Mexico's cattle or truck garden products could pursue their own stubbornly individualistic export trends, as they have been known to do in the past, without regard to the rest of Latin America.[6] More important, Mexico's incipient export trade in manufactured products — a trade which up to recently had been held down by the limited size and character of demand inside Mexico — could conceivably expand at a much accelerated rate.[7] So could the tourist trade — that much-denigrated earner of foreign exchange and generator of jobs in Mexico. Finally, the progressive development of the Latin American Free Trade Association, scheduled for a swift evolution in the decade of the 1960's, could begin to have a significant effect on the pattern of Mexico's exports.[8] But, for the remainder of the

López Mateos administration and the beginning of the regime of his successor, the sobering projections described earlier appear relevant enough.

If exports are not to provide the fillip to Mexico's growth, can we rely on import-replacement investment to do it? This is always a possibility, of course, given Mexico's substantial reliance on imports. But Mexico is at a stage in her development when further investment in import-replacing industries, though it will certainly occur, will no longer be so easy as in the past. Up to a certain point in a country's economic development — though only up to a certain point — the easiest and most obvious inducement to investment is the guarantee of protection against imports. Such protection offers domestic producers a chance to fill a vacuum in a market which is already easily measured, well developed, and clamoring for goods.

Mexico is passing that first easy stage, however. One sign of her transition appears in the fact that by the early 1960's consumer goods had come to be less than one fifth of Mexico's total imports.[9] Most of the rest consisted of capital goods and materials needed for further processing by Mexican industry. In industries that are largely foreign-owned, such as the automobile assembly plants, it might be possible to "close the border" to the supply of imported intermediate products and to impose a difficult program of import replacement upon the assemblers without rousing much effective opposition. But, contrary to the nearly universal impression in Mexico, the amounts involved in such cases by the early 1960's were no longer very great. For instance, even as early as 1957, United States-controlled manufacturing companies in the country imported only about 83 million United States dollars of intermediate goods[10] — an amount equal to only one fifth of the total materials used by those companies in that year. Also significant is the fact that these imports of United States-controlled companies were only about one tenth of Mexico's total imports of nonconsumer products, most of the rest being imported on behalf of Mexican business and Mexican government agencies. Added restrictions on imports, therefore, are likely to affect Mexican interests far more than foreign interests.

Even if the Mexican government should move vigorously to "close the border" against intermediate goods, this would not automatically evoke domestic investment in the production of such goods. Domestic investment would be far less likely than if consumer goods were the principal target. Mexico has already gone some way in substituting domestic goods for imports in certain kinds of intermediate products. Items with a standard technology and a standard final form — such as basic chemicals, artificial fibers, and various steel products — are already being produced in quantity. In many of these cases, because of the dominant position which the new plant was bound to assume in the Mexican market, the government has had a considerable hand in the creation of the facility. But in the case of many other intermediate products still imported, domestic production at this stage would be difficult even with government help. Some specialty steels, for example, demand a larger market than Mexico can now provide; oversized drill presses may demand more obscure skills than Mexico can now provide; and so on. For the present, therefore, import replacement may be slowed down by problems of scale and by technical bottlenecks.

But import replacement is not the only inducement to investment. If a Mexican entrepreneur could be reasonably sure that the internal demand for some domestic product would grow rapidly and spontaneously for other reasons, presumably he could be persuaded to invest in it. What is the likelihood that expectations of this sort will be generated among Mexican businessmen in the early and medium-term future?

No one can answer the question with assurance. Many Mexican businessmen, especially those associated with the larger industrial enterprises, are acutely aware of the limitations on the internal size of Mexican markets. The nature of Mexico's income distribution is such that, instead of thinking of 35 or 40 million people as being the object of their sales campaigns, many businessmen are obliged to think of some small fraction as the target. For instance, the urban poor, the ejidal farmers, and the small landowners — making up perhaps two thirds or three fourths of the country — may have to be regarded as simply outside the market for many modern-day products. If, by some means, businessmen could be persuaded that these groups would rapidly be pulled into their ambit, so that their markets would increase considerably faster than the total population, perhaps private expansion plans and the rate of private investment would take on a new spurt of growth.

It may be that many Mexican businessmen did take this possibility for granted in the period from 1940 on. But that state of mind requires constant reassurance, confirmed by actual performance from year to year. The slow-up of growth of the latter 1950's and the near-standstill of 1961 has obviously shaken that state of mind considerably.

It is theoretically conceivable, of course, that vigorous government action aimed at altering the distribution of income could regenerate the expectation of rapid growth in the minds of businessmen. Such measures, however, would have to take a form which businessmen would ordinarily regard as hostile and antibusiness in character, such as increases in minimum wages, increases in taxation aimed at reducing sumptuous living or idle hoards, and increases in subsidies on mass-consumed commodities and services. One is then led to ask whether the Mexican government can be expected to take vigorous measures which might be construed as being blatantly antibusiness.

The same kind of political question arises with respect to the treatment of foreign investors. If we are to assume that investment may not be forthcoming from domestic business interests, it is still possible that the necessary investment to stimulate growth might be provided from foreign sources. But this would be a real possibility only if the Mexican government felt itself in a position to permit foreign investment to enter Mexico in large volume, without inhibiting restraints. That such a policy would be exceedingly unpopular goes without saying; if continued for very long it would offend both the *técnicos* and the domestic businessmen. Only a very courageous government would take the step.

If the government should be unwilling or unable to pursue policies consistent with a high rate of private investment, then two sources of investment are left — public investment based on domestic funds and resources, and public investment based on foreign funds and resources.

The level of public domestic investment depends partly on the government's capacity and willingness to tax and partly on its ability to squeeze profits out of its decentralized enterprises. The capacity and willingness to tax are limited by many circumstances — by a long tradition of tax evasion and corruption, by technical limitations in the tax-collecting apparatus, and by a justifiable fear that high taxes will either induce capital flight or generate widespread public unrest, depending on their form. As a result, although the Mexican government still has sufficient room for maneuver to make modest tax-structure revisions of the type initiated in 1961, the government seems incapable for the present of collecting more than 10 or 11 per cent of its gross national product in the form of tax revenues. Willingness to run the national enterprises at larger profit — a result which could be achieved either by raising prices or by lowering payments to labor or both — seems even more circumscribed.

Most of the limitations on Mexico's tax-collecting or profit-generating abilities will probably relax a little with time. None of these difficulties, however, lends itself easily to rapid change. It is hard to imagine a Mexican government, operating under the present ground-rules of such governments, to depart from the slow evolutionary patterns that they have heretofore pursued in the expansion of their taxing capacities.

If government tax yields and government profits are unlikely to go up very fast, what are the chances that the government will expand its investments by domestic borrowing? The recent history of Mexico suggests that this kind of operation will continue to be kept under fairly tight control. So far, the government has had a discouraging time in its efforts to place government paper by non-inflationary means. In the end, the placement of government paper has usually required a nearly corresponding increase in the money supply. Inflationary measures of this sort have been the bugaboo of recent Mexican administrations. Although there are pressures within the government urging a more adventurous use of deficit financing, the position and the traditions of the finance ministry and the Banco de México seem sufficiently entrenched that it would be risky to assume that much change is likely to come from these quarters.

Of course, there is the possibility — even more, the probability — of increased public investment based on foreign funds. Mexican government entities were expanding their foreign borrowing at an impressive rate in the early 1960's, not only from the World Bank, the Export-Import Bank, and other public institutions, but from private foreign lenders as well. At best, however, such investment cannot add more than a percentage point or two to the proportion of Mexico's gross national product devoted to capital formation, at least during the next few years. And it cannot even continue that for many years before the limit of Mexico's public borrowing power will have been reached, at least as gauged by the usual yardsticks in vogue among public lenders.

In fact, the really strategic importance of foreign lending probably lies in the support that it gives to the Mexican balance-of-payments position, and therefore in the elbowroom that it offers to Mexican fiscal, monetary, and import policy. If Mexico were disposed to use that elbowroom imaginatively and energetically, one could envisage a surge of constructive investment in the public sector, undertaken within the limitations imposed by Mexico's balance-of-payments position. But the dominant note in Mexico's spending policies of 1962 was caution; and there was no reason to suppose that the mood would shortly change.

One last possibility for the stimulation of Mexico's economy ought not to be overlooked — the possibility that Mexico's public investment, while not changing very much in monetary terms, would change in terms of its impact upon the country's growth rates. Could it be that some large-scale projects with long gestation periods were soon to come to fruition, or that some small prospective additions to existing projects were soon to produce much larger and quicker pay-outs? Given the predilection of Mexican governments for giant monuments of concrete, given the frequent reports of irrigation works operating at 50 per cent capacity for lack of distribution channels and of roads being pushed halfway to nowhere, these possibilities were obviously not to be dismissed.

Any judgment on the income-inducing rhythm of Mexican investments demands an extraordinarily intimate knowledge of the on-going investment program of the government — a knowledge which surely does not exist outside government circles and which one has difficulty in locating within. Pieces of the puzzle are known to some; general impressions are held by others. As one tries to learn whether the government is capable of centering its fire for a time on projects which are capable of quick and heavy pay-out, he does not come away with the feeling that such a policy is very much more likely today than it has ever been. He still has to count upon the high probability that priorities will be heavily influenced by the timing of some national anniversary, by the need to show solicitude for some disgruntled section of the hinterland, by the desire to make public works large and visible, and by all the other diversions of politics which characteristically affect the public investment pattern of a nation. The net impression is, therefore, that one had better not count on an early increase in the output from government investment.

Perhaps the one factor which offers some hope for an improvement in the quality of government investment in the medium-term future is the creation in 1962 of an interministerial planning group in the Mexican government, centering on the finance ministry, whose purpose is to generate more effective public planning. One is entitled to a certain measure of skepticism about the analytical ability and wisdom of groups such as these, when confronted with the complexities of the development process. Even if the group is able and wise, one may still question whether it will find the means inside the Mexican government for imposing its advice upon the operating ministries. There are too many instances of outright failure on the part of such groups throughout the developing world to permit any observer to be sanguine about their operations. But a planning group operating in Mexico does have certain advantages over typical groups in many other countries: a going government mechanism; an energetic private sector; a margin of foreign public credit still remaining; an eager group of potential foreign private investors; and a president with the seeming power to move mountains.

Will the president be in a position to use his seeming power to increase the growth rates of Mexico? This question has arisen again and again in the preceding pages, as we have sought to project the future economic behavior of the country. To try to find an answer to the question, one has to do a certain amount of speculation about the future political process of the country.

THE POLITICAL PROCESS

The Mexican government has gradually worked itself into a position of key importance in the continued economic development of Mexico. It governs the distribution of land, water, and loans to agriculture; it mobilizes foreign credits and rations the supply of domestic credit; it imposes price ceilings, grants tax exemptions, supports private security issues, and engages in scores of other activities that directly and immediately affect the private sector. Governmental policies, therefore, are critical — critical to a degree which is not matched in many other developing economies based on a private enterprise system.

The key position of the Mexican government needs to be borne in mind in assessing the implications of its present internal political situation. The presidents of Mexico have gradually been eased — or have eased themselves — into a political strait jacket. Eschewing techniques of repression or terror, they still have striven to retain the appearance of unanimity. Fearful of the risk of losing touch with any significant element of opposition, they have tried against mounting odds to enlist the loyalty of every source of power in the country. Whereas the leaders of many other nations might feel easy even if a quarter of the national elite were disaffected with their policies and were out of communication with the government, the president of Mexico would be acutely uncomfortable in such a situation.

In a real sense, therefore, the strength of the Mexican president is a mirage. True, he need not worry about tripping over a recalcitrant Congress, being blocked by a stubborn minister, or being declared out of bounds by an independent court. But in his ceaseless effort to achieve unanimity, in his concern to extend the reach of the PRI the full distance to both the right and the left, he is held to a course of action which is zigzagging and vacillating when it is not blandly neutral.

As suggested earlier, Mexico may have reached a plateau in her upward climb and may need some new source of energy to push her into the next phase of productive investment and economic growth. Except in the unlikely event of major new exports or new import-substituting opportunities, the new stimulus will have to come from within; and that new stimulus seems likely to demand a sharp change of one sort or another in existing government policy. In a country in which the public sector was less pervasive and less restrictive in its influence, one might picture the emergence of some profound change in the private sector of the economy, sufficient to generate the new stimulus. But the control which the Mexican government exercises over the country's scarce resources — especially over credit, imports, and infrastructure — is so extensive that it is difficult to picture such a change in Mexico without an accompanying shift in public policy. Mexico's political system either must find the means to reduce the extent of its control over the economy, in hopes that the dynamic forces released by this relaxation will generate the desired growth, or it must find the means to exercise that control in a way which, by sacrificing the goal of unanimity or the appearance of legitimacy, can be more responsive to the country's changing needs.

Any shift in course would demand a certain amount of uninhibited action on the part of Mexico's president. A sharp increase in private investment in the short or medium term might conceivably take place if the restraints on foreign investment were substantially relaxed, if the controls over domestic credit were reduced, if government industrial operations were narrowed in scope, if ejidal lands were returned to private ownership, and if half a dozen other controversial steps, disturbing to the political balance, were initiated. By the same token, a sharp increase in public investment or a redistribution of income would require equally unsettling steps — a considerable rise in taxation, greater resort to deficit financing, the intrusion of public enterprise into new branches of industry, and various other disturbing policies.

So the president of Mexico, confronted with a variety of choices for resuming the upward climb, may decide to take none of them; or, just as likely, in an effort to persuade his horse to ride off in all directions at once, he may follow a jerky and erratic course toward nowhere in particular.

But if growth does not resume, the Mexican government is sure to incur the ire of many major groups of influence in Mexico, and to stimulate the discussion of a number of possible changes in the present political system.

The first of these possibilities — and the one which most Mexicans, whatever their politics, seem to prefer as a way out of their dilemma — is a reversion to the "strong" president, of the sort exemplified by Calles, Cárdenas, and Alemán. To state the position in terms consistent with our analysis, this is a preference for a president who does not insist upon unanimous consent before he makes a move. It assumes implicitly that the recent presidents of Mexico have exaggerated the risks of a neglected opposition, or that such opposition, if it *is* dangerous, should be more ruthlessly suppressed, in the interests of recapturing some direction in policy.

In the same breath with which they voice their support for a "strong" president, many Mexicans will agree that the likelihood of such a president's being nominated under the present PRI system is fairly remote, and that the most likely designee will be a man whose capacity for neutralism has been tested and proven. On this assumption, one is led to ask if the confusion and uncertainty of a multi-party system may not be preferable to the paralysis of a single party in search of unanimity.

The demonstrated capacity of business increasingly to find a common language for discourse with the *políticos* and the *técnicos* suggests that a multiparty system need not degenerate into groups so far apart in viewpoint that the concept of a loyal opposition would be impossible. For instance, one could envisage a majority party, composed of the middle and the left in the PRI structure, devoted to the proposition of a somewhat more vigorous role for the public sector, without its being utterly alienated from the business right. Alternatively, a majority party might consist of various PRI splinters plus elements of the business world, committed to a reduction in the scope of public activity and an increase in the freedom of action for the private sector — but not implacably hostile to public investment and control.

Other combinations also are possible, some of them not easily fitting into the oversimplified left-right axis of Western politics. One can envisage some of the Catholic syndicalist elements of the business world, for instance, developing an alliance — uneasy though the alliance may be — with some of the labor, agriculture, and *técnico* groups which stand for greater state intervention. It is even conceivable — though the possibility makes bold assumptions about the political maturity of Mexico — that a large center party could develop, devoted to the stimulation of a mixed economy and prepared to brave the wrath of both the left and the right.

Nonetheless, many Mexicans of intelligence and discretion recoil from the prospect of a breakdown in the PRI hegemony. They are painfully aware that no Mexican party, throughout all the 140-odd years of Mexico's independence, has ever relinquished its control of government peacefully. They recall that the last large armed revolt in Mexico was put down only a little over thirty years ago. They ask if Mexico has yet reached the stage at which it would dare to take on a multiparty system, and if the effort to move to such a system would simply culminate in a bloody show of force and repression.

One could push the questioning even further. What is the new "system" which is likely to arise in Mexico, if the threat of revolt and repression is avoided? Will it consist of two or three parties, capable of producing a clear majority in control of government, or will it degenerate into a system of many parties, on the lines of pre-Gaullist France? And even if a two-party or three-party system should emerge, what are the chances that the parties will have sufficient clarity and stability of principle to be able to lead the government on some reasonably clear-cut ideological course?

This last question is worth a moment's consideration. Ideology does not mix easily either with *machismo* or with retreatism. From time to time, ideology demands loyalty to and identification with a losing side; it demands adherence to a position in a period when there may be nothing to be gained by such adherence. Therefore, any active adherent to a given ideology is exposed; he loses some of his ability for swift-footed action. These are characteristics which are largely alien to the behavior of Mexicans since the Revolution, especially in the field of politics. "The Latin American politician," Daniel Cosío Villegas observes from his Mexican vantage point, "avoids taking a clear and firm position towards any problem because he feels that, by committing himself in public to a solution along predetermined lines, he loses maneuverability . . ." [11]

Perhaps a change will occur. If it does not, the chances of developing a stable multiparty system seem small. If a multiparty system should appear in a setting in which no conception of party loyalty existed, the in-party might begin once more to be beguiled by the effort to achieve unanimity. Suspecting that the out-party's various factions can be bought at a price, the in-party might begin looking for policies which are capable in time of capturing all the opposition. In that case, unless the traditional analysis of Mexican national character is rapidly growing obsolete, Mexico could find itself back under another version of the PRI structure — headed by a president ambitious to represent all the political currents of Mexico, and paralyzed by his desire to achieve that ambition.

Other patterns are also possible, of course, though most of them are disconcerting to contemplate. Following the precedent of the Philippines, for instance, a number of parties could develop which were almost indistinguishable in terms of ideology, and which simply acted as rallying points for various special-interest groups which felt free to jump the party fence at will. In a pattern of this sort, as in the present Mexican pattern, the government might be held in thrall by a constant need to buy the loyalties of every special-interest splinter. Hence, the government might find itself unable to follow a clear line of policy in any direction. And this indecision could have results much more disastrous than any in the Philippines, where the government's capacity either to veto or to supplement the activities of the private sector are much more limited than in Mexico.

Economists, as every layman knows, are notoriously bad prognosticators of economic developments. And when they are obliged to project political behavior as well, their reliability can hardly be expected to increase. In the case of Mexico, the problem for the prognosticator is that of predicting how long the Mexican government can continue effectively to respond to the problems its economy confronts, given the fact that those problems are changing rapidly and also that the government considers its safe responses to be sharply limited in character and in direction. At some point soon, it seems likely that the Mexican government's responses will be insufficient to remove roadblocks from the continued growth of the Mexican economy. Then Mexico's leaders will be confronted with a choice of risks. Which risks will they prefer to accept: the risks associated with inadequate economic performance or the risks associated with change in the national decision-making machinery?

APPENDIX

TABLES A-1, A-2, and A-3

TABLE A-1. *Estimates of Gross Domestic Product of*

Year	Total	Agriculture and cattle	Minerals	Oil	Power	Manufactures
1939	22,281.3	5,057.4	1,330.2	429.9	126.0	3,793.0
1940	22,216.2	4,914.7	1,288.6	415.9	130.3	3,992.2
1941	25,506.0	5,663.9	1,292.8	446.1	128.2	4,598.4
1942	26,935.3	6,172.4	1,485.4	395.3	132.5	5,247.8
1943	27,914.8	5,744.2	1,525.5	407.8	137.9	5,533.6
1944	30,037.5	5,842.3	1,377.3	439.4	138.8	5,957.9
1945	31,920.0	5,788.8	1,391.1	497.6	152.4	6,486.2
1946	34,257.9	6,234.8	1,105.7	539.6	165.4	6,893.2
1947	35,524.2	6,297.2	1,360.6	624.2	175.1	6,858.6
1948	36,801.9	7,117.8	1,249.8	623.5	195.7	7,360.8
1949	39,593.3	8,063.3	1,255.4	633.8	214.3	7,837.1
1950	43,299.0	8,919.6	1,385.6	736.1	216.5	8,659.8
1951	48,813.7	9,321.0	1,299.7	797.2	238.8	10,270.5
1952	48,455.1	9,089.1	1,435.5	824.4	260.7	9,872.2
1953	49,654.0	9,740.2	1,409.2	850.2	280.2	9,941.5
1954	54,193.5	11,559.8	1,323.2	939.3	309.8	10,469.7
1955	59,956.2	13,049.4	1,508.9	943.0	342.5	11,595.5
1956	63,001.9	12,772.9	1,477.0	1,071.0	381.5	12,523.0
1957	66,941.9	13,887.8	1,571.3	1,161.0	412.6	13,486.0
1958	69,268.2	15,056.3	1,549.1	1,368.0	449.9	13,620.0
1959	71,970.0	14,815.0	1,583.0	1,534.0	485.0	14,887.0
1960	75,270.0	14,860.0	1,680.0	1,634.0	531.0	16,474.0

Source: U.N. Economic Commission for Latin

Mexico, 1939–1960 (in millions of pesos at 1950 prices)

Construction	Commerce	Transport	Government	Other
390.1	7,077.0	987.0	1,286.0	1,804.7
367.4	7,106.2	995.1	1,228.8	1,777.0
409.2	8,579.9	1,025.6	1,321.7	2,040.2
474.6	8,273.5	1,153.8	1,445.5	2,154.5
536.5	8,886.4	1,337.0	1,571.7	2,234.2
607.4	9,995.4	1,436.7	1,838.4	2,403.9
790.2	10,827.1	1,479.4	1,964.7	2,542.5
823.8	12,475.9	1,550.7	1,728.9	2,739.9
886.6	12,899.2	1,674.8	1,907.5	2,840.4
782.0	12,607.3	1,813.2	2,107.5	2,944.3
764.7	13,526.6	1,872.2	2,259.9	3,166.0
909.3	14,591.8	2,035.0	2,381.4	3,463.9
1,272.1	17,072.4	2,061.5	2,614.8	3,865.7
1,307.6	16,736.7	2,409.4	2,643.4	3,876.1
1,072.1	17,086.9	2,492.9	2,807.7	3,973.1
1,083.9	18,473.2	2,523.4	3,174.4	4,336.8
1,226.6	20,574.4	2,808.3	3,060.1	4,797.5
1,457.6	21,843.9	2,977.0	3,458.0	5,040.0
1,567.6	22,719.4	3,185.0	3,596.0	5,355.2
1,654.9	23,171.8	3,261.0	3,595.0	5,542.2
1,753.0	23,983.0	3,424.0	3,742.0	5,764.0
1,560.0	24,985.0	3,708.0	4,085.0	5,753.0

America, based on official Mexican statistics.

TABLE A-2

Investment by Mexico's Public Sector,[a] 1939–1961

(in millions of pesos)

Year	Total	Agricultural development		Industrial development			Transportation and communication			Housing and other social investment	Other
		Irrigation	Other	Electricity	Petroleum and gas	Other	Roads	Railroads	Other[b]		
1939	233	38	1	3	24	—	51	89	4	22	1
1940	290	36	9	3	57	—	57	89	6	29	4
1941	337	57	2	4	24	—	89	94	6	54	7
1942	464	63	2	10	28	—	155	122	23	54	7
1943	568	83	3	10	26	—	181	175	31	51	8
1944	657	117	7	20	41	2	166	202	20	71	11
1945	848	140	6	16	113	3	184	250	26	91	19
1946	999	189	5	38	111	4	231	275	20	106	20
1947	1,310	228	33	76	85	7	235	417	22	181	26
1948	1,539	249	71	99	168	12	302	339	40	241	18
1949	1,956	260	199	173	247	52	333	353	72	236	31
1950	2,672	372	144	362	398	36	364	605	110	256	25
1951	2,836	502	79	263	425	44	532	544	82	345	20
1952	3,280	548	14	185	369	143	617	683	78	600	43
1953	3,076	506	58	253	456	53	544	661	139	257	149
1954	4,183	604	24	331	901	133	608	728	152	391	311
1955	4,408	602	5	369	1,055	314	591	662	169	597	44
1956	4,571	588	108	285	860	144	556	807	340	856	27
1957	5,628	641	50	294	1,283	160	788	850	380	1,058	124
1958	6,190	644	56	462	1,327	301	848	1,029	500	876	147
1959	6,532	697	151	763	996	228	1,043	1,118	513	821	202
1960	8,376	535	154	1,462	1,141	191	828	1,360	702	1,810	193
1961[c]	10,162	922	35	2,524	1,451	383	1,107	1,162	522	1,823	233

[a] The figures exclude state and local government investment.

[b] These figures include investment in oil pipe lines.

[c] 1961 data are preliminary.

Source: Communication from Secretaría de la Presidencia, Dirección de Inversiones Públicas.

TABLE A-3

Mexico: Financing of Investment, 1939–1960
(in millions of pesos at current prices)

Year	Investment		Savings		
	Public sector	Private sector	Public sector	Private sector	External[a]
1939	265	401	254	304	108
1940	336	457	216	602	−25
1941	384	608	269	565	158
1942	492	524	319	790	−93
1943	626	659	545	1,434	−694
1944	724	1,016	703	1,159	−122
1945	953	1,348	576	2,085	−360
1946	1,130	2,156	1,040	1,765	481
1947	1,431	2,726	977	2,272	908
1948	1,631	2,917	1,242	2,746	560
1949	1,964	3,087	1,980	3,300	−229
1950	2,666	3,294	2,301	3,848	−189
1951	2,981	4,677	2,448	4,280	930
1952	3,417	4,732	2,448	4,280	795
1953	3,254	4,600	2,448	4,280	977
1954	4,365	5,400	2,448	4,280	1,318
1955	4,960	7,600	2,448	4,280	336
1956	4,932	9,060	3,731	8,392	1,869
1957	5,946	10,124	3,830	9,489	2,751
1958	6,516	10,770	3,535	11,533	2,218
1959	7,130	10,944	4,814	12,864	396
1960	8,733	12,435	6,452	12,626	2,090

[a] External savings are measured by the deficit in the current accounts in Mexico's balance of payments. A surplus in current account represents dissavings and is shown with a minus sign (−).
Source: Derived from official Mexican government statistics.

Chapter 1: Mexico Today

1. In Mexico, as in most developing countries, each decennial population census probably improves somewhat in coverage over the prior census. It may be, therefore, that the rate of population growth for Mexico is systematically overstated and the increase in per capita income accordingly understated. Compare Ansley J. Coale and Edgar M. Hoover, *Population Growth and Economic Development in Low-Income Countries* (Princeton: Princeton University Press, 1958), app. B, p. 368, where some of the coverage shortcomings of the 1950 population census for Mexico are described.

2. This kind of figure should not be taken to mean that the average Mexican, in real terms, had only one ninth the living standard of the average United States resident. The official 8-cent rate by which the peso is converted into dollars undervalues the peso in terms of its purchasing power for the consumption needs of the "average" Mexican.

3. Mexico's investment figures require qualification on many counts. Here it is enough to say that the figures exclude changes in inventory, since these are not available separately for the public and private sectors. Annual inventory accumulation for both sectors combined has amounted to another 2½ per cent or so of gross national product in recent years.

4. Rich materials on the structure of agriculture are to be found in Armando González Santos, *La agricultura* (Mexico, D.F.: Fondo de Cultura Económica, 1957), and Ramón Fernández y Fernández and Ricardo Acosta, *Política agrícola* (Mexico, D.F.: Fondo de Cultura Económica, 1961).

5. See Carlos Manuel Castillo, "La economía agrícola en la región de El Bajío," in *Problemas agrícolas e industriales de México,* vol. VIII, nos. 3–4 (1956), pp. 160–162.

6. This is a statement to be taken on faith rather than statistics. The aggregate sales of manufacturing firms overtly identified with one or another of the known groups does not constitute a very large part of total manufacturing output, according to our estimates. But the identified firms do tend to dominate the list of the country's larger companies; and the affiliated banks of the identified firms tend to control much of Mexico's private credit resources.

Chapter 2: Juárez and Díaz

1. See Jesús Silva Herzog, *El pensamiento económico en México* (Mexico, D.F.: Fondo de Cultura Económica, 1947), especially the sections on Tadeo Ortíz, Esteban de Antuñano, José María Luis Mora, Miguel Lerdo de Tejada, Ignacio Ramírez, and Francisco Zarco. Also Víctor Alba, *Las ideas sociales contemporáneas en México* (Mexico, D.F.: Fondo de Cultura Económica, 1960), pp. 29–72.

2. There are numerous accounts of the mercantilist methods of the Spanish Crown before 1821. A brief well-documented version appears in Robert A. Potash, "The Banco de Avío of Mexico" (unpub. diss., Harvard University, 1953), pp. 1–22. Even more valuable for its description of the administrative methods of the Spanish Crown and the early Mexican governments is Wendell K. G. Schaeffer, "National Administration in Mexico: Its Development and Present Status" (unpub. diss., University of California, 1949), pp. 1–61.

3. Potash, "Banco de Avío," p. 29 and *passim*.

4. For an account of some of these obstacles, see Frances Calderón de la Barca, *Life in Mexico* (pp. 334–336 in Everyman's Library edition, London and New York, 1954).

5. J. Fred Rippy, *British Investments in Latin America, 1822–1949* (Minneapolis: University of Minnesota Press, 1959), pp. 17, 97–98, 103–104. The item on Mexican government bonds, 1824–1828, is from J. N. Tattersall, "The Impact of Foreign Investment in Mexico, 1876–1920" (unpub. master's thesis, University of Washington, 1956), pp. 75, 83–84. See also M. D. Bernstein, "The History and Economic Organization of the Mexican Mining Industry, 1890–1940" (unpub. diss., University of Texas, 1951), p. 1310.

6. See, for example, Daniel Cosío Villegas, *La constitución de 1857 y sus críticos* (Mexico, D.F.: Hermes, 1957); Jesús Silva Herzog, "Economic Ideas in Mexico in the Constitutional Congress of 1917," *The Social Sciences in Mexico* (published in Mexico, D.F.), vol. I, no. 1, May 1947; Ralph Roeder, *Juárez and His Mexico* (New York: Viking Press, 1947).

7. The classic work covering the economic aspects of this period of Mexican history is a volume in the monumental series *Historia moderna de México,* directed by Daniel Cosío Villegas. The relevant volume is Francisco R. Calderón, *La república restaurada: La vida económica* (Mexico, D.F.: Hermes, 1955). Of the many sources on which this chapter draws, this is the most important; but my interpretations of the events of the period are not necessarily those which Srs. Cosío Villegas and Calderón would share.

8. Andrés Molina Enríquez, in his classic, *Los grandes problemas nacionales,* offers an illuminating description of the Juárez land laws.

First published in 1908, Molina's work presents a panoramic review of the social aspects of Mexico's history. The full work is republished in *Problemas agrícolas e industriales de México,* supplement to vol. V, no. 1 (January–March 1953).

9. Speech by Limantour in the Chamber of Deputies, reported in *Boletín de la secretaría de fomento,* January 1907, p. 472. See also J. Fred Rippy, *The United States and Mexico* (New York: F. S. Crofts & Co., 1931), pp. 327–328.

10. There are various other interpretations of this event which many Mexicans prefer, including the Marxian view that Limantour was a tool of European capital in a battle against United States capital which had entrenched itself in Mexico through its investments in the railroads. See B. T. Rudenko, "México en vísperas de la revolución democrático-burguesa de 1910–1917," originally in *La revolución mexicana, cuatro estudios soviéticos* (Mexico, D.F.: Ediciones Los Insurgentes, no date), reprinted in *Anales científicos de historia moderna y contemporánea* (Moscow: Academy of Sciences of the USSR, Institute of History, 1955), vol. I.

11. The incident is described in Calderón, *La república restaurada: La vida económica,* pp. 663–665.

12. See Daniel Cosío Villegas, *La cuestión arancelaria en México* (Mexico, D.F.: A. Mijares y Hermano, 1932), pp. 18-20.

13. These estimates are only crude orders of magnitude, and are from diverse sources, with differing coverages and concepts. They are summarized by Tattersall, "Impact of Foreign Investment," table 26, p. 115.

14. The best account of this role is found in one of the as-yet unpublished books of the *Historia moderna de México* series, Fernando Rosenzweig Díaz, *El Porfiriato: La vida económica* (Mexico, D.F.: Hermes).

15. Tattersall, "Impact of Foreign Investment," p. 145.

16. This estimate appears in the Fernando Rosenzweig Díaz manuscript.

17. The gross national product estimates are found, without methodological explanation, in Enrique Pérez López, "El producto nacional," in *México, 50 años de revolución: La economía* (Mexico, D.F.: Fondo de Cultura Económica, 1960), p. 587. An index of the physical volume of production of the manufacturing industries shows a 48 per cent increase in the same decade; see Gonzalo Robles, "El desarrollo industrial," in the same source, p. 197. The population data used in the per capita calculation are from Secretaría de Economía, Dirección General de Estadística, *Estadísticas sociales del Porfiriato, 1877–1910* (Mexico, D.F.: Talleres Gráficos de la Nación, 1956), p. 7.

18. The literature on this period is extraordinary, both in quantity

and in intensity of sentiment. There are a number of works which manage to retain some measure of objectivity, however. See, for instance, George McC. McBride, *The Land Systems of Mexico* (New York: American Geographic Society, 1923), and Eyler N. Simpson, *The Ejido — Mexico's Way Out* (Chapel Hill: University of North Carolina Press, 1937). The 1908 work of Andrés Molina Enríquez, *Los grandes problemas nacionales,* cited earlier, is also most helpful in the richness of the materials it presents.

19. Secretaría de Economía, *Estadísticas sociales del Porfiriato,* table 85, p. 217.

20. Frank Tannenbaum, *Mexico, the Struggle for Peace and Bread* (New York: Knopf, 1956), pp. 137–141.

21. This was a point of view shared by intellectuals in a number of Latin American countries at the time. See Albert O. Hirschman, "Ideologies of Economic Development in Latin America," in *Latin American Issues,* ed. Albert O. Hirschman (New York: Twentieth Century Fund, 1961), pp. 4–9.

22. In the censuses of 1895, 1900, 1910, the population enumerated in each state is classified according to place of birth — whether in the state where enumerated or elsewhere. In the 1895 census, 6.5 per cent of the population was reported as having been born outside the state in which they were living; in 1900, the comparable figure was 6.9 per cent; and in 1910, 7.8 per cent. Secretaría de Economía, *Estadísticas sociales del Porfiriato,* p. 73.

23. These conclusions are suggested by data which appear in the forthcoming volume, *El Porfiriato: La vida económica* (see note 14, above).

24. Index computed by the author, using 1900–01 prices. Domestic food production is based on corn, wheat, and bean production data, after omitting doubtful data for a number of years. Imports and exports of food are based on figures in El Colegio de México, *Comercio exterior de México, 1877–1911* (Mexico, D.F.: Talleres Gráficos de Impresiones Modernas, 1960). Lest any erroneous notions develop regarding the consumption standards of the period, the figures covered by the data suggest that the intake of basic foods was less than two pounds per capita per day. No doubt, these figures missed much subsistence production, but the widespread impression that much of Mexico lived on a bare subsistence diet at the time is not controverted by the available figures.

Chapter 3: The Revolution and After, 1910–1940

1. The literature on the ideology of the Mexican Revolution is staggering in its quantity. Reasonably objective commentaries, how-

ever, have been rare until very recently. For two enlightening commentaries, see Moisés González Navarro, "La ideología de la revolución mexicana," *Historia mexicana, 40,* April–June 1961, pp. 628 ff; and Daniel Cosío Villegas, "The Mexican Revolution, Then and Now," in *Change in Latin America: The Mexican and Cuban Revolutions* (Lincoln, Neb.: University of Nebraska Press, 1961), pp. 23 ff.

2. Ironically, Daniel Cosío Villegas, pp. 26–27, attributes this result to the admiration of one of the drafters for the strong presidency of Porfirio Díaz.

3. See Víctor Alba, *Las ideas sociales contemporáneas en México* (Mexico, D.F.: Fondo de Cultura Económica, 1960), pp. 97 ff.

4. The analysis which follows makes only occasional reference to the role of the organized labor movement in Mexico's development, perhaps less than the subject deserves. For a good succinct account of the subject, see Simon Rottenberg, "México: Trabajo y desarrollo económico," *Foro internacional,* July–September 1961, pp. 85–112.

5. The anecdotal materials in Ernest Gruening, *Mexico and Its Heritage* (New York: Appleton-Century-Crofts, 1928), pp. 335–390, are of particular interest.

6. Robert E. Scott, *Mexican Government in Transition* (Urbana: University of Illinois Press, 1959), pp. 275–277.

7. Henry Bamford Parkes, *A History of Mexico* (Boston: Houghton Mifflin, 1938), pp. 384–385 and 394–395.

8. Edwin Lieuwen, *Arms and Politics in Latin America* (New York: Praeger, 1960), pp. 106–117.

9. A good description of the process is found in Frank R. Brandenburg, "Mexico: An Experiment in One-Party Democracy" (unpub. diss., University of Pennsylvania, 1955), p. 80 and *passim.*

10. See the address (University of Virginia, July 1935) of Ramón Beteta, then an official in the Cárdenas administration, entitled "Economic Aspects of the Six-Year Plan," reproduced both in Spanish and English in *Programa económico y social de México (una controversia):* *Economic and Social Program of Mexico (a Controversy),* ed. Ramón Beteta (Mexico, D.F., 1935), esp. pp. 44 ff.

11. For a succinct history of Mexico's land reform program, see Edmundo Flores, *Tratado de economía agrícola* (Mexico, D.F.: Fondo de Cultura Económica, 1961), pp. 300–345. Also Salomon Eckstein, "Collective Farming in Mexico" (unpub. diss., Harvard University, 1961), esp. pp. 65–187.

12. William P. Tucker, *The Mexican Government Today* (Minneapolis: University of Minnesota Press, 1957), p. 31; and Parkes, pp. 400–401.

13. A comprehensive summary of the disputes will be found in J. Richard Powell, *The Mexican Petroleum Industry* (Berkeley: University of California Press, 1956). For an eloquent summary of the

Mexican viewpoint see Jesús Silva Herzog, *Nueve estudios mexicanos* (Mexico, D.F.: Imprenta Universitaria, 1953), pp. 139–221.

14. José E. Iturriaga, *La estructura social y cultural de México* (Mexico, D.F.: Fondo de Cultura Económica, 1951), pp. 28, 60. The existence of this trend was not always apparent to contemporary observers; see Marjorie Ruth Clark, *Organized Labor in Mexico* (Chapel Hill: University of North Carolina Press, 1934), p. 152.

15. The official data on production of corn are found in Joaquín Loredo Goytortua, "Producción y productividad agrícolas," in *México, 50 años de revolución: La economía* (Mexico, D.F.: Fondo de Cultura Económica, 1960), p. 122. The data on the agricultural sector as a whole appear at p. 587 of the same book in an article by Enrique Pérez López, "El producto nacional."

16. Same book, p. 197, in an article by Gonzalo Robles, "El desarrollo industrial."

17. The growth of manufacturing in the 1920's was considerable, but one dare not be too precise about the amount. In the book just cited, one official source (Gonzalo Robles, "El desarrollo industrial," table 1, p. 197) reports a 40 per cent increase and another official source (Enrique Pérez López, "El producto nacional," table 3, p. 587) reports a 100 per cent increase.

18. For an interesting account of the role of the Monterrey community in this process, see Mary Catherine McGee, *Monterrey, Mexico: Internal Patterns and External Relations,* University of Chicago Department of Geography, December 1958.

19. Systematic studies of this phenomenon in Mexico relate to a somewhat later period, principally the 1940's. For an account of the cultural ties to the land, see Oscar Lewis, *Tepotzlan, Village in Mexico* (New York: Henry Holt, 1960), p. 61. For an analysis of the causes of the drift from the land, see Wilbert E. Moore, *Industrialization and Labor — Social Aspects of Economic Development* (Ithaca, N.Y.: Cornell University Press, 1951); also Comisión de Planeación Industrial de la Cámara Nacional de la Industria de Transformación, *Proceso ocupacional* (Mexico, D.F.: published by CNIT, 1956), pp. 131, 156, 162–163.

20. U.N. Economic Commission for Latin America, *Economic Survey of Latin America, 1949* (New York: United Nations, 1951), table 6, p. 414.

21. The regeneration of agricultural output may have been a good deal stronger than the official figures indicate. Or else the reopening of internal transportation in Mexico may have made it possible to stretch a given output much further. In any event, between 1925 and 1940, during a period when public health measures were still in their infancy, the mortality rate of children under one year of age dropped

from over 200 to about 110 per thousand, suggesting the existence of a greater food supply.

22. *Trimestre de barómetros económicos,* March 1948, tables 7, 8, and 9, pp. 47–49.

23. U.N., *Economic Survey of Latin America, 1949,* table 10A, p. 424.

Chapter 4: Economic Policies and Performance since 1940

1. For an invaluable guide to available data on the Mexican economy, see Secretaría de Industria y Comercio, Dirección General de Estadística, *Catálogo general de las estadísticas nacionales* (Mexico, D.F.: Talleres Gráficos de la Nación, 1960).

2. Of all the figures making up Mexico's gross product data, those on "commerce" seem the least reliable. There are some indications, for instance, that the "commerce" data given in Appendix Table A-1 and shown graphically in Chart 2 grossly overstate the importance of that sector in the Mexican economy for 1950. See I. M. Navarrete, *La distribución del ingreso y el desarrollo económico de México* (Mexico, D.F.: Universidad Nacional, 1960), table 1, p. 43. Her table shows that the contribution of "commerce" to the gross domestic product of Mexico in 1950 was about 22 per cent of the total, whereas the figures in our Table A-1 show "commerce" as contributing about 34 per cent to Mexico's gross product. Unofficial judgments inside Mexican government circles are that the actual facts lie somewhere between these two limits. If the "commerce" figures in Table A-1 are overstated for 1950 they are overstated for all the other years, in view of the method of construction of the commerce series.

3. For a summary of data on the subject, see Xavier de la Riva Rodríguez, "Salubridad y asistencia médico-social," in *México, 50 años de revolución: La vida social* (Mexico, D.F.: Fondo de Cultura Económica, 1961), pp. 420–424.

4. Between 1939 and 1949, nominal wages in 24 Mexican industries went up 160 per cent while the Mexico City cost-of-living index (the only cost-of-living index available in Mexico) went up about 225 per cent. See D. G. López and J. F. Noyola Vásquez, "Los salarios reales en México, 1939–1950," *El trimestre económico,* April–June 1951, pp. 201–209. Also Adolf Sturmthal, "Economic Development, Income Distribution, and Capital Formation in Mexico," *Journal of Political Economy,* June 1955, pp. 183–201. Neither the cost-of-living index nor the nominal wage measure is to be taken too literally, since both measures are riddled with statistical pitfalls. For instance, the wage measures took no account of increasing fringe benefits, and the cost-of-living index took no account of the differences between the

official ceiling prices and actual prices in some articles. It is not easy to say where the net bias lies.

5. Between 1951 and 1959, in fifteen industries — comprising 80 per cent of the payrolls and employment of the 24-industry group mentioned in the preceding note — wages rose by 125 per cent. In the same period, the Mexico City cost-of-living index went up 90 per cent.

6. Figures on the labor force come from Víctor L. Urquidi, "Problemas fundamentales de la economía mexicana," *Cuadernos americanos,* no. 1 of 1961, p. 99. Somewhat different figures are provided by Nacional Financiera, the difference apparently being due to questions of definition.

7. A test of the effects of shifts in industry mix and salary-worker mix for 15 manufacturing industries was undertaken for the period 1951 to 1959. If the 1951 mix had been retained in 1959, the total nominal compensation paid by these industries would have been about 15 per cent lower than it, in fact, proved to be — a difference which was largely due to the shift toward the salaried sector.

8. I. M. Navarrete, *La distribución del ingreso y el desarrollo económico de México,* tables 6 and 7, pp. 72–73.

9. P. Lamartine Yates, *El desarrollo regional de México* (Mexico, D.F.: Banco de México, 1961), tables 14 and 15, pp. 70–71. The Yates figures show that the 1960 per capita gross product in Mexico's poorest state, Oaxaca, was about one tenth that of the Federal District, which contains Mexico City. It is doubtful that the difference in welfare terms is that large, in view of the inadequate way in which imputed income is handled in calculations of this sort; but no one can question the existence of very large differences.

10. The Navarrete data, dealing with income classes, are equivocal on the question whether Mexico's income distribution was growing more egalitarian; they show that an upper-middle-income group between 1950 and 1957 was expanding in numbers at a rate faster than the richest or the poorest segments of the income distribution. The Navarrete study graphically underlines two problems which exist in any analysis of changes in the income distribution of developing countries. First, the consumption habits of the low-income groups are so utterly different from those of the upper-income groups that it is almost useless to deflate the incomes of the different groups by the same price deflator; yet, as in the Navarrete study, this is what the investigator is usually forced to do because of the absence of adequate price and consumption data. Second, the problem of imputed income, which is of great importance at the low end of the income scale, cannot be dealt with at all and, in the Navarrete study, simply has to be neglected.

11. See Yates, tables 43 and 44, pp. 137, 146. His table 43 presents the results of an ingenious calculation of "welfare," based on mortality

rates, literacy, teacher availability, and similar factors, showing once more that there has been a slight catching-up of welfare levels in the poorer areas.

12. An analysis of Mexico's export and import pattern in this period appears in U.N. Economic Commission for Latin America, *Economic Survey of Latin America, 1949* (New York: United Nations, 1951), chap. ix, pp. 391–487, and in "La industrialización de México," *Trimestre de barómetros económicos,* March 1948, pp. 36–57.

13. From 1939 to 1945, the reported net movement of capital was an inflow of 135 million United States dollars. At the same time, "errors and omissions" in Mexico's balance of payments — which in such a period usually consists of concealed capital movements — came to over $290 million. The figures for this period are based on the *Combined Mexican Working Party Report of the International Bank for Reconstruction and Development* (Baltimore: Johns Hopkins Press, 1953). The data are summarized in Barry N. Siegel, *Inflación y desarrollo: Las experiencias de México* (Mexico, D.F.: Centro de Estudios Monetarios Latinoamericanos, 1960), table V, p. 92.

14. For data on the sources of change in Mexico's money supplies, see Siegel, *Inflación y desarrollo,* pp. 84, 91.

15. For an account of this period, see Víctor L. Urquidi, "Tres lustros de experiencia monetaria en México: Algunas enseñanzas," in *Memoria del segundo congreso mexicano de ciencias sociales,* Oct. 22, 1945, Mexico, D.F., pp. 423–511.

16. A revealing source on the problems and policies of this era is the addresses of Mexico's finance ministers before national bankers' conventions. These have been assembled in a single volume for the period 1934 to 1958 and published by the ministry in 1958 under the title *Discursos* (Mexico, D.F.: Secretaría de Hacienda y Crédito Público, 1958).

17. For some illuminating comments on these points, see Simon Rottenberg, "México: Trabajo y desarrollo económico," *Foro internacional,* July–September 1961, pp. 94–101.

18. A brief review of tariff protection in Mexico from Cárdenas to Alemán appears in Sanford A. Mosk, *Industrial Revolution in Mexico* (Berkeley: University of California Press, 1950), pp. 69–71.

19. Adolfo Orive Alba, "Las obras de irrigación," in *México, 50 años de revolución: La economía* (Mexico, D.F.: Fondo de Cultura Económica, 1960), table 6, p. 354.

20. This impression was sharpened by some figures produced in 1953 by the IBRD Combined Mexican Working Party, purporting to show that profits in the Mexican economy had risen from 27 per cent of national income in 1940 to 41 per cent in 1950. See p. 87 of the *Combined Mexican Working Party Report,* cited earlier. Later on, more complete information indicated that the relative importance of

profits probably had not changed during the decade after all. See. I. M. Navarrete (our note 2, above), table 4, p. 56.

21. This conclusion is stated with some reservation. The technical problems of measuring gross-product change of a country such as Mexico are so great that any comparisons of long-term growth rates are exceedingly vulnerable. The reader should not be utterly surprised, therefore, if some subsequent revision of Mexico's gross-product data increases the growth rate for this period. The important point here, however, is that the Mexican government and the Mexican public believed by 1958 that its growth rate had slowed considerably. This belief was important in the shaping of policies in the administration that followed.

22. Contemporary journals were filled with reactions to the devaluation. Illustrative of the current comment of the time was the May 1954 issue of *Siempre* which was crowded with references to what one author called the "disillusion, disgust, and almost desperation of the people."

23. Data supplied by Secretaría de Agricultura y Ganadería, Dirección de Economía Agrícola.

24. The calculation is based on data produced by the U.N. Economic Commission for Latin America.

25. U.S. Department of Commerce, *U.S. Business Investments in Foreign Countries* (Washington: Government Printing Office, 1960), p. 110, shows that in 1957 the manufacturing subsidiaries and branches of United States companies in Mexico sold 643 million U.S. dollars worth of goods. Data on p. 115 of the same publication afford a basis for estimating that about 257 million of the total was value added by these companies. Meanwhile, the total value added by Mexico's manufacturing industry in 1957 appears to have been 1,598 million U.S. dollars, according to Banco de México data.

26. In a study of the technical ties between Mexican and foreign firms undertaken in 1960–61, W. Paul Strassman found that of 35 firms which were not United States subsidiaries, 13 had technical assistance contracts with a foreign manufacturer and 10 had contracts with foreign consulting engineers or consulting scientists. The Strassman sample is deliberately weighted in favor of the more modern and technologically progressive Mexican enterprises.

27. For example, in 1957, United States-controlled plants in Mexico imported less than 83 millions of the 406 millions of materials, measured in United States dollars, which they bought in that year. *U.S. Business Investments*, pp. 118–121.

28. *Joint International Business Ventures*, ed. Wolfgang G. Friedmann and George Kalmanoff (New York: Columbia University Press, 1961), pp. 27–28, 46–50. The tendency was most evident in manufacturing, where the pressure by the government was greatest.

29. Stanford G. Ross and John B. Christensen, *Tax Incentives for Industry in Mexico* (Cambridge, Mass.: Harvard University Law School, 1959), pp. 52–54.

30. A good indication of the government's concern over the inflationary consequences of these expenditures is found in the presentations of Antonio Ortiz Mena, Secretario de Hacienda y Crédito Público, in his speeches before the annual bankers' conventions of 1959, 1960, and 1961, published in separate pamphlets by the ministry's Dirección General de Prensa and regularly printed in *Comercio exterior*, the monthly review of the Banco Nacional de Comercio Exterior.

31. A word of caution is in order here, however. The figures officially labeled "public investment" probably represent sums authorized rather than sums actually spent. This could constitute a considerable source of year-to-year error and may even be a major source of error over the longer run.

32. Summaries of these measures appear in *Business Week*, March 4, 1961, pp. 84–87.

33. Illustrations of the way in which various United States firms have responded to these pressures are provided in *Business International*, Aug. 25, 1961, pp. 1–3.

34. For typical illustrations of efforts to reassure Mexico's business groups, see the Mexican newspaper *Excelsior*, March 15, 1961, p. 1, reporting a speech by the minister of finance; *Excelsior*, March 21, 1961, p. 1, reporting a speech by the minister of commerce and industry; *Excelsior*, May 10, 1961, p. 1, a similar speech by the minister in charge of the *Patrimonio* ministry; *Novedades*, Aug. 2, 1961, p. 1, reporting a like speech by a director of Nacional Financiera; and *Excelsior*, Aug. 4, 1961, another speech by the minister of commerce and industry, made expressly in the name of the president.

Chapter 5: The *Políticos* and the *Técnicos* since 1940

1. He is much less likely to voice this heresy publicly than privately. But even public expressions of this viewpoint are encountered from time to time. See Moisés González Navarro, "La ideología de la revolución mexicana," *Historia mexicana*, April–June 1961, pp. 635–636; Jan Bazant, "Tres revoluciones mexicanas," *Historia mexicana*, October–December 1960; also an interview with Jesús Silva Herzog, reported in *Novedades*, supplement, Nov. 1, 1960, p. 2.

2. President López Mateos' redistributions of land promise to go well above 10 million hectares by the end of his administration.

3. See President López Mateos' *Informe a la nación* of Sept. 1, 1960; the relevant passages on the problem of corruption in the

agrarian reform program are reproduced in Edmundo Flores, *Tratado de economía agrícola* (Mexico, D.F.: Fondo de Cultura Económica, 1961), p. 323. See also the President's references to the same subject in a speech in Michoacán, reported in *Excelsior*, Aug. 6, 1962, p. 1.

4. One of the common devices is for the *de facto* owner of a large tract of land to break it up into parcels of legal size, register the parcels in the names of nominees, and accept irrevocable powers of attorney from these nominees.

5. The number of rural schools went up from 17,561 in 1940 to 24,566 in 1959; but the number of pupils did not increase as much. Besides, the drop-out rate between the first and sixth grades of the rural schools continued disconcertingly high, so that the number in the sixth grade was less than 3 per cent of that in the first. Secretaría de Industria y Comercio, Dirección General de Estadística, *Anuario estadístico de los Estados Unidos Mexicanos 1958–1959* (Mexico, D.F.: Talleres Gráficos de la Nación, 1960), table 94, p. 177.

6. Wendell K. G. Schaeffer's account of the degree of autonomy of the ministries and the decentralized agencies of the Mexican government during the 1940's is most illuminating. See his work, "National Administration in Mexico: Its Development and Present Status" (unpub. diss., University of California, 1949), p. 88 and *passim*.

7. See Sanford A. Mosk, *Industrial Revolution in Mexico* (Berkeley: University of California Press, 1950), pp. 89–91.

8. The section on the parties and the presidents has drawn upon Schaeffer's dissertation and the following other sources: Robert E. Scott, *Mexican Government in Transition* (Urbana: University of Illinois Press, 1959); William P. Tucker, *The Mexican Government Today* (Minneapolis: University of Minnesota Press, 1957); Frank R. Brandenburg, "Mexico: An Experiment in One-Party Democracy" (unpub. diss., University of Pennsylvania, 1955); Leon V. Padgett, "Popular Participation in the Mexican One-Party System" (unpub. diss., Northwestern University, 1955).

9. The difference between claimed membership and actual membership is obviously considerable. Compare Scott, *Mexican Government in Transition,* pp. 171–172.

10. A much harsher description of the separation between the technician and the politician in Mexico appears in Schaeffer, "National Administration in Mexico," p. 135: "The administrator has been smothered with routine, blocked by ignorance, and benumbed by the knowledge that initiative will go unrewarded unless it happens to coincide with the political plans of the small coterie of officials surrounding the president." Schaeffer's description, however, was written in 1949 and is somewhat more appropriate to the 1940's and 1950's than to the 1960's.

11. In 1961, Prebisch floated a series of new elaborations which

have begun to be assimilated into the policy preferences of most Mexican technicians. Among these are proposals for promoting Latin American exports in manufactured products by increased investment and subsidy, for promoting import substitution by domestic subsidy instead of import restriction, and various other ideas. The views of Prebisch pre-1961 will be found in U.N. Economic Commission for Latin America, *Economic Survey of Latin America, 1949* (New York: United Nations, 1951), chaps. i to v, and *Economic Survey of Latin America, 1954* (New York: United Nations, 1955), pp. 3–22. The most important elaboration of 1961 appears in a signed article entitled "Economic Development or Monetary Stability: The False Dilemma," in the U.N. periodical *Economic Bulletin for Latin America,* vol. VI, no. 1, March 1961.

12. For a sampling of the views of Mexico's leading *técnicos,* see Víctor L. Urquidi, *Viabilidad económica de América Latina* (Mexico, D.F.: Fondo de Cultura Económica, 1962); Horacio Flores de la Peña, "Estabilidad y desarrollo," *El trimestre económico,* July–September 1957, p. 247; Alfredo Navarrete, Jr., "El crecimiento económico de México: Perspectivas y problemas," *El trimestre económico,* April–June 1958, p. 204; *Problemas del desarrollo económico mexicano, mesa redonda,* ed. Jorge Espinosa de los Reyes (Mexico, D.F.: Editorial Cultura, 1958); and Ernesto Fernández Hurtado, "A propósito de 'el peso mexicano,' " *Problemas agrícolas e industriales de México,* vol. V, no. 1 (January–March 1953), esp. p. 141.

13. A somewhat similar point is made regarding Latin American economic technicians in general by Daniel Cosío Villegas in his "Política y política económica en América Latina," *Foro internacional,* April–June 1961. He says in part: ". . . the Latin American economist is not in general a man of deep convictions . . . Besides, if one has to judge by what one sees directly in his own country, there are grounds for fearing that the great majority of the Latin American economists have been just as much opportunists as the politicians they serve . . ." (p. 510). Although this judgment is somewhat harsher than any to which I would subscribe with respect to the Mexican *técnicos,* it obviously supports the validity of the assumption in the text.

14. A characteristic article appears in *Mañana,* July 18, 1959, p. 22, under the title, as translated, "The Dishonesty of Public Officials." The article reproduces the prologue of Mexico's "beautiful law" — the Law of the Responsibilities of the Functionaries and Employees of the Federation — and alludes to the 72 crimes listed in the law. After noting that only minor employees such as mailmen and watchmen are ever tried under the law, the article claims: "But judicial proceedings against important officers and employees are very rare, even though the daily systematic commission of at least 60 of the 72 crimes listed in the law is palpable." An earlier work which dwells on the subject —

a classic — is Lucio Mendieta y Núñez, *La administración pública en México* (Mexico, D.F.: Imprenta Universitaria, 1942).

Chapter 6: Leadership Ideology in the Private Sector since 1940

1. The official census figures show that in both 1910 and 1950, the foreign-born population was less than 1 per cent of Mexico's total population.

2. These findings correspond nicely with an analysis of the characteristics of England's innovators during its Industrial Revolution, presented in Everett E. Hagen, *On the Theory of Social Change* (Homewood, Ill.: Dorsey Press, 1962), table 13-3, p. 301.

3. It is a sad fact that most current descriptions of the upper-class business executive in Mexico do not go beyond the Diego Rivera murals of thirty years ago, either in subtlety or documentation. A characteristic profile appears in an article by Arturo González Cosío, "Clases y estratos sociales," in *México, 50 años de revolución: La vida social* (Mexico, D.F.: Fondo de Cultura Económica, 1961), esp. pp. 72–74. See also Carlos Fuentes, *Where the Air Is Clear,* trans. Sam Hileman (New York: Ivan Obolensky, 1960), pp. 71–90, 215–222, and Luis Spota, *Casi el paraíso,* 6th ed. (Mexico, D.F.: Fondo de Cultura Económica, 1960), pp. 150–163, 332–336, 348–359, 393–395. One of the sketches in Oscar Lewis, *Five Families* (New York: Basic Books, 1959), pp. 293–350, though not claiming to be "representative," is also in this vein. An occasional work, however, does try to deal with the Mexican businessman's personality as a serious subject for study and generalization. See Francisco González Pineda, *El mexicano: Psicología de su destructividad* (Mexico, D.F.: Editorial Pax, 1961), pp. 232 ff.

4. The discussion of leadership characteristics draws heavily on Francisco González Pineda, just cited, pp. 62–63, 67–68, 258–259; Samuel Ramos, *El perfil del hombre y la cultura de México* (Mexico, D.F.: Espasa-Calpe Argentina, 1951), pp. 54–56; Aniceto Aramoni, *Psicoanálisis de la dinámica de un pueblo* (Mexico, D.F.: Imprenta Universitaria, 1961), pp. 125, 133–141, 163–169; Santiago Ramírez, *El mexicano: Psicología de sus motivaciones,* 3rd ed. (Mexico, D.F.: Editorial Pax, 1961), pp. 62, 67, 85, 98; and Octavio Paz, *The Labyrinth of Solitude* (New York: Grove Press, 1961).

5. This reaction is not dissimilar to the behavior of immigrant groups in any new — therefore, presumptively hostile — environment. It was characteristic, for instance, throughout the nineteenth and early twentieth centuries in the United States.

6. The pattern portrayed above is summed up by Octavio Paz, *Labyrinth of Solitude,* discussing the loneliness and sense of solitude of the Mexican.

7. A full development of the characteristics of the entrepreneur and his environment as they relate to the development process will be found in Hagen's *On the Theory of Social Change.* Hagen's work is unusual in the degree of emphasis it places on noneconomic factors as the explanation for economic change. His bibliography is especially helpful for economists who wish to become familiar with the work of sociologists, anthropologists, and historians in this field.

8. From an informal memorandum in 1961 from W. Paul Strassman to Benjamin Higgins, Professor of Economics, University of Texas.

9. A word of caution is needed here. Francisco González Pineda, in his work cited earlier, offers no such optimistic view of trends in Mexico. His descriptions of Mexican society in general stress a "growing tendency" toward instability (pp. 134–135); and his description of the psychology of the businessman is innocent of any of Strassman's emphases (pp. 232 ff).

10. *Conferencias de mesa redonda,* ed. Manuel Germán Parra (Mexico, D.F.: Cooperativa Talleres de la Nación, 1949).

11. Merle Kling, in his *A Mexican Interest Group in Action* (Englewood Cliffs, N.J.: Prentice-Hall, 1961), p. 10, reports that a "leading member" of the staff of a right-wing Mexican business group, Instituto de Investigaciones Sociales y Económicas, explicitly endorsed this tactic.

12. See, for instance, Confederación de Cámaras Nacionales de Comercio e Industria (CONCANACOIN), *Análisis económico nacional, 1934–1940.* This document expresses very well the viewpoint not only of the industrial and commercial groups but also of the bankers. During the Cárdenas administration, CONCANACO and CONCAMIN had been required to merge into the single organization cited in the title, but they became separate groups again in 1940.

13. See CONCANACOIN, *La situación real de los ferrocarriles nacionales de México* (Mexico, D. F., 1938).

14. See CONCANACO, *Problemas derivados de la intervención del estado en la economía* (Mexico, D.F., 1946). The document was the outcome of a convention organized by CONCANACO with the participation of the Asociación de Banqueros de México.

15. *Ibid.,* pp. 7–8. At a slightly later stage, in 1953, some of the ideological leaders of CONCANACO formed the Instituto de Investigaciones Sociales y Económicas, a small group devoted to propaganda in favor of an almost naïve form of political liberalism. See Kling, *Mexican Interest Group,* cited above.

16. This is more a summary than a translation of a specific passage. The Patronal position appears in Confederación Patronal de la República Mexicana, *La organización patronal en México* (Mexico, D.F., 1947). A summary of the Patronal position is given by Isaac

Guzmán Valdivia, "El movimiento patronal," in *México, 50 años de revolución: La vida social* (Mexico, D.F.: Fondo de Cultura Económica, 1961), pp. 312–313.

17. For some years, the issue practically paralyzed the work of the Instituto de Investigaciones Sociales y Económicas, mentioned in note 15, above. Eventually, however, the liberals won out. See Kling, *Mexican Interest Group*, p. 2.

18. A fairly good guide to the preoccupations of CONCANACO is provided by the contents of its weekly letter, *Carta semanal*. My observations are based in part upon a perusal and analysis of the contents of these weekly letters after 1950.

19. Illustrative of CONCANACO's repeated condemnations of state intervention was its comprehensive statement entitled "Puntos de vista institucionales sobre la intervención del estado en actividades comerciales," in its *Carta semanal* of June 27, 1953, pp. 6–8.

20. *Revista de economía*, Nov. 15, 1945, pp. 5–6.

21. However, note Sanford A. Mosk's description of the CNIT, in which he suggests the rise of a new and hitherto unfamiliar type of businessman, the "New Group of Mexico," genuinely devoted to the prosecution of Revolutionary goals. See his *Industrial Revolution in Mexico* (Berkeley: University of California Press, 1950), pp. 21–52. Writing in the late 1940's, Mosk foresaw a rapid growth in the influence of this group, which even then he regarded as considerable.

22. CONCANACO, *Carta semanal*, July 3, 1954, p. 8; reiterated in substance in the issue of Dec. 18, 1954, p. 2.

23. CONCANACO, *Carta semanal*, Sept. 29, 1956, pp. 1, 5.

24. Summarized in *Mañana*, Nov. 18, 1961, pp. 22–23.

25. Reported in *El universal*, May 22, 1962, p. 1.

26. José Luis Ceceña, "Las inversiones norteamericanas en nuestro país," *Siempre*, May 30, 1962, supplement no. 15.

27. CONCANACO, *Carta semanal*, Sept. 24, 1955, p. 7. CONCANACO's decision to oppose uncontrolled foreign investment in commercial activities established a clear ideological difference between that organization and the political liberals on the right. The latter, speaking through their Instituto de Investigaciones Sociales y Económicas, continued to welcome foreign commercial capital. To emphasize the disinterested ideological character of its position, the Instituto spoke through the voice of its vice-president, who headed one of Mexico's principal department stores and was one of the main competitors of Sears Roebuck & Company in Mexico.

28. CONCANACO, *Carta semanal*, Jan. 21, 1956; also Daniel Morales, "Deben reglamentarse las inversiones extranjeras en México," in *Mañana*, May 9, 1959, pp. 18 ff.

29. For the CONCAMIN position, see "La iniciativa privada," interview with Juan Sánchez Navarro in *Novedades*, Supplement: Nov. 19,

1960, p. 8; also Morales, just cited, p. 20. For CNIT, see José Domingo Lavín, "Revisión del problema de las inversiones extranjeras directas," *Ciencias políticas y sociales,* October–December 1959, pp. 545–564.

30. The ratio of Mexico's foreign trade to its domestic output of goods in fact grew considerably from the early 1940's to the early 1950's, then declined somewhat in the next ten years. But the more important trend contributing to the growing interest of organized business in domestic markets may be the rapidly improving organization and widening opportunities for increasing returns to scale in those markets.

Chapter 7: The Mexican Dilemma

1. U.N. Economic Commission for Europe, *Economic Survey of Europe in 1957* (Geneva: United Nations, 1958), chap. v, p. 8, table 5 ("Imports of raw materials . . .").

2. U.N. Economic Commission for Latin America, *The Latin American Common Market* (United Nations, 1959), table 4, p. 59.

3. Louis O. Delwart, *The Future of Latin American Exports to the United States: 1965 and 1970* (Washington: National Planning Association, 1960), table 15, p. 43.

4. *Latin American Common Market,* table 4, p. 59; and *Economic Survey of Europe in 1957,* chap. v, p. 6, table 4 ("Imports of foodstuffs . . .").

5. All three sources cited in the above notes offer such estimates. See *Economic Survey of Europe in 1957,* chap. v, p. 11, table 6; *Latin American Common Market,* table 3, p. 58; Delwart, *Future of Latin American Exports,* tables 4, 6, and 8, pp. 20, 23, and 25.

6. Delwart (p. 58) makes relatively optimistic comments on the subject.

7. An eloquent and informed analysis of Mexico's export opportunities in manufactured goods appears in a talk by Calvin P. Blair, "United States Economic Growth and Markets for Mexican Exports," before the Second Annual United States–Mexico Trade and Investment Institute, San Antonio, Tex., mimeo., Oct. 21, 1960.

8. See Víctor L. Urquidi, *Viabilidad económica de América Latina* (Mexico, D.F.: Fondo de Cultura Económica, 1962), pp. 125–136.

9. These figures exclude the imports of the frontier areas and the free zones. In the long run, these areas may be denied their easy access to United States products, in which case another wave of import-substitution may be possible. But for the present it is safer to assume that the near-impossibility of policing the Mexican–United States border and the high overland costs of servicing these areas from the Mexican center will operate to leave these areas in their present status.

10. U.S. Department of Commerce, *U.S. Business Investments in Foreign Countries* (Washington: Government Printing Office, 1960), pp. 115, 118, 121.

11. Daniel Cosío Villegas, "Política y política económica en América Latina," *Foro internacional,* April–June 1961, p. 503.

Index

Abegglan, James C., 156
Agriculture: output by *1960*, 5; public investment in, 7, 198; and private sector, 15–18, 86; credit, 16–17, 55, 83; U.S. investment, 22; under Díaz, 38, 49, 52, 53; reform in *1920's*, 71; and *1917* constitution, 75; output *1910–1920*, 79, 80–81; output in *1930's*, 82–84; output *1940–1960*, 90–91, 124–125, 126, 196; under Alemán, 102–103, 111, 124–125; and *técnicos*, 137, 144; relation between public and private sectors, 154; exports, 180–181. *See also* Ejidal farmers; Hacienda system; Land policy
Aguascalientes, 34
Alemán, Miguel: term of office, 66; his presidency, 99–108, 109, 114, 116, 123–124, 190; agrarian program, 124–125; welfare program, 125–127; and foreign investment, 127–128; and private sector, 161–162
Alliance for Progress, 8
Altos Hornos de México, S.A., 96
Apizaco, 41
Argentina, 1, 4
Army, 59, 66, 67, 69
Asociación de Banqueros, 18, 19, 170–171
Avila Camacho, Manuel: term of office, 66; his presidency, 94–99, 101–103, 107, 116, 123; agrarian program, 124–125; welfare program, 125–127; and foreign investment, 127–128; and political organization, 129–130; and the

Church, 134; attitude of business to, 164

Bailleres, Raúl, 20
Baja California, 49
Balance of payments: from *1939* to *1961*, 105, 106, 112, 113, 122; and CONCANACO, 169; and foreign lending, 186
Banco de Crédito Ejidal, 72
Banco de Londres y México, 18, 20
Banco de México: and credit, 18, 101, 151; its creation, 68, 74; under Cárdenas, 72; and private sector, 86, 178; and Second World War, 98; and balance of payments, 105, 106; under Ruiz Cortines, 109; and *técnicos*, 137; and economic prospects, 186
Banco Nacional de Comercio Exterior, 72
Banco Nacional de México, 18, 20, 171
Banking: its relation to the government, 18–19, 164, 170–171; Díaz reform of, 52; and credit, 55; after Revolution, 59; and relation of public and private sectors, 86; and foreign investment, 156
Border trade, 105, 106, 112
Brazil, 4, 155
Bulnes, Francisco, 42
Business: its relation to the government, 18, 19–21; under Cárdenas, 74–78; *1940–1960* output, 89–90, 197; under Alemán, 101–102; characteristics of leaders, 154–162; ideology of leaders, 163–175

BOOKS PREPARED UNDER THE AUSPICES OF THE CENTER
FOR INTERNATIONAL AFFAIRS, HARVARD UNIVERSITY

PUBLISHED BY HARVARD UNIVERSITY PRESS

The Soviet Bloc, by Zbigniew K. Brzezinski, 1960 (sponsored jointly with Russian Research Center).

Rift and Revolt in Hungary, by Ferenc A. Váli, 1961

The Economy of Cyprus, by A. J. Meyer, with Simos Vassiliou, 1962 (jointly with Center for Middle Eastern Studies).

Entrepreneurs of Lebanon, by Yusif A. Sayigh, 1962 (jointly with Center for Middle Eastern Studies).

Communist China 1955–1959, with a foreword by Robert R. Bowie and John K. Fairbank, 1962 (jointly with East Asian Research Center).

In Search of France, by Stanley Hoffmann, Charles P. Kindleberger, Laurence Wylie, Jesse R. Pitts, Jean-Baptiste Duroselle, and François Goguel, 1963.

Somali Nationalism, by Saadia Touval, 1963.

The Dilemma of Mexico's Development, by Raymond Vernon, 1963.

The Arms Debate, by Robert A. Levine, 1963.

AVAILABLE FROM OTHER PUBLISHERS

The Necessity for Choice, by Henry A. Kissinger, 1961. Harper & Brothers.

Strategy and Arms Control, by Thomas C. Schelling and Morton H. Halperin, 1961. Twentieth Century Fund.

United States Manufacturing Investment in Brazil, by Lincoln Gordon and Engelbert L. Grommers, 1962. Harvard Business School.

Limited War in the Nuclear Age, by Morton H. Halperin, 1963. John Wiley & Sons.

OCCASIONAL PAPERS IN INTERNATIONAL AFFAIRS, PUBLISHED BY CENTER FOR INTERNATIONAL AFFAIRS

1. *A Plan for Planning: The Need for a Better Method of Assisting Under-developed Countries on Their Economic Policies,* by Gustav F. Papanek, 1961.
2. *The Flow of Resources from Rich to Poor,* by Alan D. Neale, 1961.
3. *Limited War: An Essay on the Development of the Theory and an Annotated Bibliography,* by Morton H. Halperin, 1962.
4. *Reflections on the Failure of the First West Indian Federation,* by Hugh W. Springer, 1962.
5. *On the Interaction of Opposing Forces under Possible Arms Agreements,* by Glenn A. Kent, 1963.